THE SECRETS OF AVALON

Published by Avalonia

BM Avalonia
London
WC1N 3XX
England, UK

www.avaloniabooks.co.uk

The Secrets of Avalon
Copyright © August Hunt 2010

ISBN-10: 1-905297-32-7
ISBN-13: 978-1-905297-32-0

First Edition, May 2010
Design by Satori

Cover Art *"The Bard"* by Thomas Jones. With kind permission of the National Museum Wales; Amgueddfa Cymru.

British Library Cataloguing in Publication Data. A catalogue record for this book is available from the British Library.

ABOUT THIS AUTHOR

August Hunt has a lifelong passion for the Arthurian myths and has been studying them since his youth, which is also when his passion for writing first emerged. His first short stories appeared in his high school newspaper in the 1970's, and since then he has received scholarships and literary prizes for his fictional work, and has written numerous magazine articles, books, novels and screenplays.

He has lectured extensively on the Arthurian myths and related Dark Age topics at colleges and events, and has acted as consultant on television documentaries about King Arthur for the Discovery Channel and National Geographic. His works on the Arthurian mythos and other Dark Age topics are also featured on various websites.

Drawing on his considerable knowledge of folklore, Celtic myth, onomastics and Dark Age history, August Hunt is providing new and challenging material which illuminates many of the previously shadowy areas of the Arthurian tradition, including his own theory on the historical identity of King Arthur, discussed in his work *Shadows in the Mist: The Life and Death of King Arthur.*

August holds a degree in Celtic and Germanic Studies, and is a member of the International Arthurian Society. When he is not engaged in his research and writing, he enjoys hiking and landscaping, with unusual passions such as designing and erecting modern stone circles and monuments which reproduce the solar equinoctial and solstitial alignments of their ancient European counterparts.

He lives in the Pacific Northwest of the United States of America with his fiancée, a dog, several fish and two lizards affectionately referred to as the *'family dragons'.*

His other books include:

Shadows in the Mist: The Life and Death of King Arthur, 2005, Hayloft Publishing

From Within the Mist (anthology), 2004, Double Dragon

Doomstone, 2002, Double Dragon

You can write to the Author:

August Hunt,

c/o Avalonia, BM Avalonia, London, WC1N 3XX, England, UK

Also see: www.secretsofavalon.co.uk

ACKNOWLEDGMENTS

My thanks to the following correspondents, without whose help most of the more difficult etymological and archaeological problems could not have been resolved:

Robert Vermaat, Tim Padley of the Tullie House Museum, Carlisle, Dr. Graham Isaac of the National University of Ireland, Galway, Dr. Ranko Matasovic, author of the Proto-Celtic Etymological Dictionary, Dr. Garrett Olmsted, Dr. Ken Dark of Reading, Huw Pryce, School of History and Welsh History, University of Wales, Bangor, Dr. Graham Thomas, Senior Assistant Archivist, Department of Manuscripts and Records, The National Library of Wales, Dafydd Price Jones and Andrew Hawke of the Geiriadur Prifsygol Cymru, Dr. David Howlett of Oxford, Tom Lane of the Society of Lincolnshire History and Archaeology, Phil Parkes, ACR, of the School of History and Archaeology, Cardiff University, Neil Fairburn, Archaeology Project Manager, Milford Haven to Brecon Pipeline, NACAP Land & Marine JV on behalf of National Grid, Adam Gwilt, Curator of the Bronze & Iron Age Collections, Department of Archaeology & Numismatics, The National Museum Wales, Dr. Nina Steele, Historic Environment Record Archaeologist, Gwynedd Archaeological Trust, Dr. Frances Lynch, Dr Paul Robinson, Curator, Wiltshire Heritage Museum, Alison Taylor, Institute of Field Archaeologists, SHES, University of Reading, Dr. Catherine M. Hills. Cambridge University, Jacqueline I. McKinley, Senior Project Officer, Wessex Archaeology, Amanda Ravlick, a graduate student at Florida State University, Professor Charles Murgia, Department of Classics, University of California, Berkeley, Julia Crick of the University of Exeter, Department of History, Christopher Gwinn, G. Vernon Price, Dr. Linda Malcor, Professor O'Riain of University College, Cork, Dr. Betty O'Brien, Professor John Waddell of the Department of Archaeology at the National University of Ireland, Galway, John Bradley, Mariah Elaine Smith, University of Kansas graduate student, Alfred Stuckelberger, Georgina Plowright, Curator, English Heritage Hadrian's Wall Museums.

Any conclusions I have reached based upon information supplied to me by these correspondents do not necessarily represent the opinions of the correspondents themselves. As the majority of academics are trained to avoid speculation of any sort, I suspect many would disagree with my findings or the spirit of my findings. Errors of extrapolation or other variety are entirely my own.

Thomas Jones, The Bard
With the kind permission of the National Museum of Wales

THE SECRETS OF AVALON

AN INTRODUCTION TO ARTHURIAN DRUIDISM

FOREWORD BY JOHN MATTHEWS

AUGUST HUNT

Published by Avalonia

LIST OF IMAGES

Figure 1 - Merlin advising Arthur, Gustav Dore 10
Figure 2 - Mayburgh Henge Stone 14
Figure 3 - St Michael's Church, Burgh-by-Sands 24
Figure 4 - Latis altar at Aballava 37
Figure 5 - Eildon Walk 43
Figure 6 - Belatucadros Carving 65
Figure 7 - Clackmannan Stone 100
Figure 8 - Double Vase Cremation Burial 120
Figure 9 - Magister Draconum 130
Figure 10 - Tintagel Head 133
Figure 11 - Epona Stone, Maryport 146
Figure 12 - King Arthur Cross, Glastonbury 163
Figure 13 - Bryn Celli Ddu 174
Figure 14 - The Capon Tree 189
Figure 15 - St Anne's Well, Buxton 220

TABLE OF CONTENTS

Foreword by John Matthews 11

Introduction...15
Where is Avalon? 25
The Goddesses of Avalon..............................30
The Lady of the Lake....................................35
Myrddin at Avalon..39
The Horned God..64
Other Gods and Goddesses...........................68
Arthur and Uther..108
The Genius of Britain....................................124
The Mother of Arthur 132
The Grail of the Mare and the Raven............145
The Lightning and the Stone 160
The Everlasting Battle and Avalon................169
The Spiritual Avalon 179

Appendices

The Trees of Avalon: A New Interpretation of the Ogam
Alphabet 188
The Thirteen Treasures of the Island of Britain and Their
Ritual Uses 209
Zodiacal Correspondences of Arthur's Battles 219
Bibliography 225
Index 231

Figure 1 - Merlin advising Arthur, Gustav Dore
Illustration by Gustav Dore for Tennyson's work *Idylls of the King*.

FOREWORD

BY JOHN MATTHEWS

Theories concerning the origins and history of the British hero Arthur (better known to the world as *'King'* Arthur) and of the existence and practice of Druidry abound. We have been reliably informed, over the years, of a surprisingly large number of people who, it is claimed, were the historic Arthur, or the mythic Arthur, or the totally invented Arthur, and so on. In the same way we have heard numerous accounts of the origins of Druidry, of the practices, traditions and history of this remarkable group of priests, shamans and history-keepers of the ancient Celtic and pre-Celtic world.

Despite many attempts by writers from every discipline, from the extremely academic to the lunatic fringe, as yet no one has succeeded in defining the truth about either Arthur or the Druids. Even more rarely do we see any attempt to connect the two. And herein lies the strength and originality of August Hunt's book. Not only does he delve very deeply indeed into the mythic and historic background of the Arthur stories, he also applies his considerable knowledge of folklore, onomastics, and Dark Age history to illuminate the connections between the traditions of both Arthur and the Druids. The result is an important book that really does break new ground, casting fresh light into many dark and obscure place and passage in the vast panoply of Arthurian and Celtic traditions.

The second important aspect of the research (most of it truly original) is to throw light on the most mysterious character in both Celtic and Arthurian literature and tradition: Merlin. The very name induces a shiver of interest. Much ink has been spilled in an effort to decipher the many strands of belief and tradition which have gone into the creation of this fascinating character; but few have succeeded in illuminating his origins, life, and acts to any positive degree. Writers such as R.J. Stewart and I have suggested that Merlin was more than just a magical adviser to King Arthur, and that he was much more than a Druid. Among other things it has been suggested that the accounts of Merlin's life can only be properly understood in the light of a magical or shamanic tradition that predates the Dark Ages by many eons. Others have shown that there is a very strong case for Merlin as an historical character who lived, in fact, shortly after the period that many now refer to as Arthurian.

This last is important precisely because it does much to back up the existence of Arthur himself – a claim still hotly debated by many people both within and outside the academic community. August Hunt is the first writer to really attempt a synthesis from the rich heritage of documents, the riddles found in landscape, and the mythic and spiritual background from which Merlin emerges.

If this were not enough he finally scales the highest cliff of all – the identification of places connected with Arthur, Merlin and a whole collection of heroes, gods and goddesses, who at one time were familiar figures in the inner landscape of the people of Britain, but who have since slipped into obscurity and become almost forgotten. August Hunt sets out to find them in the landscape itself, in the echoes of place names and the fragmented folklore and local traditions in which the last glimmering traces of these important figures may be traced.

In all, this is a fascinating book, which challenges many strongly held beliefs, both in the academic community and that of the spiritual followers of both Celtic and Druidic tradition. Some will doubtless be aggrieved by certain of his findings, but most, if they are honest, will greet this groundbreaking book with a hearty cheer.

I, for one, look forward to the whole of the projected Avalon series, which will offer a range of exciting and provocative ideas to set all who love the matter of Arthur talking and, perhaps, revising their own beliefs about these endlessly intriguing subjects.

John Matthews
Oxford, 2009
www.hallowquest.org.uk

Figure 2 - Mayburgh Henge Stone
Standing Stone close to the henge called King Arthur's Round Table,
Mayburgh, Cumbria.

INTRODUCTION

TOWARDS A DEFINITION OF ARTHURIAN DRUIDISM

Arthurian Druidism is an ambiguous religion, the further development of which has been hampered by several factors. Chief among these is the modern, almost universal refusal to acknowledge that there was a historical Arthur. Coupled with this refusal is a stubborn insistence on viewing Merlin (Welsh Myrddin) as either a prophesying madman roaming the Scottish woods or as a master wizard casting spells in romantic fictions. It did not help that early antiquarians, with insufficient grounds for doing so, sought to imaginatively convert Merlin into a druidic priest. Further obfuscating matters is the unceasing debate over whether or not Arthur was Christian (those who demand that he was ignore the complex set of cultural conditions existing in North Britain during the Post-Roman period of the 5th-6th centuries CE).

The few attempts made to present to the world a true picture of Arthurian Druidism have failed because they relied too heavily on creative intuition or outright fraud. None have sought to properly balance a speculative approach to the subject with a sound, reasonable application of facts derived from scientific studies such as onomastics (the study of place-names), archaeology, history and folklore. Unprofessional comparative methods have been wielded loose and free, producing countless falsehoods, some of which have, unfortunately, seeped their way into the popular consciousness. Dubious resources touted as revelatory in nature are routinely consulted for research purposes, resulting in the promulgation of unsubstantiated claims and the birth and perpetuation of pseudo-traditions.

I have, with sadness, witnessed the nascent neopagan movement flounder under its own excesses. There has as yet been no collapse; instead, I would describe it as a waning of youthful enthusiasm. People moving away from established monolithic religions in a quest for spiritual fulfilment or a sense of belonging more intimately to nature have become disenchanted with the alternative paths self-proclaimed (and often thoroughly unqualified) *'gurus'* have laid out for them. They have become justifiably suspicious of cults and crafts invented whole-cloth. The non-pagan public, whose respect (and not merely toleration) needs to be gained, has had its doubts, criticisms and even disparagements all too often confirmed.

In my opinion, to save neopaganism, to prevent it from again becoming a creed adhered to only by a scattering of secretive, solitary practitioners, the originators of the movement must reappraise their own motives and methods and take responsibility for the sacred trust that falls upon the shoulders of anyone seeking to guide the lives of others. These originators must develop a new respect for the ancient materials which they have in the past so glibly treated, acknowledging as they do the scant remains of these materials and arriving at satisfactory parameters for the hypothetical amplification of such religious relics.

Another challenge to modern-day pagans is how to reconcile their religious beliefs and practices with the prevailing scientific world view. For example, pagans tend to personify the sun as a deity. Implicit in such a personification is the notion that the sun is a conscious entity. But science, while it still has much to explain regarding the origin and nature of the sun, presents this object as merely a giant thermonuclear reactor, devoid of any kind of consciousness. If the scientists are right (and I, for one, find that this is usually the case), how can a pagan justify praying to the Sun? Or making offerings to the Sun? Or seeking protection or bounty from the Sun? Or engaging in often elaborate rituals to celebrate the seasonal transformations of the Sun?

I think the solution to this dilemma is actually rather simple: when overwhelming evidence demands that they do so, pagans must embrace the findings of science. To do otherwise would be to engage in the same kind of anti-progressive activism that characterizes so much of the Catholic Church's defensive history. Such an acceptance of facts or even valid theory proven conclusively by science does not mean, however, that pagan belief must be supplanted. Instead, pagans must develop the ability to interpret their cherished deities or other objects of devotion *as symbolic representations of more profound truths*. For the Universe, as now partially understood by science, is far more complicated, far stranger and more wonderful than anything conceived of by our pagan ancestors. Indeed, no existing religious or philosophical system of thought comes close to comparing with the mathematically-derived views espoused by theoretical physicists! Just because many of us cannot understand those views unless they are explained in layman's terms does not mean that we should reject them. No pagan, despite his or her hankering for the *'good old days'* of our ancestors, should be part of a movement whose expressed goal is to foster a new Dark Age in which the light of intellectualism is extinguished in favour of mandatory superstition.

And, finally, neopagans must decide if a group with such disparate spiritual beliefs and practices can – or even should – reunify into some kind of cohesive alliance. To truly organise pagans into some kind of all-inclusive church with the power to interact politically in the events of the modern world may not be desirable and, indeed, may go against cherished precepts founded in a need for freedom of individual thought and action. But the creation of a *spiritual body* exhibiting solidarity and long-term growth potential, whose leaders strive to attain and promote stability and strength in numbers, rather than the chaotic flux and the weakness inherent in glorified support groups, could contribute much of value to our troubled times.

It is my hope that the current book will go a considerable distance toward remedying these problems. Utilizing the same analytical tools I did for my previous book, *Shadows In The Mist: The Life And Death Of King Arthur* (Hayloft, 2005), and subsequent revision essays published on the award-winning Vortigern Studies Website of Robert Vermaat, I plan on establishing the legitimacy of the figure of Merlin, as he is pivotal to any discussion of Arthurian Druidism. I will also delve into other aspects of the religion, not the least of which is the symbolic significance of Arthur himself, his battles and his sojourn in Avalon. Along the way the gods, goddesses, sacred places, belief systems and rituals of the Northern Britons of Arthur's time will be sketched in broad outline. Future books in the series will further explore and expand upon those critical elements of the tradition that could only superficially be treated of here.

So what is druidism? Simply put, it is the religion system of the ancient Celtic druids. A definition, of course, which naturally leads to the next question: *'What is a druid?'*

Many definitions for the word *druid* have been proposed, yet the most viable remains *dru-vid* or *'oak-knowing'*. By extension, a druid is an *'oak-knower'*. But what is meant by someone who *'knows the oak'*? It has been supposed that such a person, anciently the member of a cast of priests, had considerable knowledge of trees and perhaps of a sacred tree alphabet and calendar. This is an overly simplistic view and does not acknowledge the symbolism implicit in the oak tree.

The oak was the tree of the sky and of the sky-father. This sky-father went under many names among different peoples in different times. We tend to think of him, usually, in his Classical guises of Zeus and Jupiter, or of his Germanic counterpart, Thunor or Thor. The Celtic peoples also had sky-fathers, one of whom was called Taranis, the *'Thunderer'*. The oak tree's spreading branches, high up in the canopy of the forest, represented the sky itself and the god himself.

There is no site in Europe that better displays the importance of the oak in the ancient religious system inherited by the druids than Seahenge at Holme-next-to-Sea in Norfolk, England. This monument is composed of 55 wooden posts arranged in a circle around an upturned oak tree. Such wooden henge monuments formed the models for the later monuments in stone, such as the famous Stonehenge on Salisbury Plain in Wiltshire.

Seahenge allows us to understand not only the significance of the oak to the druids, but the true nature of the interior sacred space of a wooden or stone circle. The oak at Seahenge is upturned, with its spreading roots pointed upward towards the sky. Why? Because the space within the circle was conceived of as a mirror-reflection of the sky itself. By entering the precinct a priest was, essentially, standing upon or in the heavens. His position relative to the upturned oak proved that this was so on a symbolic level. The roots of the oak were to be conceived of as holding the sky-supporting trunk of the tree fast in the earth; its branches, being the sky itself, covered the surface of the enclosure.

This mirror-image of the sky found within the wooden posts or standing stones of a druidic circle was called a nemeton. This name for a holy enclosure is illuminating in and of itself, for it comes from *nemeto-*, meaning '*sacred place, sanctuary*', itself from *nemos*, '*heaven, sky*'. Thus the nemeton was the sky.

A druid, then, was a priest whose special training had given him a profound knowledge of the sky and everything that pertained to the sky. Such knowledge would have concentrated on the observation and prediction of heavenly events, chiefly concerning itself with the annual motion of the planets and stars. Agricultural festivals originally (before the slipping of the calendar) coincided with solstices and equinoxes. The ability to foretell eclipses, meteor showers, cometary appearances and the like would have given the druids immense power and prestige. Like heavenly bodies themselves, the druids rose from the earth into the sky as they set foot into the nemeton, and fell back to earth when they left the sacred enclosure. The planet Jupiter rises and sets and, in this respect, a druid was not only an '*oak-knower*', but a human incarnation of the sky-father himself, the '*Knowing oak*'.

Arthurian Druidism makes use of these principles, merely applying them specifically to an Arthurian context. This context is composed of those traditions preserved by the Welsh which treat of Arthur himself and his family, divine heroes or deities brought into his orbit and places legitimately associated with him. We must take it on faith that these traditions record genuine vestiges of ancient British druidic worship and ritual practices and that they were not merely invented, as some scholars contend, as oral or literary entertainment. We must also be willing to subscribe to the view that Christianity in its purest form did not entirely prevail in the North of Britain in the century or two after the Roman withdrawal. In truth, the evangelizing efforts of native, Continental and Irish saints during this period would not have been necessary had large portions of the population not lapsed into paganism.

An aspect of Arthurian Druidism which I will be constantly emphasizing is what I term 'correspondences'. Astrologers reading this statement will immediately know exactly what I'm talking about – so, too, will practitioners of magic and Wicca. The old adage 'As above, so below' certainly applies. For while Arthur was a real human being, who ruled a real kingdom, fought at real places, and was buried in a real place, within the confines of druidic belief he was also a divine king with his own celestial counterpart, whose life and death provides us with an ideal vision of heroic striving towards a selfless, beneficent purpose.

Another recurring theme – perhaps the central tenet - in my treatment of Arthurian Druidism will be seasonal transformation imagery. To the early Britons, nothing was more important than the regular rotation of the seasons. Their lives depended on the natural cycles and rhythms of Nature without which crops would not grow and livestock would not prosper. And their only escape from the finality of death lay in their ability to acknowledge their unity with eternal heavenly entities – entities like the sun, whose passage through the solar year dictated seasonal change. The sun might seem to die at midwinter, but it was always reborn.

Some readers may be disappointed that some elements of Arthurian Druidism do not appear to conform to the more mystical strain prevalent in current Celtic Reconstructionist thought. Others will object that cherished relics like the Holy Grail, which has been subject to Christian appropriation and sublimation for centuries, have become somehow less mysterious, less magical, less miraculous. Yet there was a refreshing honesty at the root of British pagan religion, an honesty that despite its often complex iconography and secretive poetic language, never demanded its adherents devote themselves to an Other or Other-world or Other-state-of-existence that was patently unknowable.

Pagans are a common-sense lot. They believe in the here and now, but recognize that eternity resides in the same place at the same time. They prefer their gods and goddesses to be of the here and now, and place no reliance on alien divinities who exist in uncaring fashion beyond the physical universe. They celebrate the passing of a loved one in the same way they celebrate the passing of a season, with sorrow for loss and joy in the prospect of cyclic rebirth.

Not for the pagan is an obsessive dwelling on unanswerable theological questions, or the raging fanaticism that leads one to persecute or murder those who do not hold the same subjective Truth. Pagans have the wisdom to avoid becoming enmeshed in metaphysical philosophies that serve no purpose other than that of intellectual masturbation, but at the same time they are avid students of any science whose findings amplify rather than diminish the wonders of Nature. They may, on occasion, be attracted to the unique promise of a pseudo-science, but eventually develop a power of discernment that protects them from being exploited by con-artists and potentially dangerous cult leaders.

Finally, pagans – at least the ones I have personally known – want to do good. They want to serve their fellow Man, they want to work for the welfare of animals, they want to make the world a better place to live in, for us and future generations. Many pagans are now members of the military, and in the United States, at least, their religious preference is officially recognized and, supposedly, condoned. One of my pagan friends is in health care, while another works in emergency services and a third is a county sheriff. Long gone is the clichéd misconception that a pagan by definition is someone lacking intelligence or sensitivity, who is lazy, irresponsible, has no discipline or lacks commitment to anything save unbridled freedom, who dresses like a hippy or Goth and is body-decorated with multiple piercings and tattoos, whose life is filled with uninterrupted chaos or organised anarchy, who is a follower not a leader, is weak, whiny and needy, has an addictive personality and pursues only pleasure and self-aggrandizement.

Today's pagans are for the most part indistinguishable from the mainstream population. They have become, as it were, integrated into modern society. This does not mean that they have sold out. Rather, they have been successful in adapting to changing conditions. Most pagans are monogamous; they did not adopt their faith as an excuse for, or justification of, indiscriminate sex. If they are polyamorous, they have strict codes of moral conduct to guide them in their lifestyle. Modern pagans are unlikely to be found in careers where the primary reward is financial. Instead they are interested in enriching the lives of others and find fulfilment in being stewards of the environment. They have Nature-respecting and otherwise well-adjusted children who attend good schools.

This being so, what role in the lives of today's pagans can Arthurian Druidism play? How would embarking on the path of Arthurian Druidism benefit them?

Granted, there are many paths available to the modern pagan. But only one puts forward as its central figure the prototypical saviour hero upon whom, directly or indirectly, most of today's literary and cinematic heroes are patterned. The 'White Knight' of our movies, fantasy novels and comic books, in no matter what guise he appears, is beneath his costume of anonymity none other than Arthur, or perhaps one of Arthur's knights. While this White Knight is not, strictly speaking, the early Celtic Arthur of pagan Britain, but instead the Arthur of medieval Christian romance, he is Arthur, nonetheless.

One might think that our increasing obsession with the cult of the superhero in our entertainment media is in direct reverse-proportion to the number of genuine heroes in our society. But this is not at all the case. We have a preponderance of heroes – they merely go unsung, being unrecognized and unrewarded because our materialistic culture is more interested in accruing money, possessions and empty fame. As long as status is determined by such superficial, meaningless things, and the majority of our attention is focused on pursuing them, genuine as opposed to imaginary heroes will remain under- or unappreciated.

To save or rescue something or someone in any positive sense should be the joint goal of our society. Perhaps what is called for is a new order of Arthurian knighthood composed of dedicated pagan servants of the community and the world, and most particularly of Nature. The Round Table might yet again become fashionable as a symbol of Equality and Solidarity. A Myrddin (the later Merlin of Arthurian romance) or even a council of Myrddins could be elected to advise the Round Table on matters pertaining to future projections and planning and to oversee the Nemeton. The Quest as the search for all things needed to help Man excel as a species and as the chief caretaker of this world might once again come to the fore as a viable pagan calling. Even the Grail could be evoked as that which is essential to sustaining spiritual and physical life and well-being. The Nine Queens of Avalon might become the guardians of the feminine principle and everything pertaining to it, as well as of the Otherworld of Eternal Summer.

And how, exactly, would prospective Arthurian druids go about implementing such an ambitious plan?

Well, the first step is to sufficiently familiarize ourselves with the precepts of Arthurian Druidism. And that is the aim of this simple primer. As for the rest, I leave that up to the readers of this book.

Figure 3 - St Michael's Church, Burgh-by-Sands
11th century church built inside the site of the Roman fort of Aballava on
Hadrian's Wall, Cumbria.

CHAPTER 1

WHERE IS AVALON?

The tradition that the Arthur of legend was buried at Glastonbury in Somerset, England, is a well-established one. But certain problems regarding the account of the exhumation of the great king's bones in 1190 CE have called into question the veracity of the tradition. That it was politically expedient for Henry II to quell rumours among his Welsh and Cornish subjects of Arthur's imminent return is undeniable. It now seems unlikely that Glastonbury, while still an ancient sacred site, is the real Isle of Avalon, and that we had best look elsewhere in Britain for this Celtic Otherworld localization.

Some odd details surround the *'discovery'* of King Arthur's grave at Glastonbury. These details have been discussed at length before by scholars, but the conclusions drawn from them have varied. First, a 6th century Arthur (the usual date ascribed to his floruit) would not have been buried in a hollowed oak, as the account of Gerald of Wales insists. The skeleton found in such a coffin would have been of the Bronze Age. We may compare the Bronze Age warrior found buried in a dugout canoe, another canoe covering the first, in the barrow at Loose Howe on Danby High Moor in the North York Moors. As Glastonbury was surrounded by extensive marshland, the *'hollowed oak'* was almost certainly a dugout.

Second, a 6th century Arthur would have had his grave marked by a stone bearing Roman capitals. The formula of the inscription would have been something like:

HIC SEPVLTVS IACIT ARTVRIVS

'Here buried lies Arthur'

Instead, the monks at Glastonbury claimed to have found a lead cross buried beneath the coffin cover. Drawings of this cross reveal the form and content of the inscription (HIC IACET SEPVLTVS INCLITUS REX ARTVRIVS IN INSULA AVALONIA/ *'Here lies buried the famous king Arthur in the isle of Avalon'*) to be of the tenth century, not the sixth century. This would seem puzzling, were it not for the fact that 12th century monks could easily forge an inscription in such a way as to make it seem to be from an earlier period. We know that they did this with manuscripts.

An alternate theory has been proposed: that the grave was originally discovered in 945 CE, when St. Dunstan, the Abbot of Glastonbury, erected a masonry wall around the cemetery and had the area raised. At this time the original stone marker would have been removed, and the lead cross fashioned and placed inside the coffin. The whole was then covered over and forgotten, only to be rediscovered in 1190 CE.

The objection to this theory is that so remarkable a discovery in the 10th century would certainly have been recorded. Furthermore, the grave of a worthy such as Arthur would have been marked in such a way as to be readily noticeable to future generations, i.e. it would not have been left unmarked with a mere lead cross placed within the coffin. That St. Dunstan and his monks would have had some reason to keep the location of Arthur's grave secret again makes no sense, as Dunstan was himself English, not British. Furthermore, I've been unable to find other recorded instances in which such a cross or similar inscribed memorial object has been found inside an ancient coffin.

All in all, the theory that Arthur was reburied, but his grave left unmarked, is unacceptable. This being the case, we must reluctantly admit that in all likelihood the Glastonbury burial of King Arthur is a forgery. The possible financial reason for committing such a forgery has been mentioned elsewhere. Primarily, the monks were interested in attracting more pilgrims to Glastonbury, as there had been a disastrous fire and money was badly needed for rebuilding.

On Hadrian's Wall, which forms the dividing line between England and Lowland Scotland, there are two Roman forts of particular interest to students of Arthurian legend. One, at Castlesteads, was called *Camboglanna*. This Old Celtic name lies at the root of the Welsh place name Camlann or Camlan, the site of Arthur's death in 537 CE according to the *Welsh Annals*. If Camboglanna is where Arthur died, then it is certainly not a coincidence that the only place in Britain known anciently as Avalon is located just under 14 miles west along the Wall at Burgh-by-Sands.

The Aballava Roman fort, now on the edge of marshland near the Solway Firth, was referred to in the early *Ravenna Cosmography* as *Avalana*. This place name means, literally, the *'place of apples'*. Camboglanna is on the Irthing, a tributary of the Eden River. The Eden empties into the Solway Firth very near this fort. A dedication to the goddess Latis was found at Aballava. She is the goddess of open bodies of fresh water, a literal *'Lady of the Lake'*. What we appear to have with Arthur at Avalon with the Lady of the Lake is Arthur at Aballava/Avalana with Dea Latis. I will have more on the Lady of the Lake in Chapter 3.

Urien Rheged, whose father Cynfarch was Arthur's cousin, was married to Modron, i.e. Matrona, the Mother Goddess, daughter of Aballach, a personification of the Irish Ablach, from Emhain Ablach, the apple tree otherworld. Aballach was thought of as the founding king of Avalon, i.e. of the Aballava fort at the west end of Hadrian's Wall, just across the Solway from the homeland of Urien.

Emain Ablach, chiefly because it was associated in Irish tradition with the god Manannan mac Lir, was wrongly identified with the Isle of Man. Another theory holds that Emain Ablach is, in reality, the island of Arran. However, the only important *'apple-place'* which actually bears an apple name is Aballava, which is geographically situated roughly between the Isle of Man and Arran. Emain has been connected with the word for *twins* in ancient Irish, as the folk etymology story attached to the Irish royal site of Emhain Macha makes clear. But as we shall see in Chapter 6, Emain Macha actually means *'the Swift One [Imona] of the*

Plain', a name for a horse goddess. Emain Ablach is the thus the *'apple-place of Imona'*.

An Arthur who fell at Camboglanna could have been brought down the river system in this region or carted along the Roman road to the Avalon that was Burgh-By-Sands. The actual Roman period cemetery at Burgh-By-Sands/Aballava is said to have been to the south of the fort. Fragments of a tombstone of one *'Julius Pi[ ]linus... a Dacian tribesman...'* were found there.

Alas, a location of the cemetery to the south of the fort puts it near the vallum, possibly destroyed by the building of the modern canal and railway. Two other tombstone fragments were found at Burgh-By-Sands. They were in the care of Tullie House Museum when they disappeared.

While it is impossible to know whether Arthur was buried in the Roman period cemetery of the Aballava fort, this place must remain a primary candidate for the location of his grave.

According to the early 12th century *History of the Kings of Britain* by Geoffrey of Monmouth, the author responsible for the first, full version of the Arthur tale, there may have been yet another Avalon. Geoffrey placed Arthur's final battle of Camlann on the Camel River in Cornwall. He may have been aware of the Old Cornish word *auallen*, *'Apple-tree'*. Old Welsh has *aballen* and Breton *aualen*. The forms *auallen* and *aballenn* are recorded from the 12th century. Most importantly, Geoffrey never identifies his *'Avallonis'* with Glastonbury.

If we follow the Cornish coast north from the Camel and pass by Tintagel, the birthplace of Arthur according to Geoffrey's account, we arrive eventually at Appledore in Devon, situated on a neck of land or headland jutting out into the confluence of the Taw and Torridge Rivers. This town was *le Apildore* in 1335 CE. The name is Old English and means *'Apple-tree'*.

Obviously, Geoffrey's Avalon, if derived from the Cornish, was a suitable substitute for the English name Appledore. The *'Insula'* or island of Avalon/Appledore would have been used in the same sense as *'isle'* is used in Isle of

Purbeck, Isle of Portland, or Isle of Thanet. In other words, Geoffrey's Isle of Avalon may well be the neck of land or headland of Appledore.

If so, Appledore was merely Geoffrey's substitute for the real Avalon in the North – the Roman fort of Aballava at Burgh-By-Sands. The latter is the only Avalon actually called such that was near a Camlann site. None of the Cam-river or town names in southwest England preserve a form that could have become the Camlann of the *Welsh Annals*.

CHAPTER TWO

THE GODDESSES OF AVALON

The nine sisters placed on Avalon by Geoffrey of Monmouth are known Irish goddesses. I have identified these sisters as follows:

Geoffrey's Nine Sisters	Irish Goddesses
Morgen	Morrigan
Moronoe	Muireann, mother of Fionn mac Cumhail
Mazoe	Macha (Imona / Emain)
Gliten Glitonea Gliton	Clidna triplicated
Tyronoe	Tuireann, sister of Muireann or Fionn's sister
Thiten Thiten cithara notissima, 'lyre-famous'	Dechtine (the –ch- is silent), here duplicated and wrongly linked to Irish tet, theoit, teoid, ted. 'harp-string', mother of Cuchulainn

The argument has been made for Morgen – the later Morgan le Fay or Morgan *'the Fairy'* – being a native Welsh goddess. However, not a single source mentions such a goddess prior to Geoffrey of Monmouth's *Life of Merlin*. The Morgens found in an early Welsh genealogy featuring Glast, a fictional eponymous founder of Glastonbury, are male princes and cannot, therefore, be Morgen.

Geoffrey describes Morgen thus:

> *"The one who is first among them has greater skill in healing, as her beauty surpasses that of her sisters. Her name is Morgen, and she has learned the uses of all plants in curing the ills of the body. She knows, too, the art of changing her shape, of flying through the air, like Daedalus, on strange*

wings. At will, she is now at Brest, now at Chartres, now at Pavia; and at will she glides down from the sky on to your shores. They say she had taught astrology to her sisters..."

The bird-form assumed by Morgen is, of course, the crow aspect of the Irish Morrigan, the *'Spirit-Queen'*. And there is now no reason to doubt that Geoffrey merely substituted the familiar Welsh name Morgen for Morrigan. The Morrigan was the preeminent battle goddess of the ancient Irish, but she is also known for being present at the death of the greatest of the Irish heroes, Cuchulainn. This last fact may have been Geoffrey's inspiration for having Morgen appear to ferry away the dying Arthur. *'The Morrigan'*, as she was sometimes referred to, also tried to seduce Cuchulainn and this sexual motif may have contributed to Morgan le Fay's sleeping with her brother, Arthur (see *'Anu'* in Chapter 6).

The Spirit-Queen resided not in Emain Ablach, but in the frightful Otherworld Cave of Cruachan at Rathcroghan near Tulsk, Co. Roscommon. Of course, all otherworlds are Avalon, which could be a place of both dread and delight, emotions engendered in us by our conflicting view of places of burial as both houses for the dead and portals to the happy afterlife. For anyone who has ever ventured into an ancient passage grave, the sensation of exposure to numinous power is evident. Apprehension and anticipation go hand in hand when exploring these kinds of funeral monuments.

Muireann was the mother of Fionn and the divine wife of Cumhail, i.e. the god Camulos (see Chapter 6). Fionn and his fiana or *'warrior band'* are in many ways the Irish counterpart of Arthur and his champions. The word *fiana* contains the same ancient root as Latin *venatio*, *'hunting'*, and so we find Fionn as Gwyn the mighty hunter in the Arthurian tale *Culhwch and Olwen*. In Welsh tradition, Gwyn became the lord of the Otherworld.

Macha (see Imona in Chapter 6) was an important Irish horse goddess. We have seen above that Emain Ablach belonged to her.

The goddess Clidna was worshipped in Co. Cork. She came from Tir Tairngire or the 'Land of Promise', a designation for the Otherworld, and she owned three magical birds that ate apples from a sacred tree. We may compare these birds with those belonging to the Welsh goddess, Rhiannon.

Tyronoe is Tuireann or Uirne, variously the sister of Muireann or Fionn's sister, whom has a spell cast upon her while she is pregnant which transforms her into a bitch. She gives birth to twin hounds, Bran and Sceolang, who become Fionn's prized hunting dogs.

Dechtine, the mother of Cuchulainn by Lugh Lamhfota or Lugh of the Long-hand, is said to come from the Newgrange passage grave on the Boyne, an Otherworld house that belonged to Aonghus Og or Mac Og, the Irish equivalent of the Welsh Mabon the Divine Son.

What are we to make of the fact that Geoffrey of Monmouth inhabited Arthur's Avalon with Irish goddesses? Some would doubtless say that this was proof that Avalon was a concept borrowed from the Irish. Others would go even further and claim that if Avalon has as its denizens Irish goddesses, then Avalon itself must be an Irish island.

I would counter both of these statements by saying that none of the Irish sources place all of these goddesses on Avalon. In fact, only Macha (= Imona) is expressly associated with the Isle of Apple-trees. It seems fairly certain, therefore, that Geoffrey selected these various goddesses from disparate Irish sources because he lacked the names of corresponding British goddesses. The existence of the Irish goddesses was known to him and so it was convenient to have them preside over Arthur's Otherworld-island.

However, having said this, it is true that Geoffrey's Avalon goddesses remind us to an uncanny degree of the Gallizenas of the island of Sena, modern Ile de Sein, off Pointe du Raz on the western coast of Brittany, mentioned by Pomponius Mela in c. 40 CE:

"Sena in the British sea, opposite the Ossismician coast, is remarkable for an oracle of the Gallic God. Its priestesses, holy in perpetual virginity, are said to be nine in number. They are called Gallizenas, and are thought to be endowed with singular powers, so as to raise by their charms the winds and seas, to turn themselves into what animals they will, to cure wounds and diseases incurable by others, to know and predict the future; but this they do only to navigators who go thither purposely to consult them."

Various origins for the term Gallizenas have been sought, but I think none of them very satisfactory. This is, rather transparently, a form of Old Irish *caillech* or *caillechan*, 'crone, elderly woman, hag, witch', but also *'nun'*, as the word originally meant *'veiled one'*. And if I am right, then the placement of this island off the coast of Brittany is likely an error for Inis Cathach, modern Scattery Island at the mouth of the Shannon River in Ireland. Shannon or Sionainn is a river-goddess name. It comes from *seno-ona* and means *'Old Goddess'*. Sena, the ancient name of the Ile de Sein, would appear to have the same root (cf. Senuna, Sena, Senua, as a goddess name on votive plaques found near Baldock, Hertfordshire).

The island of Inis Cathach was taken over by the Christian Saint Senan (whose own name, probably not coincidentally, is a diminutive of the same root found in Sionainn and means *'old'*) in the 6th century. A strict misogynist rule was imposed that no woman could ever set foot on the island. This was doubtless a Christian reaction to the fact that pagan priestesses or caillechan had once inhabited the place.

A couple of interesting legends regarding pagan worship by priestesses on Scattery Island have been preserved. First in importance is that which concerns the *péist* (*'beast'*) *'Cata'* or Cathach, a water monster similar to the female Caoranach of Lough Derg. St. Senan (about 500 CE) found this monster dwelling on Scattery Island. The Cata devoured the saint's smith, Narach, but Senan brought him forth again alive. In the subsequent combat between priest and péist, the latter advanced with *'its eyes flashing flame, with fiery breath, spitting venom and opening its horrible jaws,'* but Senan made the sign of the cross, and the beast collapsed, was chained and then thrown into Doolough near Mount Callan (the black lake, *'Nigricantis aquae juxta montem Callain in Tuamonia'*). In the oldest (metrical) *Life of Senan*, the péist appears as the *'immanis bellua'* (*monstrous beast*) or *'bestia,'* while Iniscatha is rendered *'Belluanam Insulam'* (*island of the beast*). The legend is alluded to even in the late eighth-century *Calendar of Oengus* under March 8th, *'Senan of Inis Cathaig gibbeted Naroch's foe.'* The story is remembered widely, and among all classes at Scattery and along both banks of the river, at Kilkee, Kilmihil, and round Doolough and Miltown Malbay. In the fifteenth-century details of the *'Cathedral'* of Scattery a large-eyed dragon with crocodile jaws is conspicuous; there was another carving at Kilrush; and a third, - the *'pattern-stone'* removed from Scattery and until lately at Kilkee,—showed the Cata as *'the amphibious beast of this blessed Isle,'* a nondescript creature with spiked back, scales, fish tail, nose curling up spirally, and clawed forefeet.

After Senan had expelled the Cathach, a local chieftain called MacTail, or Mactal, hired a druid to put a spell on the saint. However, as the druid landed on a nearby island, a tidal wave enveloped him and swept him to his death. The island is still pointed out as *'Carraig a Draoi'* or *The Druid's Rock*. It lies between Hog Island and Scattery, and can be seen at low tide.

The *'Lady's Grave'* is found at the low tide mark to the west of Rinn Eanaigh. It is said to cover the grave of a young lady called Connara whose advances Senan had repulsed. Connara is described as an Irish princess or the *'holy nun'* who founded the convent of *Cill na gCailleach* (Church of the Caillech) on the side of Poulnasherry Bay on the mainland.

In Chapter 9, we will examine the nine Otherworld goddesses who appear in the early Arthurian poem *The Spoils of Annwn*. These goddesses are the keepers of a magical cauldron, the prototype of the later Holy Grail.

CHAPTER THREE

THE LADY OF THE LAKE

We have seen above that the Arthurian *'Lady of the Lake'* was, in reality, Dea Latis of the Avalon Roman fort at Burgh-By-Sands, Cumbria. But later Arthurian romance would further identify her as Niviane or Viviane. Where did the French romance authors get this name for the lake goddess?

In Welsh tradition, Nyfain (variants Nyuein, Nyven, Nevyn) daughter of Brychan is the name given to the mother of Urien. This Brychan is said to be the famous Irish chieftain known to have founded the Welsh kingdom of Brycheiniog and to have fathered eleven sons and twenty-four daughters. However, there was also a Northern Brychan, whom the Welsh sources associate with a Manaw, supposedly either Manau Gododdin at the head of the Firth of Forth, or the Manau that was the Isle of Man. The tomb of this Northern Brychan is either on an island called the Island of Brychan, which is near or bordering on Manaw, or is at a place called the Valley of Brychan within Manaw itself.

No satisfactory site has been identified fitting these descriptions. However, as Gaelic *corrie* means *'valley'*, the Valley of Brychan is certainly an error for the *Coire* or *'Cauldron'* of Breccan, i.e. the Corrievreckan, the name of a whirlpool situated between the Inner Hebridean islands of Jura and Scarba. Today this location is marked on maps by the Gulf of Corryvreckan.

In the *Metrical Dindshenchas* (Part 18), we are told the following about Breccan's fate in the whirlpool:

1. *"No generous chieftain that reached it ever returned hither again from its white-paven floor, since Breccán of Bérre went his way.*
2. *Breccán son of Partholan, that seer of old, drank no wholesome draught: he was drowned here with his fifty ships by the crowding waves of the whirlpool.*
3. *I know the tale sages tell of the mighty whirlpool's home, whence comes, to denote it perpetually, the familiar name and its clear reason.*
4. *I have heard of famous Breccán, whose is the loud-roaring grave—him that enriched every hearth of Uí Néill, busily plying in his vessel a brisk trade.*
5. *Breccán son of Maine, rich in graces, the Cauldron drowned with its red spray, and he lies under the heavy high-piled strand with his ship and his valiant following.*
6. *Though it has buried unforgotten Breccán, his name endures in story with his bark and its burthen that lie beneath the whirlpool's stormy water."*

Maine was a son of Niall, and so this tale provides the names of different Breccans whose names became attached to the whirlpool. I would suggest that the name Maine here accounts for the *'Manaw'* associated with the Northern Brychan in the Welsh sources.

The Corrievreckan is also linked to the Cailleach, the goddess in her aged form, and is considered to be a portal to the Otherworld.

Nyfain's name cannot, as some have thought, be an eponym for the ancient Novantae tribe, whose territory (roughly Dumfries and Galloway) was ruled over by Urien. The identification is etymologically impossible. But the name could very easily represent the Irish goddess Nemhain. Nemhain was one of the premiere battle-goddesses of Ireland, and was often paired with Macha, Morrigan and Badb.

Figure 4 - Latis altar at Aballava
Altar dedicated to the goddess Latis at the Roman site of
Aballava on Hadrian's Wall, Cumbria.

In the Vulgate *Merlin*, the forest name of the Lady of the Lake is first given as the Forest of Briosque and only later as Broceliande, the name used by Chretien de Troyes. While Broceliande has been sought in various places, none of the candidates work geographically or etymologically. I would derive the Old French *'Briosque'* from the *–fries* component of Dumfries, the town situated just West-Southwest of Lochmaben in Dumfriesshire. While once thought to be the *'Fort of the Frisians'*, authorities now correctly identify *–fries* with Gaelic *preas*, Angl. Pres(s), gen. *phris*, Angl. *–fries*, gen. pl. *preas*, *(b)p(h)reasach*, *'bush, copse, thicket'*. Spellings such as Dunfreisch, Droonfreisch, and Drumfriesche occasionally occur in old documents.

It makes a great deal of sense to envisage Merlin and Viviane in the Dumfries region, as this was the home stomping grounds of Myrddin, the Welsh prototype for Geoffrey of Monmouth's Merlin. Broceliande, then, is simply Briosque + land.

In the context of any discussion of Myrddin and Nemhain in southwest Scotland, it is necessary to mention the Locus Maponi or *'place of [the god] Maponus'*, identifiable with Lochmaben in Dumfries (or perhaps the Ladyward Roman fort near Lochmaben, or even with the Clochmabenstane just south at Gretna Green; see the listing for Mabon in Chapter 6). As is well known, Mabon was the son of Modron, i.e. Matrona, the Divine Mother. This is the same Modron who is presented as the wife of Urien, son of Nyfain/Nemhain.

While it is tempting to give Modron the Divine Mother the name Nemhain, we are not justified in making this assumption. And, indeed, given the proximity of Lochmaben to the Annan River, and the presence of a St. Ann's on a tributary of the Annan which has its confluence with the latter river at Lochmaben, it makes more sense to associate Modron/Matrona *'the Divine Mother'* with a British version of the Irish goddess Anu. Annan is the genitive of *anau*, cognate with Welsh *anaw 'riches'*, Gaelic *Anu* the name of the Irish goddess of prosperity. Geoffrey of Monmouth made this goddess, in the guise of *'Anna'*, the sister of Arthur.

On the other hand, when we discuss Myrddin's sister Gwenddydd, whom Geoffrey of Monmouth called Ganieda, we will see that there may be a good reason to identify *her* with Nemhain.

For Nefyn or Nemhain in the early Welsh poem *Cad Godeu*, see the listing for Achren in Chapter 6.

CHAPTER FOUR

MYRDDIN AT AVALON

Who was Merlin – or, rather, *what* was Merlin?

This question has intrigued and vexed countless students of the Arthurian tradition for centuries. Was he someone who panicked and ran away from the Battle of Arfderydd? Who lost his sanity in the battle and lived like a wild beast in the woods? Had he really been a great bard of the chieftain Gwenddolau? If he were a madman, by what mechanism did his insane pronouncements become recognized as prophecies? Why was he also called Llallogan or Llallawg? Why was he dealt a triple sacrificial death akin to that meted out to the god Lugh (Gaulish Lugos, Welsh Lleu)?

These questions are important in and of themselves, of course. But for our purposes they take on a more profound significance. When we answer them in an objective way, can we say definitively that Merlin had belonged to a class of druidic priests? Or that he had performed some vital function for such a priesthood?

In Geoffrey of Monmouth's *History of the Kings of Britain*, Merlin, the Welsh Myrddin, is associated with Amesbury's Stonehenge on Salisbury Plain and with Mount Killaraus (= Killare next to the Hill of Uisneach, the centre of Ireland), while in Geoffrey's *Life of Merlin* the great sage is placed atop a mountain in the Scottish Caledonian Wood.

Fragments of the *Life of St. Kentigern* tell of a madman/prophet named Lailoken, who is explicitly identified with Merlin, and who is found on a 'rock' at Mellodonor (modern Molindinar Burn) within sight of Glasgow and at Drumelzier (modern Dunmeller) in Scottish

Borders. Lailoken is said to have been buried near Drumelzier.

Before Geoffrey introduced Merlin into the Arthurian saga by substituting him for Ambrosius of Dinas Emrys, a hill-fort in Gwynedd, Wales, and of Wallop, Hampshire (see below), the madman/prophet had divided his time between Carwinelow, the fort of his lord Gwenddolau, near Longtown in Liddesdale (known now as the Moat of Liddel), nearby Arthuret, the scene of the Battle of Arfderydd, in which his lord was slain and he went mad, the Lowland Caledonian Wood with its mountain and the court of King Rhydderch Hen/Hael. Rhydderch belongs at Dumbarton in Strathclyde, although Geoffrey makes him a Cumbrian king.

In Geoffrey the Caledonian mountain remains unnamed. This is unfortunate, in that by finding this mountain we might learn a great deal more about Merlin's identity. And, incidentally, we would have a much firmer fix on the location of Arthur's seventh battle, which occurred in the Caledonian Wood.

Merlin's Caledonian Wood mountain is mentioned in one other source: the 13th century French verse romance by Guillaume Le Clerc entitled *Fergus of Galloway*. The *Fergus* romance is distinguished by the author's knowledge of Scottish geography. To quote from Cedric E. Pickford in *Arthurian Literature in the Middle Ages*:

> "His [Guillaume's] Scottish geography is remarkably accurate... In the whole range of Arthurian romance there is no instance of a more detailed, more realistic geographical setting."

The modern translator of *Fergus*, the late D.D.R. Owen, has made similar remarks on this romance. The notes and synopses in his translation also remind the reader that various elements of the *Fergus* mountain episode were adapted from Chretien's *Yvain and Perceval* and the *Continuations* of the latter.

But it remains true that only *Fergus* actually names Merlin's mountain and purports to give us directions on how to get there. The hero Fergus starts his journey to the mountain not as Nikolai Tolstoy (in his *The Quest for Merlin*) claims at the Moat of Liddel, where Merlin fought and fled in madness, but at Liddel Castle at Newcastleton in Liddesdale. Tolstoy uses 1) Guillaume's directions and the placement of King Rhydderch at Dumbarton 2) Merlin's affinity with the stag in Geoffrey's *Life of Merlin* 3) the incorrect positioning of Merlin's Galabes springs (see below) and 4) the great height of the hill to select Hart Fell at the head of Annandale as Merlin's mountain.

There are marked problems with each of these guidelines used by Tolstoy. Firstly, the directions given are incredibly vague and hence can be used to chart a course from the Moat of Liddel to just about anywhere:

> *"[Fergus] comes riding along the edge of a mighty forest... Fergus comes onto a very wide plain between two hills. On he rode past hillocks and valleys until he saw a mountain appear that reached up to the clouds and supported the entire sky..."*

Secondly, Fergus' mountain is given two names, neither of which match that of Hart Fell: Noquetran (variants Nouquetran, Noquetrant) and *'Black Mountain'*. The latter is obviously a poetic designation only, the primary name being Noquetran.

And thirdly, there is no edifice of any kind atop or on the flanks of Hart Fell which could have been referred to as *'Merlin's Chapel'*. As described in the *Fergus* romance, this edifice must be an ancient chambered cairn. Such monuments are often associated with Arthurian characters.

The hill-name Noquetran is obviously a Norman French attempt at a Gaelic hill-name, with the first component being *cnoc*, English *knock*, *'hill'*. As the French render English bank as banque and check as cheque, *Cnoc/Knock* became *Noque-*.

The secret to correctly interpreting the *–tran* component of Noquetran lies in a closer examination of Professor Owen's notes on the *Fergus* romance. For lines 773-93 he writes:

"This adventure [of the Noquetran] is largely developed from elements in C.II [the Second Continuation of Chretien's Perceval]. There Perceval fights and defeats a Black Knight in mysterious circumstances. Earlier, he had found a fine horn hanging by a sash from a castle door. On it he gave three great blasts, whereupon he was challenged by a knight, the horn's owner, whose shield was emblazoned with a white lion. Perceval vanquished this Chevalier du Cor and sent him to surrender to Arthur. At his castle he learned of a high mountain, the Mont Dolorous, on whose summit was a marvellous pillar... fashioned long ago by Merlin."

For lines 4460 ff, Owen writes:
"Mont Dolorous, which also appears in C.II (see note to II. 773-93 above), is here associated with Melrose and is probably to be identified with the nearby Eildon Hills..."

In the *Fergus* romance, the Noquetran episode comes first. The horn hangs from a white lion (cf. the lion on the knight's shield in the *Perceval Continuation*) in the Noquetran chapel, where Merlin had spent many a year. In front of the chapel is a bronze giant, apparently a statue, whose arms are broken off by Fergus, causing the giant's great bronze hammer to fall to the ground. Later in the romance, Fergus goes to the Dolorous Mountain or the Eildons and encounters there a club-wielding giant in the Castle of the Dark Rock (reminiscent of the 'Black Mountain' name applied to the Noquetran).

As it happens, the Eildons are noteworthy for having three major ancient monuments atop two of their three hills. On the Eildon North Hill is the largest hill fort in Scotland, the probable oppidum of the Selgovae tribe. Here also is a Roman signal station.

But on Eildon Mid Hill is a large Bronze Age cairn. This ancient burial mound is situated on the Southwest flank of Eildon Mid Hill about 30m below the summit, at a height of some 395m OD. It has been much robbed and now appears as a low, irregular mound of stones, about 15m in diameter, from which a few boulders protrude to indicate the possible former presence of a cist.

Figure 5 - Eildon Walk
Site of a Bronze Age cairn.

More remarkable was the presence below the cairn of a group of seven bronze socketed axes. These axes are now in the Royal Museum of Scotland.

This group of seven socketed axes was found in 1982 on the lower western slopes of Eildon Mid Hill, Ettrick and Lauderdale District, Borders Region. Although recovered from redeposited soil, the axes probably represent a hoard of the Ewart Park phase of the late Bronze Age. The find reinforces what appears to be a significant local concentration of contemporary metalwork around the Eildon Hills.

In view of their discovery in redeposited soil we cannot be absolutely certain how the axes were originally deposited. However, their number, their proximity and their similar condition all suggest that they came from a hoard, probably close to their eventual find-spot. Whether the seven axes recovered in August 1982 comprised the whole hoard remains uncertain. On the other hand, it is possible, though less likely, that more than one separate deposit was originally involved.

These bronze axes immediately remind us of the bronze hammer in the *Fergus* romance's account of Merlin's Chapel. This being so, I would see in the name *'Noquetran'* or Noquetrant a Gaelic *cnoc* or Anglicized *'knock'* plus one of the following:

G. *dreann* – grief, pain (cf. Irish *drean*, sorrow, pain, melancholy); or

G. *treana, treannadh* – lamentation, wailing.

In other words, Noquetran is merely a Gaelic rendering of the Old French Mont Dolorous, the famous Dolorous Mountain of Arthurian romance!

The bronze hammer Fergus causes to be dropped near Merlin's Chapel on the Noquetran is a folk memory of a bronze socketed axe being deposited on the slope below the Eildon Mid Hill cairn or, more probably, of such an axe being found on the site prior to Guillaume Le Clerc's writing of the *Fergus* romance. Merlin's Noquetran chapel is the Eildon Mid Hill Bronze Age cairn.

Melrose Mountain, Black Mountain and Castle of the Dark Rock are all designations for the Eildons. The hill-name Eildon is found in 1130 as Eldunum and in 1150 as Eldune. While various etymologies have been proposed, the most commonly favoured one is G. *aill*, *'a rock, cliff'*, plus OE *dun*, *'a hill'*. The *Fergus* romance's *'Castle of the Dark Rock'* (Li Chastiaus de la Roce Bise) may stand for the hill-fort on Eildon North Hill, with Eildon being perceived as composed of *aill*, rock, plus not *dun*, *'hill'*, but instead OE *dun*, a colour partaking of brown and black; ME *dunne, donne*, dark-coloured: Ir. *Dunn*, a dun colour: Wel. *dwn, dun*, swarthy, dusky: Gael. *Donn*, brown-coloured.

So why were the Eildons identified with the Dolorous Mountain/Noquetran? The answer may lie in part with Nikolai Tolstoy's astute observation that the lion Fergus thinks should be roaming over the mountain-top, but which he finds inside the *'chapel'* is an error or substitution for the god Lugos (Welsh Lleu, Irish Lugh). In Welsh, Lleu's name could sometimes be spelled Llew, and the latter is the normal spelling for the Welsh word *'lion'*. Merlin's associations with Lleu will be briefly discussed below. For now, suffice it to say that the Dolorous Mountain undoubtedly got its name because the divine name Lugos or Lugh was at some point wrongly linked to Latin *lugeo*, '*to mourn, to lament, bewail*'. Such mistakes in language could easily have occurred when going from Celtic to Old French. It may even be that in preferring lugeo to Lugos, a pagan religious secret was being disguised and thus protected.

The Dolorous Mountain is then, properly, '*Lugos Mountain*'. And the Lugos/Lugh/Lleu mountain in particular is Eildon Mid Hill, the highest of the Eildons, with its Bronze Age cairn. Such an identification of the Dolorous Mountain has implications for the Dolorous Garde of Lancelot, especially given that Lancelot himself is a late literary manifestation of the god Lugh, something first discussed long ago by the noted Arthurian scholar Roger Sherman Loomis.

We know of five Lugh forts in Britain, four known and one unlocated. Of the former there is Dinas Dinlle in Gwynedd, Loudoun in East Ayrshire, Luguvalium or Carlisle in Cumbria and Lleuddiniawn or '*Lothian*', land of the Fort of Lugh. Din Eidyn, modern Edinburgh, the capital of Lothian, preserves the name of Lugh's mother in Irish tradition, Eithne. Luguvalium has been interpreted as containing a personal name *Lugovalos*, '*Lugos-strong*', but I believe this name is instead a descriptive of the fort itself as being '*Strong as Lugh*'.

Then there is the Lugudunum or '*Hill-fort of Lugh*' of the *Ravenna Cosmography*. This place, according to Rivet and Smith's *The Place-Names of Roman Britain*, is situated somewhere roughly between Chester-le-Street and South Shields. The only good candidate would seem to be Penshaw Hill, which the Brigantes Nation Website calls *"the only triple rampart Iron Age hill-fort known to exist in the north of England."* Penshaw Hill is associated with the famous Lambton Worm, a monster not unlike the two worms or dragons of Lleu's hill-fort of Dinas Emrys in Gwynedd, Wales.

The Eildons are noted for the stories of '*Canobie*' or Canonbie Dick and Thomas the Rhymer of Ercildoune.

Canonbie is close to both the Carwinley of Myrddin's/Merlin's lord Gwenddolau and Arthuret Knowes, the scene of the Battle of Arfderydd in which Myrddin was driven mad. The 13th century Thomas is credited with meeting an elf-woman under the Eildon Tree (whose location is now marked by a stone) and being taken under the Eildons to the land of Faery. He is also credited with a prophecy concerning Merlin's grave at Drumelzier:

> *"When Tweed and Powsail meet at Merlin's grave,*
> *Scotland and England that day ae king shall have."*

The story of Canonbie Dick presents Thomas as a wizard from past days, and I will quote it in full:

> *"A long time ago in the Borders Region there lived a Horse Cowper called Canobie Dick. He was both admired and feared for his bold courage and rash temper. One evening he was riding over Bowden Moor on the West side of the Eildon Hills. It was very late and the moon was already high in the night sky.*
>
> *He had been to market but trade that day had been poor and he had with him a brace of horses, which he had not been able to sell. Suddenly, he saw ahead of him on the moonlit road, a stranger. The stranger was dressed in a fashion that had not been seen for many centuries. The stranger politely asked the price of the horses.*
>
> *Now Canobie Dick liked to bargain, and was not worried by the strange man's looks. Why, he would have sold his horses to the devil himself, and cheated him as well, given half a chance. They agreed a price which the stranger promptly paid.*
>
> *The only puzzle was that the gold coins he used to pay were as ancient as his dress. They were in the shape of unicorns and bonnet pieces. However, Canobie Dick shrugged his shoulders. Gold was gold. He smiled to himself, thinking that he would get a better bargain for the coins than the stranger had got for the horses.*
>
> *When the stranger asked if he could meet him again at the same place, Canobie Dick was happy to agree. But the stranger had one condition: that he should always come by night and always alone.*
>
> *After several more meetings, Canobie Dick became curious to learn more about his secret buyer. He suggested that 'dry*

bargains' were unlucky bargains and that they should seal the business with a drink at the buyer's home.

'You may see my dwelling if you wish,' said the stranger; 'but if you lose courage at what you see there, you will regret it all your life.'

Canobie Dick was scornful of the warning, after all he was well known for his courage and the stranger seemed harmless enough. The stranger led the way along a narrow footpath, which led into the hills between the Southern and central peaks to a place called the Lucken Hare. Canobie Dick followed but was amazed to see an enormous entrance into the hillside. He knew the area well but had never seen before such an opening or heard any mention of it.

They dismounted and tethered their horses. His guide stopped and fixed his gaze on Canobie Dick. 'You may still return,' he said. Not wanting to be seen as a coward, Canobie Dick shook his head, squared his shoulders and followed the man along the passage into a great hall cut out of the rock.

As they walked, they passed many rows of stables. In every stall there was a coal black horse, and by every horse lay a knight in jet black armour, with a drawn sword in each hand. They were as still as stone, as if they had been carved from marble.

In the great hall were many burning torches. But their fiery light only made the hall more gloomy. There was a strange stillness in the air, like a hot day before a storm. At last they arrived at the far end of the Hall. On an antique oak table lay a sword, still sheathed, and a horn. The stranger revealed that he was Thomas of Ercildoun [Thomas the Rhymer] the famous prophet who had disappeared many centuries ago.

Turning to Canobie Dick he said, 'It is foretold that: 'He that sounds the horn and draws that sword, shall, if his heart fails him not, be king over all broad Britain. But all depends on courage, and whether the sword or horn is taken first. So speaks the tongue that cannot lie.''

The stillness of the air felt heavy. Canobie Dick wanted to take the sword but he was struck by a supernatural terror, such as he had never felt before. What, he thought, would happen if he drew the sword; would such a daring act annoy the powers of the mountain?

Instead he took the horn and with trembling hands put it to his lips. He let out a feeble blast that echoed around the hall.

*It produced a terrible answer. Thunder rolled and with a cry
and a clash of armour the knights arose from their slumber
and the horses snorted and tossed their manes.*

*A dreadful army rose before him. Terrified, Canobie Dick
snatched the sword and tried to free it from its scabbard. At
this a voice boomed:*

'Woe to the Coward, that ever he was born,

Who did not draw the sword before he blew the horn'

*Then he heard the fury of a great whirlwind as he was lifted
from his feet and blasted from the cavern. He tumbled down
steep banks of stones until he hit the ground. Canobie Dick
was found the next morning by local shepherds. He had just
enough trembling breath to tell his fearful tale, before he
died."*

A similar story is told of Alderley Edge in Cheshire, only
in that version the wizard is Merlin and the sleeping knights
are King Arthur and his men.   My guess is that in the case
of the Canonbie Dick story, Thomas the Rhymer has taken
the place of Merlin.   This is not a new supposition, but
combined with my identification of Myrddin's Noquetran
with Eildon Mid Hill as the Dolorous Mountain, the
argument is significantly strengthened. *Fergus* was written
around 1200 CE, while Thomas is thought to have lived c.
1220-1298.   At some point Thomas was substituted for
Merlin at his chapel/cairn on Eildon Mid Hill.

If I am right and the Eildons are Merlin's Mountain at
the centre of the great Celyddon Wood, then we can allow for
the Celyddon as being thought of as the ancient woodland
which covered much of the area surrounding the Eildons.
When we combine this with the fact that Merlin was
obviously wandering in the wood in the vicinity of
Drumelzier when he was captured by Meldred, it is fairly
obvious that the Celyddon, which in this context means
merely a great forest of the Scottish Lowlands, extended for
a considerable distance.

Indeed, we know there were four great ancient forests
surrounding the Eildon Hills: the Jedforest, whose Capon
Tree oak is one of the oldest such trees in all of Britain;
Teviotdale itself, which was covered by huge oaks and ash

trees in the 12th century; the Ettrick Forest of Selkirkshire; and the Lauder Forest, an immense forested track encompassing Lauderdale that still existed up until the 17th century. Apples, or rather crab-apples, the very species of tree Merlin takes refuge under in the early Welsh poetry, were also present in this region. The St. Boswell's Apple is thought to be 150 years old and is the largest of its kind in Scotland. Thomas the Rhymer, taken to Fairyland at the Eildons, is given an apple by the Queen of Fairy.

In my online Vortigern Studies essay on Arthur's battles, I was able to precisely pinpoint the location of Arthur's Coed Celyddon battle. Geoffrey of Monmouth actually provides us with the clue we need to find the battle site in the great Scottish wood. Although he has been justly criticized for producing fictional tales of early British kings rather than historical biographies, we cannot discount the possibility that at least occasionally his account of Arthur's reign may preserve accurate historical traditions. When he has Arthur face the Saxons in the Caledonian Wood, he tells us that:

> "Arthur... ordered the trees round that part of the [Caledonian] wood to be cut down and their trunks to be placed in a circle, so that every way out was barred to the enemy."

This circular palisade Arthur constructs in the Caledonian Wood is none other than the Catrail or 'Fort-fence', a discontinuous linear earthwork which runs from Robert's Linn to Hosecoteshiel and embraces the entire head of the Teviot basin from the Slitrig to beyond the Borthwick Water. The Catrail runs through what was the great Ettrick Forest and functioned as a large scale territorial boundary. In association with other natural features, it may have functioned in respect of the hill fort of North Eildon Hill in the same role as the earthwork called 'The Dorsey' seems to have functioned in respect of the royal Irish site of Emain Macha.

We can say, then, that Arthur's circular palisade in the Caledonian Wood was quite likely the Catrail, and that this dyke is to be brought into connection with the oppidum of the Selgovae on Eildon North Hill, as well as Merlin's Chapel, the Bronze Age cairn atop Eildon Mid Hill.

THE NAME MYRDDIN

The attested name Myrddin reflects an earlier, not directly attested *Myr-ddyn, with the second element *dyn* 'man, person', and the first element *Myr-* which is found in the name of the Old Irish goddess-type figure *Morrigan* (who also prophesies), and in English night-*mare*, and also in several Slavic words. The basic meaning was *'supernatural being, elf, goblin, phantom'* or the like. So *Myrddin was originally something like *'Elf-man'*. His father's name was Morfryn or Mor-bryn, literally *'Elf-hill'*.

This Myr-ddyn > Myrddin is a much more satisfactory explanation than the previously offered theory that Myrddin was derived from the city name of Carmarthen, ancient Caerfyrddin, Roman Moridunum, *'Sea-fort'*. This last notion derives from the fanciful *History of the Kings of Britain* by Geoffrey of Monmouth. In this source, Myrddin is found as a boy at Carmarthen. The whole story is Geoffrey's alteration of Nennius' tale of the boy Ambrosius being found at Campus Elleti in Glamorgan.

THE CELYDDON WOOD AS THE LAND OF SPIRITS

The ancient Classical writer Procopius (in his 6th century CE *History Of The Wars*, VIII, XX. 42-48) said:

> *"Now in this island of Britain the men of ancient times built a long wall, cutting off a large part of it; and the climate and the soil and everything else is not alike on the two sides of it. For to the south of the wall there is a salubrious air, changing with the seasons, being moderately warm in summer and cool in winter... But on the north side everything is the reverse of this, so that it is actually impossible for a man to survive there even a half-hour, but countless snakes and serpents and every other kind of wild creature occupy this area as their own. And, strangest of all, the inhabitants say that if a man crosses this wall and goes to the other side, he dies straightway... They say, then, that the souls of men who die are always conveyed to this place."*

From the Welsh poem *The Dialogue of Myrddin and Taliesin* (*Black Book of Carmarthen*), we learn that at Myrddin's Battle of Arfderydd:

> "Seven score chieftains became gwyllon;
> In the Wood of Celyddon they died."

Gwyllon or 'Wild Ones' is a word deriving from *gwyllt*, 'wild'. The Welsh epithet for Myrddin is, of course, Gwyllt. Myrddin Gwyllt is Myrddin 'the Wild'.

But as Tolstoy pointed out, there is something odd about these two lines. The gwyllon or 'Wild Ones' are equated with the warriors who died in the battle! The word 'died' in the poem's second line is Middle Welsh *daruuan*, i.e. *darfuan*. Modern Welsh has *darfyddaf* or *darfod*, which according to the authoritative *Geiriadur Prifysgol Cymru* Welsh dictionary has the following meanings:

> 'To come to an end, end, conclude, finish, complete, terminate, cease; expire, die, languish, weaken, fail, fade, decline, perish'

Darfod is an interesting word. It is from the prefix *dar-*, roughly 'across', and *bod*, 'to be', with the regular lenition of b>f. So literally 'to be across', possibly in the same sense in which we say of a dead person 'he has crossed over'.

There is thus no ambiguity in the poetic passage we are considering. The warriors who became 'Wild Ones' did not go mad – they *died*. In this context, then, to become gwyllon means to become a roving spirit that has left its battle-slain body behind. To exist as a 'Wild One' is to exist in spirit-form after the death of the body.

The Christian medieval mind either could not accept this notion of wandering spirits or, just as likely, misunderstood it. The gwyllon were transformed into *living* madmen who leapt or flitted about the forest much as did their Irish counterpart, Suibhne Geilt.

In another Myrddin poem, *Greetings* (*Black Book of Carmarthen*), we are told by Myrddin himself:

> "The hwimleian speaks to me strange tidings,
> And I prophesy a summer of strife."

Hwimleian or *'Grey Wanderer'* is yet another word for a spirit or spectre. Myrddin *'the Wild'*, as he is portrayed in Welsh tradition, is thus the soul of a dead man, wondering the woods of Celyddon. We must presume that it was believed that certain individuals with psychic powers could communicate with or perhaps even channel such spirits - the gwyllon or hwimleian – and thereby extract from them information only available to the dead, e.g. prophetic utterances.

Difficult as it is for us to believe in this modern age, ancestral spirits were once worshipped and even placated with offerings. *'Dis Manibus'* or *'For the Divine Spirits of the Dead'* was a common heading for Roman period memorial stones. Morddyn or Myrddin the *'Elf-Man'* may have been such a spirit of the dead.

In the case of Merlin, then, we have a warrior-bard whose divine patron was Lugh. He was slain in battle at Arfderydd and his spirit wandered the Lowland Scottish forest, but had its proper home atop the Lugh Mountain of Eildon Mid Hill. There, in *'Merlin's Chapel'*, the spirits of the dead congregated.

But this is not all that can be said about Myrddin, for we have yet to consider his other name, Llallawc or Llallogan/Lailoken, and account for his triple-death at Drumelzier on the Tweed.

LAILOKEN

It has been customary to agree with the identification of Myrddin with the madman Lailoken, W. *Llallogan* or *Llallawc*. In his edition of Geoffrey of Monmouth's *Life of Merlin*, Basil Clarke proposes that Myrddin was originally a certain Llallawg or Llallogan who went mad at Arfderydd.

The crux of the issue is found in the Welsh poem, *The Prophecy of Myrddin and Gwenddydd, His Sister*. There Gwenddydd addresses her brother Myrddin as both Llallogan (once) and Llallawc (several times). The 15th century MS. *Cotton Titus A. XIX* contains the tales of

Kentigern and Lailoken and Meldred and Lailoken. Jocelyn's 12th century *Life of St. Kentigern* also mentions Lailoken in its last chapter. In both of these sources, Lailoken is identified with Merlin. The question then is: are we to see Llallogan/Llallawc as merely a term of endearment applied to Myrddin or as a separate person with whom Myrddin was wrongly identified?

In the story of Meldred and Lailoken, Merlin suffers a triple death at the hands of Meldred's shepherds. The triple death is a motif found in Celtic literature and was a special kind of death meted out to kings, heroes and gods alike. It is, in essence, a form of human sacrifice, made sacred by the use of three simultaneous methods of killing. It has been hypothesized that each method of killing was sacred to a specific god. The three Celtic divinities in question have been tentatively identified with Taranis the thunder god, Esus the lord and master and Teutates, the overall god of the people.

Nikolai Tolstoy used the example of Lailoken's triple death to more closely link Merlin with the god Lleu/Lugh, as Lleu in Welsh tradition also suffers a triple death.

That such a form of human sacrifice was actually practiced has been proven by examination of the Lindow Man, who was struck in the head by an axe, choked with a garrotte and drowned in a pool. By undergoing such a sacred killing, the Lindow Man was acting the role of a god like Lleu. And by acting such a role, he became the god – a sun god who was seasonally killed and reborn.

The corollary of the three-fold death was, of course, resurrection. The god Lleu, who in death is represented as an eagle in an oak tree, was brought back to life by Gwydion. The Lindow Man as Lleu, by dying, helped ensure the seasonal rebirth of the sun god.

The true importance of Lailoken's triple death on the Tweed near the Dunmeller of Meldred has been overlooked, however. For it clearly demonstrates that by the time of the composition of the *Life of St. Kentigern*, Merlin's true death at Arfderydd and his roaming the Caledonian Wood as a spirit had been forgotten or concealed. Inserted in its place was the notion that the battle had driven him mad. And because his state of madness was taken literally, a version of another madman's death was borrowed to provide a fitting conclusion to his life story.

The model for Myrddin's death at Dunmeller was taken from that of another *'elf'* figure. In Welsh tradition we find a character called Gwerthmwl Wledig or Gwerthmwl the Ruler (variants Gyrthmwl, Gwrthmwl, etc.). In the first of the *Welsh Triads*, he is mentioned as Chief Elder of Penrhyn Rhionydd in the North. Penrhyn Rhionydd has been very plausibly identified with the Rhinns of Galloway. Arthur is Chief Prince of the same place, while Cynderyn Garthwys, i.e. St. Kentigern, is the Chief Bishop. We have seen above that Lailoken was brought into connection with Kentigern.

In *Triad 44*, immediately after mention of the Arfderydd battle is made, Gwerthmwl's sons are said to have ridden onto Allt or Rhiw Faelawr or Faelwr in Ceredigion on the west coast of Wales. This is the site of the fort known as Dinas Maelawr (modern Pendinas), the home of the legendary Maelor Gawr or Maelor *'the Giant'*. Dinas Maelawr is also called Castell Maylor and was built upon a high hill or ridge beside the river Ystwyth. Gwerthmwl's sons ride up the hill to avenge their father, whom Maelor is said to have killed. Clearly there is something very wrong with this tale: Gwerthmwl does not belong in Ceredigion, but in the far North of Britain. It is obvious that his story has been relocated to Wales.

The chieftain Gwerthmwl in *Triad 63* is referred to as 'Ellyll Gwerthmwl Wledig', the word *ellyll* meaning *'spirit, phantom, ghost, goblin, elf, fairy'*. In her note to *Triad 63*, Rachel Bromwich suggests that the word *ellyll* in this context may be related to that of the Gwyllt epithet used for Myrddin and the Irish Geilt epithet used for the madman Suibhne.

To quote the relevant Triad in full:

"Tri Tharv Ellyll Ynys Brydein:
Ellyll Gvidawl
Ac Ellyll Llyr Marini
Ac Ellyll Gyrthmvl Wledic"

"Three Bull-Spectres of the Island of Britain:
The Spectre of Gwidawl
The Spectre of Llyr Marini
And the Spectre of Gyrthmwl Wledig."

Ellyll is cognate with Irish Ailill, a personal name with the same meaning. Rather remarkably, the best etymology for ellyll and Ailill is a reduplicated form of *ail/eil*, *'other'*. The name Llallawc/Llallogan is derived from W. *llall*, *'other'*, yet another reduplicated form of *ail/eil*.

I would add that Alladhan, the name given to Llallogan in the Irish Suibhne Geilt story, is from Irish *allaid*, *'wild'*. The most likely etymology for *allaid* is the same *al-* root, as an *'Other'* is someone who lived beyond the civilized world and was hence barbarous or *'wild'*, a stranger or foreigner or an enemy, i.e. someone deemed dangerous because he did not belong to one's native land.

Gwerthmwl of the Rhinns of Galloway, when we remember that the Welsh render an initial F- as Gw-, is the 8th century Bishop of Whithorn, Frithuwald. The discrepancy in date between Bishop Frithuwald and St. Kentigern (d. 603) is probably due to Nennius' statement that the Bernician chieftain *'Friodo(l)guald'*, i.e. Frithuwald, was ruling in the last quarter of the 6th century. This Friodo(l)guald is mentioned along with Deoric son of Ida, Hussa, Urien Rheged, Rhydderch Hen, Gwallawg and Morgan.

Now Frithuwald in Old English means either *'Peace-ruler'* or *'Protection-ruler'*. But Gwerthmwl Wledic (Welsh *wledic* or *'ruler'* plainly suggests the Old English *wald*) may well have been interpreted by the Welsh as *'Ffridd'*-ruler, i.e. *'Forest-ruler'*. Irish has *frith*, *'a wild, mountainous place, a forest, a deer forest'*, Welsh has *ffridd*, *'wood, wooded land, a mountain pasture, a sheep walk'* and ME has *frid*, *'deer park'*, from AS *fyrhth(e)*, *'wood, woodland'*.

Triad 63, which refers to Frithuwald/Gyrthmwl as a *'tharv ellyll'* or *'bull-spectre'*, also has a variant, wherein the phrase *'charw ellyll'* or *'stag-spectre'* is substituted. If *'stag-spectre'* is the more proper form, then we would have yet another reason why Gyrthmwl's death story was borrowed for that of Myrddin, as Geoffrey of Monmouth tells us that Merlin took the form of a stag.

One might hypothesize that the Bernician chieftain Frithuwald was captured by British enemies based at Dunmeller. As often happened with war captives, he was selected because of his high political status to be given up as a triple sacrifice. Probably the sacrifice was intended to bring good fortune in battle against the Saxons. By dying a triple death, Frithuwald became an incarnation of the god Lugh, who as we have seen underwent a seasonal death and rebirth.

To sum up: it seems fairly certain that the story of Gwerthmwl the Ellyll's death at Dinas Maelawr on the Ystwyth belongs properly at Dunmeller on the Tweed, and was borrowed in order to provide Merlin, who had actually died at Arfderydd/Arthuret, with a suitable death-story.

a) Frithuwald/Gwerthmwl being killed at Dinas Maelawr on the Ystwyth =

b) Lailoken being killed at Dunmeller on the Tweed

An ellyll, as well as a llallawc or llallogan, must in this context be related to the gwyllon and hwimleian. All were used to describe the spirit of either a warrior slain in battle – a warrior who was sacred to the god Lugh – or of a person who had been offered up as a triple-sacrifice to Lugh.

MERLIN AND THE GOD ALLETIOS

Camelot derives via the Old French from an earlier Romano-British Campus Alletio. Alletios is the name of a god whose name contains the same *ail/eil* root as ellyll, Alladhan and Llallawc/Llallogan. Anne Ross has suggested Alletios may be the *'God of the Otherworld'*. This god name is found only at the Corbridge Roman fort on Dere Street just south of Hadrian's Wall.

Camelot, as is made plain by Chretien de Troyes' use of the term and his placement of it near Caerleon and *'Castle Vagan'*, i.e. Welsh Castell Sain Ffagan, is an Old French attempt at the Campus Elleti of Ambrosius, mentioned in the *Historia Brittonum* of Nennius. This place has usually been situated somewhere in the Ely Valley, but as I have demonstrated in an online article at the Vortigern Studies Website, there is an excellent linguistic reason for considering this a relocation.

That Campus Alletio or Camelot could well have been in the vicinity of the Corbridge fort is suggested by another interesting place-name at this location. From the Venerable Bede:

> *"The place is called in English Heavenfield, and in Latin Caelestis campus, a name which it certainly received in days of old as an omen of future happenings; it signified that the heavenly sign was to be erected there, a heavenly victory won, and that heavenly miracles were to take place there continuing to this day"*

Bede clearly indicates that Oswald's campsite was known as Heavenfield long before he erected the cross and prayed there. Therefore, it was an old pagan holy site. And Bede's Caelestis not only means *'heavenly'*, but can refer to a deity as well.

We know that an altar was dedicated to Caelistis Brigantia at Corbridge. As campus Caelestis is near Corbridge, I would propose that this is the field of Caelestis Brigantia and that, as such, it was an *'Otherworld'* location. The same would have been true of a campus Alletio at Corbridge.

The most recent scholarly work on Alletios has sought to associate him with native British smith gods and thunder gods who bear lightning hammers. We are once again reminded of the bronze hammer in the *Fergus* romance and the bronze axes found below *'Merlin's Chapel'* on Eildon Mid Hill. While the Welsh smith god was Gofannon (cf. the Irish Goibhniu), we must not forget that one of Lugh's epithet's was *'Skillful-hand'*. In Irish mythology, Lugh was master of many trades, including smithcraft.

Knowing that all these *'fairy'* designations – ellyll, Alladhan, Llallawc/Llallogan – have to do with spirits of human heroes who were deemed holy due their relationship with the god Lugh, I believe that Alletios is a byname for Lugh himself. Lugh Alletios was the supreme *'other'*, the god of the Otherworld who received in his divine mountain the spirits of those slain in his honour, either on the battlefield or during sacrificial rituals. These spirits became *'Others'* like him.

SOME OTHER MYSTERIOUS PLACES ASSOCIATED WITH MERLIN

There are some other Merlin sites whose locations are uncertain. Five of them are the Fountain of Barenton, another tomb of Merlin, the spring of Galabes, Merlin's esplumoir and the Green Chapel of the Gawain poem.

The Fountain of Barenton is none other than the mineral springs of Berrington (Berinton) near Tenbury Wells in Herefordshire.

A previously unlocated grave of Merlin is said by the *Prose Lancelot* to be in the Perilous Forest of Darnantes atop a mountain. Darnantes or Dar-nantes is the River Dore, which flows through the Golden Valley in the Black Mountains of Wales. Dore is either from French *D'ore*, *'golden'*, or W. *dwr*, *'water'*, while *–nantes* is from W. *nant*, *'stream, brook'*. The Perilous Forest of the Dore River must be in this area, which is still forested to this day. Only a couple of miles west of the Dore is Mynydd Merddin, *'Myrddin's Mountain'*, one of the traditional Welsh sites of Merlin's tomb. However, as Mynydd Merddin is an outlier of the Black Mountains, this could well be a relocation of Merlin's mountain at the Eildons in the North.

As for Merlin's spring or springs of Galabes, Geoffrey of Monmouth places this site in the region of the Gewisse. In a note to his *The Quest for Merlin* (pp. 270-271), Tolstoy suggests that Geoffrey may have substituted the Gewisse for Nennius' Guunessi. This would mean, of course, that Galabes would be found in Guunessi. Tolstoy is mistaken here. Merlin's Galabes is plainly Nennius' Guoloph, i.e.

Wallop, the site of a battle between Aurelius Ambrosius and Vitalinus. Now there is a Wallop stream in the Shropshire of Vortigern, but there is another in Hampshire, the Wallop Brook, site of the villages known as the Wallops. Hampshire is within the territory of the Gewisse.

The Cair Guorthirgin of Guunessi has been identified with a site at Nant Gwrtheyrn near the northwest coast of Llyn between Yr Eifl and Nefyn. Guunessi (Gwnnws, Gwynnys) is now a farm two miles south of Nant Gwrtheyrn.

Now to treat briefly of the famous *'esplumoir'* or *'esplumeor'* of Merlin, which the *Didot Perceval* places next to the Grail Castle of Bron and Perceval:

> *"...and I wish to make a lodging outside your palace and to dwell there... And all those who will see my lodging will name it the esplumoir of Merlin ['si le clameront l'esplumoir Merlin']. Then Merlin left them and made his esplumoir and entered within and never since then has he been seen in the world."*

Raoul de Houdenc's *Meraugis de Portlesguez* identifies the esplumoir as a high rock upon which are twelve damsels forever prophesying. These *'twelve damsels'* are in reality a stone circle. They are akin to various stone circles named for maidens or witches, e.g. Boleigh's Merry Maidens, Bosscawen-Un's Nine Maidens, Little Selkeld's Long Meg and Her Daughters, Harthill Moor's Grey Ladies, Stanton's Nine Ladies.

The best guess to date as to the meaning of esplumoir is *'moulting cage'*, but this is usually considered unsatisfactory. The word is otherwise unknown in Old French.

The *es-* of esplumoir is a prefix such as that added to caliber to form Escalibur or Excalibur, the name of Arthur's sword in later romance. As such, it can be dropped, leaving us with a word spelled *'plumoir'* or *'plumeor'*. I would see in either of these an obvious Old French attempt at Old Breton *ploe*, *'parish'*, plus *meur*, *'great'*. There are four Ploemeur place-names in Brittany: Pleumeur-Bodou and Pleumeur-Gautier in Cotes d'Armor, Plomeur in Finistere and

Ploemeur in Morbihan. Plomeur in Finistere is home to the Kerugou dolmen.

Suppose, however, that *'great parish'* is not being used in this context as a genuine place-name, but as a description of a type of district? I believe this, is in fact, what the author of the *Didot Perceval* intends here. He was availing himself of two traditions. One, which is known to come from before the 12th century, is the designation of the island of Britain as *'Clas Merdin'*. Clas, according to the *Geiriadur Prifysgol Cymru*, has the meanings *'monastic community, monastica classis, cloister, people of the same country, band or community of fellow-countrymen'*. The second strand of tradition comes from Geoffrey of Monmouth, who makes Amesbury the scene of a famous monastery, the so-called Cloister of Ambrius (or Emrys, the Welsh form of the Latin name Ambrosius). This monastery may be referred to in the *Welsh Triads* under its name Caer Caradoc, one of the three eternal choirs of the island of Britain. This again is due to Geoffrey, who refers to Salisbury near Stonehenge and Amesbury as Caer Caradoc.

Geoffrey, furthermore, places Stonehenge or the Giants' Dance atop a hill next to the parish of Amesbury, supposedly the *'Fort of Ambrosius'*. For Geoffrey, and anyone reading him in the Middle Ages, Ambrosius was merely another name for Merlin himself.

The *'Great Parish'* of Merlin, i.e. of Ambrosius, would be the parish of Amesbury with its stone circle. Again according to Geoffrey, Ambrosius brother of Uther was buried within the Giant's Dance. Since Merlin bears the Ambrosius name as well, the *Didot Perceval* author placed Merlin's Otherworld *'lodging'* or tomb at Stonehenge.

But if the Esplumeor Merlin = the *'great parish'* of Amesbury, the nearby Grail Castle obviously was not Corbenic or Castell Dinas Bran in North Wales (see Chapter 9 below), a tradition recorded in other Arthurian romances. Then what is the Grail Castle next to the Great Parish of Ambrosius?

The best guess would be Amesbury's neighbouring hill-fort Vespasian's Camp, only 1.2 miles east of Stonehenge.

The name of this camp is due to the Elizabethan antiquarian Camden. In reality, the fort pre-dates the Romans. However, I think it is not a coincidence that Geoffrey of Monmouth calls Salisbury Caer Caradoc after the British chieftain Caractacus who was defeated by the Roman Vespasian. We have no record of Salisbury ever being referred to as the fort of Caractacus; the ancient name of Old Sarum next to Salisbury was Sorviodunum.

Could not Geoffrey have mistaken Salisbury the town for Caer Caradoc, when in reality Caer Caradoc was the name of the hill-fort on Salisbury Plain? Camden might well have replaced the name of the defeated British chieftain with that of the Roman conqueror, Vespasian. If so, the *'eternal choir'* of Caer Caradoc mentioned in the *Welsh Triads* is another name for the Cloister of Ambrosius at Amesbury. And as far as the author of the *Didot Perceval* was concerned, Vespasian's Camp next to the Esplumeor Merlin or Great Parish of Amesbury was the Grail Castle.

Another Arthurian site has always intrigued me; that of the Green Chapel in the 14th century epic poem *Sir Gawain and the Green Knight*. While it is not immediately apparent that the Green Chapel has anything to do with Merlin, we will see that it actually belongs to the great enchanter.

The poem leaves no doubt as to what the Green Chapel really is:

> *"... a hillock of sorts, A smooth-surfaced barrow on a slope beside a stream... All hollow it was within, only an old cavern..." (Lines 2171-82)*

This chambered barrow is *'hardly two miles'* from the castle of the Green Knight, who calls himself Bertilak of Hautdesert (High Desert). The directions to this castle are unknown; we are only told that Gawain is going north by way of the Gwynedd coast opposite Anglesey and the Wirral Peninsula. After this the description of his route becomes increasingly vague.

Bertilak represents the Bertholais of the *Arthurian Vulgate*. Indeed, the English translation of the *Vulgate* renders Bertholais as Bertilak. This Bertholais is associated with Gawain, but does not bear any of the characteristics later ascribed to Bertilak. In the *Vulgate*, Bertholais and the False Guinevere (whose champion the former was) are exiled to the hinterlands. The suggestion has been made that Bertilak's beautiful wife, the temptress of Gawain, is actually the False Guinevere. Because the poet put Morgan le Fay in Bertilak's house, it is also possible that the Green Knight's wife is an aspect of Morgen, i.e. the Morrigan.

Speaking purely from a phonological standpoint, Bertholais may owe his name to the Britaelis of Geoffrey of Monmouth's *History*. Significantly, Britaelis was Gorlois' servant whose form was assumed by none other than Merlin in the story of Ygerna's seduction by Uther.

If Bertholais is Merlin, it is surely significant that the *Life of St. Kentigern* has Lailoken/Myrddin/Merlin buried 'not far from the green chapel where the brook Pausayl flows into the River Tweed.' In other words, the 'Green Chapel' is none other than the Northern Merlin's supposed grave.

MYRDDIN AND THE JOURNEY TO AVALON

The very first account of Arthur's conveyance to Avalon differs remarkably from that found in late sources such as the *Morte D'Arthur* of Sir Thomas Malory. It is Geoffrey of Monmouth's *Life of Merlin* that tells us how Arthur was brought by boat from Camlann to Avalon, with Merlin a passenger and Barinthus the steersman. As has been recognized for some time, this Barinthis is Geoffrey's spelling for the famous Irish St. Brendan the Navigator, originally Breanainn, who set out from Ireland to find Tir Tairngire or the Land of Promise in the west.

The typical Celtic triad of Arthur, Merlin/Myrddin and Barinthus/Brendan is replaced in the romances by various numbers of 'queens', i.e. goddesses of Avalon, who ferry Arthur away to the Otherworld without any masculine assistance. Morgan (= the Morrigan) is often listed as one of these 'queens', as is the Lady of the Lake (= the Dea Latis Nemhain), of course.

Breanainn is a borrowing from the Welsh and is a name based on *brenin*, *'king'*. Brenin itself derives from the name of the goddess Brigantia, specifically from **brigantinos*, a term which identified the king or *'exalted one'* as consort of the tutelary goddess of the Brigantes tribe. As the Camlann that was Castlesteads and the Avalon that was Burgh-By-Sands are both in Carvetii territory, and the Carvetii were part of the Brigantian confederation, it is particularly appropriate that the pilot of the boat should bear this name.

Of course, we are talking about ancient religious symbolism here – not physical fact. It is well known that Myrddin lived – and died – well after Arthur's time. He could not, therefore, have been personally present in the funeral barge that took Arthur to Avalon. But as Myrddin was a divine spirit of a slain warrior-bard, he may be emblematic of the other slain champions who perished with Arthur at Camlann and who, presumably, also were taken to Avalon.

CHAPTER FIVE

THE HORNED GOD

At the very heart of the kingdom of the Carvetii or *'Deer-people'* are the three henges at Eamont: the great Mayburgh or *'Maiden's Fort'* Henge, King Arthur's Round Table and the Little Round Table. Eamont is from Anglo-Saxon *ea-gemot* or *'water-meet'*, signifying the river confluence at this location. Eamont replaced the earlier Cumbrian place-name Echwydd or *'Out-water'* which is mentioned in the Taliesin poems as a site the Rheged kings ruled over. Echwydd or *'Out-water'* is a reference to the Eamont River, which flows out of the large, natural lake of Ullswater, the second largest body of water in the Lake District.

Because a large concentration of dedications to the British god Belatucadros were found at the Roman fort of Brovacum, modern Brougham, next to Eamont, it has been assumed that the three henges belonged anciently to him. Next to one of the Belatucadros dedications was found a carving of a horned god. As the *'Deer-people'* would certainly have worshipped a deer god, this carving is usually considered to be a depiction of Belatucadros himself. Belatucadros inscriptions are found at other sites in northwest England, chiefly along the western half of Hadrian's Wall, including at the Avalon fort of Burgh-By-Sands.

The name Belatucadros is from *belatu-*, *'striking'* or *'slaying'*, and *cadro*, *'beautiful'*, *'good'*, *'fair'* or *'shining'*, and means, therefore, something like *'He who is beautiful in slaying'*. The Romans identified him with their own war god Mars. This is a fitting name for a god whose animal form was that of a noble and potentially fiercesome red stag.

Figure 6 - Belatucadros Carving
Altar carving from the Roman fort at Aballava of
the Horned God Belatucadros of the Carvetii tribe.

During the rut of September and October, red stags engage in regular combats in competition for harems of hinds. The combats are composed of a period in which the two contestants walk in parallel with each other, roar and finally strike at each other, locking antlers and pushing until one animal is pushed backwards or gives way and retreats. Serious injury and even death can result.

The ancient Britons, observing such combats, could not have helped but to have compared them to the fighting of human warriors, who locked weapons and similarly strove to injure or kill their opponents or force them into retreat. The red stag thus became not only a manifestation of the deity, but the totem animal of the Carvetii tribe.

The horned god, however, also had a clear celestial aspect. While the King Arthur's Round Table and Little Round Table henges at Eamont have no distinguishing features, much more impressive Mayburgh Henge has more to tell us about the worship of the heavenly Belatucadros.

The earthwork is defined by an almost circular bank which is up to 45 metres wide and 7.3 metres high, surrounding an internal area up to 90 metres in diameter. The bank is made up almost entirely of water-worn stones obtained from the River Eamont, 110 metres to the north. There is no ditch. A single entrance exists on the eastern side. The interior is level, and a single standing stone is located near the centre. There may have been a narrow ditch surrounding the inner side of the bank. Various pit-like features could indicate burials or votive deposits or the positions of former stone settings. One group of these pits is clustered to the south east of the single remaining 2.8 metre tall standing stone, in an area where Dugdale recorded a stone setting in the later 17th century. The earliest account of the site was by this Dugdale, who noted only four stones in the interior and two more standing just outside the entrance. William Stukeley, writing in 1725, claimed that there had been two circles of huge stones within the rampart, one immediately inside the bank, the other with a diameter of 15m to which the remaining stone belonged. He said that only four stones had survived, and that three of these had been blown up just before 1725. Thomas Pennant, in his *Tour of Scotland* 1796, said four stones stood in the centre and four more flanked the entrance, two on each side.

Regardless of what the original stone circle at Mayburgh may have looked like, it was obviously a nemeton whose opening faced the rising sun in the east. While the oak tree of the druids symbolized both the sky and the sky-god, the multiple tines of a great stag's spreading antlers stood for the heavenly lightning of the same god. The classic image of Cernunnos or the *'Divine Horned One'* on the Gundestrup cauldron depicts an anthropomorphic god with antlers. In one hand he holds the horned (= crescent) lunar serpent, and in the other a sun-torc. He also wears a similar torc. Animals of various kinds surround him like loyal subjects; these may once have represented constellations or other planetary and stellar bodies. Such iconography serves to show the divinity not only as the royal stag, the *'king of the beasts'* of the forest, but also as Jupiter the king of the gods and of heaven. Thus the Roman interpretation of Belatucadros as Mars had been based solely on the obvious martial function of the former, and not on the true nature of this particular Horned God.

Belatucadros found his way into Arthurian story as the white stag who so often is utilized as the starting point of a quest. We have seen that the *cadro-* portion of Belatucadros' name meant *'beautiful, good, fair, shining'*. The ancient Carvetii people would have perceived their god in the same way: as a magnificent stag whose pelt was bright as the light-filled sky precisely because he was the sky.

We will see in Chapter 6 below that Gwyn, the Welsh god of the Otherworld whose name means *'white, fair, blessed'*, appears to have been the Horned God in another guise.

CHAPTER SIX

OTHER GODS AND GODDESSES

(A DEVOTIONAL CATALOGUE)

The following list of Arthurian deities is by no means exhaustive. Instead, it is inclusive only of those divine personages I personally deemed the most important, and so must be considered a representative sampling of the rich store of names and attributes found embedded in Romano-British inscriptions, early Welsh poems and prose compilations such as the *Mabinogion*.

ACHREN

To know who Achren is, we must start at the Fort of Nefyn the Tall, Nefyn being the Welsh way of spelling the Irish Nemhain. In our time the fort is called Carn Bod-Buan or Boduan, which stands over the town of Nefyn on the Lleyn Peninsula in Gwynedd, Wales.

Long ago, at the foot of this fort, there occurred a famous battle among the tribe of the Gangani, the men of 'The Branch', as they called the headland at the end of the Lleyn Peninsula. It was because of this battle that the Welsh poets centuries later told of a battle fought between the trees of the forest. For the poets thought that the battle of the Men of the Branch was a battle of the branches of trees, and this they called the Battle of Godeu.

Godeu (or Goddeu) is *not* the word for wood, which in Welsh is *coed* (in Latin sources, *coit*). It is instead a short form of Gododdin, that kingdom in the North of Britain that lay along the Firth of Forth in Scotland. In the early medieval period, it was thought that men of Manau Gododdin, or that part of Gododdin at the head of the Firth of Forth, had come down to Gwynedd to rule. The ruler of these men was called Cunedda. But in truth Cunedda did not come from Manau Gododdin. He actually came from Drumanagh in Ireland, directly across from the Lleyn Peninsula. He was known to the Irish as Chuinnedha or Cuindedha.

Achren has been thought of as a goddess. She is mentioned as fighting in the Battle of Godeu. But the manuscript that speaks of her is very late – in fact, from the 17th century! We are told in this late source that the god Bran was also in the battle, and that if anyone could guess either her name or his, then the side that person was on would win the battle. Bran had with him sprigs of alder (or alder depicted on his shield), and it was because of this that Gwydion was able to guess his name. For was not Bran's son named Gwern, which in Welsh is *'Alder'*?

But Achren herself was not a goddess – she was a divine bird from Annwn, the Otherworld. In the *Welsh Triads* we are told that the cause of the Battle of Godeu was the theft of a plover, white roebuck and a whelp from Arawn, Lord of Annwn, by Amaethon son of Don. When the tale is told in the 17th century, only the white roebuck and whelp are said to be the cause of the battle. The plover is oddly missing.

So what happened to the plover? This bird in the early Welsh tongue was *'chornugil'*, and in the text of the *Triads* *chornugil* is preceded by *'a'*. Achren is nothing more than a corruption for *'a chornugil'*. In other words, Achren is the plover of Annwn.

This is why she is paired with Bran, whose name means *'Raven'*. They were both sacred birds of the Gangani or *'Branch'* people. The plover migrates very long distances, and often does so without stopping along the way. Its flight is rapid, and it also is quick to give alarm calls, and so is the sentinel for other shorebirds. One should invoke the spirit and essence of the plover when long trips are planned or when it is necessary to be unusually vigilant.

AMAETHON

This god's name means *'He who Drives Around the Plough'*. He is the Welsh god of agriculture, corresponding to the Roman Saturn. The farmer ploughing in his field is an embodiment of Amaethon, and the farmer should call upon this god to aid him in preparing the field for planting. So, too, should the gardener, who uses only the hoe to prepare the earth for seed.

ANU

She was the goddess of the river Annan in Dumfriesshire of the Scottish Lowlands. Geoffrey of Monmouth made her into *'Anna'*, daughter of Uther and Eigr. In the Irish sources, Anu is identified with the Morrigan, and is also made the sister of Badb and Macha. We have seen above in Chapter 2 that while the Welsh name Morgan (as in Morgan le Fey) meant *'Sea-born'*, she was a substitute for the Irish Morrigan or *'Spirit-queen'*. Thus Anna or Anu, sister of Arthur, who was identified by the Irish with the Morrigan, became Morgan le Fey, sister of Arthur. Anu's name means *'riches'* and she should be called upon whenever emotional or physical prosperity is sought. Anna in the early Welsh genealogies is the wife of Beli Mawr (q.v.), and the father of Afallach, the Welsh form of Irish Ablach, the apple Otherworld also known as Avalon. We have seen that Avalon is the Burgh-By-Sands Roman fort of that name, which was right across the Solway from the Anann River.

ARIANRHOD

Arianrhod or Aranrhod is the *'Silver Wheel'*, an apt description for the full moon, envisioned as a wheel rolling through the heavens. It is from Arianrhod that Lleu the sun god receives his name and weapons. Thus she should be called upon for the naming of children and for the wisdom to choose those tools or skills which will most assist children during the course of their lives. A Welsh word for moon is *'lleuad'*, because Lleu's name meant *'Light'* and it was the sun's light reflecting from the moon that made the goddess *arian* or *'silver'*.

That Arianrhod is actually tricked by Gwydion into bestowing a name and weapons upon Lleu I take to be late patriarchal interference in what was originally a matriarchal custom.

ARAWN

Arawn is the Welsh form of Orion the Hunter, a borrowing from Classical mythology. Some have thought to see the Biblical Aaron in this god name, but Arawn's relationship to Hafgan (q.v.), as well as his being a hunter in Welsh tradition, confirms the identification with Orion. Annwn is the pagan Otherworld, specifically the underworld, which prior to Christianity did not have negative connotations. The word itself either means *'very deep place'* or the *'not-world'*. It became identified with the Christian Hell.

The real king of Annwn is Gwyn son of Nudd (q.v.). In the *Life of St. Collen*, the entrance to Annwn is at Glastonbury Tor, and the king of Annwn is expressly stated to be Gwyn. The great hunter in Welsh tradition was Mabon, as is made clear in the *Mabinogion*. There we are told that no one can hunt the monstrous boar Twrch Trwyth without Mabon, who is the only one who can handle the hound Drudwyn. Mabon was Apollo Maponus, and at Nettleton Scrub Apollo Cunomaglos was the *'Hound-prince'*.

Because Orion was the constellation of Winter, call upon him during the cold season for help when pursuing worthy objectives or when honouring ancestors.

For another Celtic deity who may have been associated with Orion, see the listing for Vitiris below.

ARNEMETIA

'*She who is next to/by/in front of/across from the Sacred Grove*' was the goddess worshipped at Aquae Arnemetia, the Baths of Arnemetia, modern-day Buxton in the Peak District of Derbyshire. In my book *Shadows in the Mist*, I supplied my argument for this place being the site of Arthur's Mount Badon battle.

Her name presents us with a bit of a problem, for it suggests the goddess did not reside in the nemeton or sacred grove itself, but rather somewhere not too far outside of it. The waters at Buxton were considered sacred to her precisely because of their proximity to the nemeton. Doubtless the grove, wherever its precise location, was part of what came to be known under the Normans as the '*Royal Forest of the Peak*', a region bordered by the rivers Goyt, Etherow, Derwent and Wye. The '*Frith*' of Chapel-en-le-Frith, under a half down miles north of Buxton, is from the Anglo-Saxon word for '*woodland*', a reference to the Peak Forest.

The waters of Arnemetia were rededicated to the Christian St. Anne, mother of Mary. We have seen above that Anne was herself often a substitute for the goddess Anu.

The Roman Diana Nemorensis or Diana '*of the Sacred Grove*', whose temple stood on Lake Nemi, can be compared with Arnemetia. In this Classical context, a lake and grove are found in close conjunction with each other. The same relationship may have existed between the natural springs of Arnemetia and her nemeton. Various types of water-loving trees grow in abundance on the banks of lakes, rivers and springs. Such trees help protect the spring from drying up during the hot part of the year. There is thus a symbiotic relationship of sorts between a spring and its nemeton. Experts in early British religion have not neglected to notice that a goddess Nemetona, literally '*Divine One of the Sacred Grove*', received a dedication at Bath, the Romano-British Aquae Sulis.

Arnemetia, then, is the goddess who presides over springs that are sheltered by trees. She is the guardian deity of such places as well as being manifest in the healing qualities of the water. She should be called upon when water cures are administered and when refuge from negative forces is sought. Any nemeton dedicated to her can be viewed as an inviolable sanctuary.

BELI MAWR

Beli Mawr or Beli *'the Great'* is Apollo Belenos, Apollo the Bright or Shining One. The earliest Welsh genealogies make his father one Afallach, who as we have seen can be equated with the Irish Ablach of Emain Ablach, the Apple Orchard Otherworld. His mother was *'Anna'*, i.e. the goddess Anu.

In Arthurian romance Beli Mawr is called Pellinore. In the 12th century, Johannes Cornubiensis identified Caer Beli or the Fort of Beli with Ashbury Camp near Week St. Mary in Cornwall. This fort he also termed the *'Fatale Castrum'* or Deadly Castle. However, this is an error, as Ashbury Camp is an unremarkable hill-fort. Instead, Ashbury, Oxfordshire is the actual site of the original Cair Beli. This is where we find the famous Neolithic chambered tomb now known as Wayland's Smithy. Wayland was the smith-god of the invading Saxons. The Smithy is near the Uffington White Horse and one of the primary symbols of Belenos in Gaul is the horse.

Beli as Apollo is associated with Stonehenge, as Geoffrey of Monmouth has the Britons slain by the Saxons at this great ritual centre on May 1st or Beltane, the day of *'Beli's Fire'*. Stonehenge, of course, is just a little south of the Wayland's Smithy chambered tomb and the Uffington White Horse.

As Stonehenge was a great astronomical observatory concerned primarily with the motion of the sun through the year, a motion which defines our measurement of time, Beli should be invoked for any matter that is time sensitive or requires calculations and computations. He is the horse that unfailingly gallops across the sky 365 days a year. As such, he is also useful for purposes of steadfastness and determination or single-mindedness of purpose. He is a prophet in the sense that like the future, the course of the sun is always predictable. Finally, he is the god of resurrection, as the sun is reborn every Winter Solstice. Archaeo-astronomers have confirmed that the Winter Solstice was observed annually at Stonehenge.

BEDWYR

It was once claimed that Bedwyr was the *'Birch-king'*, but this etymology does not work. He was instead anciently Bodvorix or *'Battle-king'*. Because of his martial name, and the fact that he is said to have only one arm, we can identify Bedwyr as a byname of the Romano-British god Mars Nodens. Nodens, known to the Welsh as Nudd or Lludd, and to the Irish as Nuadha, lost his solar arm and had it replaced by a silver lunar arm fashioned by a divine smith. Because of the loss of his solar arm, he was not qualified for kingship over the gods and his place was taken by the sun god Lugh (= Welsh Lleu). The Norse Odin similarly loses his solar eye, and Tyr his solar hand. We will see below that the Arthurian hero Cai or Cei, the later Sir Kay of the romances, was made a constant companion of Bedwyr for a very good reason. Bedwyr is the god of war. He should not be invoked lightly, for he brings with him the horrific violence of manslaughter on a massive scale, with all of its dire consequences. Simply put, he is the soldier's god.

BLODEUWEDD

'Flower-aspect', as she is known, brings about the death of her lover Lleu at Midwinter. The goat and bathtub of Lleu's death scene represent, respectively, the goat of Capricorn and the water-bearer of Aquarius; in 3000 BCE, the sun was between these two signs on the Winter Solstice.

Because of the precession of the equinoxes, the sun was between these two signs on Imbolc of 1 February in the year 1650 CE. While it is difficult to assign an Imbolc death for Lleu, his being slain on the shortest day of the year, when the sun is at its weakest, makes a great deal of sense. If he did die on the Winter Solstice, this would be a very ancient tradition indeed!

Lleu's solar twin, Goronwy Pebr, 'the Radiant', would himself be killed by his resurrected rival either on Lughnasadh or August 1 (assuming an Imbolc death for Lleu) or on the Summer Solstice (assuming a Winter Solstice death for Lleu). Blodeuwedd's sacred bird was the barn owl, a nocturnal bird whose round, white face symbolized the moon. Thus she is the same goddess as Arianrhod, who gives the young Lleu his name and weapons.

BRAN

Bran means 'Raven' in Welsh, and this is a nickname for the Welsh Lleu (q.v.). In Gaul Lugos (= Lleu and the Irish Lugh) was frequently depicted with ravens, and it is thought possible by some that a Proto-Indo-European word meaning 'blackness, dimness, darkness' produced an otherwise unattested word in Gaul for raven that resembled Lugos' name. The blessed head of Bran, a symbol for Lleu himself, is a solar symbol. It is also the grain of the wheat, cut off at harvest. Harvest coincided with Lughnasadh, the festival of Lugh on August 1. The burying of the head of Bran signifies that the planting season has begun on Beltane, May 1. On the negative side, the raven is a scavenger bird that frequents battle fields in search of corpses to feed upon. The appearance of the raven can, therefore, presage conflict. Yet, ironically, as the sacred warrior can embody Bran as a raven or war-god, his consumption as a battlefield corpse by Bran the raven is akin to Christ's consuming of the bread and wine at the Last Supper – the same bread and wine which symbolized Christ's own body and blood. The Irish war goddesses took the form of crows and, indeed, the goddess name Badb means *'Crow'*. Like the Norse Valkyries who carried slain warriors to Valholl, the crow or raven can be viewed as a divine bird that eats and then carries the dead to the Otherworld in its gizzard. The body of a human being is not unlike a seed; it must be planted in the earth before it can be reborn. We will discuss Bran's magical cauldron in Chapter 9.

BRIGANTIA

This was the great goddess of the Brigantes tribe whose name means *'the High One'* (in the sense of being *'Exalted'*). We know from Romano-British inscriptions that she had a male consort named Bregans, who seems to have been of minor importance. The territory of the Brigantes covered a wide area of northern England. The Carvetii or People of the Deer were a northeastern confederate tribe of the Brigantes. We have seen that Arthur's power centre lay at Stanwix next to Carlisle, the latter being the capital of the Carvetii in the earlier Roman period. In Gaul the Romans equated Brigantia with Minerva. In Britain her name is preserved in river and hill place-names. For example, in southwest England Brigantia's name is present at Brent Knoll, a hill-fort in Somerset where Edern (or Yder), one of Arthur's knights, is said to battle three giants. These three giants are obviously a triune British deity and can only be Bregans, consort of Brigantia. And this goddess continues to be worshipped to this day by Christians in the form of St. Bridget or Bride, although in some cases this last represents a later import of the Irish St. Brighid, herself originally Brigantia. Kirkbride or the *'Church of Brigid'* is only a couple of dozen miles southwest of the Avalon that is Burgh-By-Sands. Bridekirk is further south in Cumbria and there are other St. Bride churches in the region, e.g. at Moresby, Brigham, Beckermet and Ponsonby. Some of these Bride churches evince early dedications to this goddess-turned-saint. Brigantia was worshipped at the Corbridge Roman fort, the Camelot of Arthur. There an altar was set up to her as Caelestis Brigantia or *'Heavenly Brigantia'*.

Brigantia's or Bridget's cult is well-developed and complex. Her feast day on February 1 corresponds with the pagan festival of Imbolc (*'In the Belly'*, a designation for pregnant ewes) or Oimelc (*'Ewe's Milk'*, for lactating ewes), which celebrated the birth of the new lambs and their suckling nourishment from their mothers. St. Brigid's Cross, woven of rushes, was originally a solar symbol and stood for the goddess herself. The same was true of her doll, which was constructed of sheaves of wheat and placed in a bed. This doll stood for the goddess as the seed that was planted in the soil and then sprouted and grew, just as the sun set in the earth in the evening only to rise from it in the morning. A club was burned with the bed and its outline sought in the ashes as this was considered a sign of a successful harvest in the coming year. This club was phallic, the lightning of the god, the strike of which burned the field and thus fertilized it. It was also symbolic of the plough, with the outline it left in the ashes representing the furrow in which the seed would be planted. Not surprisingly, this pre-eminent mother goddess was also a triple goddess who provided feasts of plenty and presided over holy wells, a perpetual fire (symbolic of the sun), prophecy, healing, crafts and poetry. The depiction of Brigantia on a carved stone at Birrens, Dumfriesshire, shows her as Minerva, replete with spear and shield. Minerva was the Roman version of the Greek Athena, a fierce warrior goddess whose rampages in the *Iliad* of Homer are well known. This means that the ancient goddess Brigantia was quite different from the Christian saint she became, who is decidedly pacifistic in nature. In a very real sense, then, Brigantia or Bridget was the most *'full-spectrum'* of all the goddesses in the Celtic pantheon. Those who accept her as their patron deity can invoke her for almost anything imaginable.

CAI

He is the constant companion of Bedwyr. The name Cai is not from Latin Caius or Gaius. His father's name is Cynyr, the ancient Cunorix or *'Hound-king'*. At the Lydney Park shrine of Mars Nodens, whose Bodvorix epithet yields Bedwyr, the most common ritual deposits were images *of dogs*. Some of these images have specifically been described as representing an animal akin to the Irish wolfhound. The dog can be faithful and loving, as well as protective, but it can also hunt and kill animals, or fiercely attack and savage humans. Like its cousin the wolf, it can feed upon carrion. In Classical religion, the three-headed dog Cerberus guarded the entrance to Hades and wolves in Norse myth were the steeds of Valkyries. The monstrous lunar animal Fenrir swallowed Tyr's solar hand during an eclipse. The dog was also associated with healing shrines because it was believed to be able to heal its own wounds with saliva. Certainly the dog of Bedwyr or Mars Nodens was primarily a dog of war. As such, it should be seen as merely the animal form of Bedwyr himself.

The other possible derivation of Cai's name is Celtic *cagio*, *'hedge, fence'*. This survives in the Welsh word *cae*, *'hedge, fence, enclosure, field'*. The meaning of *cae* changed over time from *'that which encloses'*, i.e. a fence, to *'that which is enclosed'*. A wooden fence or palisade was commonly erected atop the earthen mound produced by digging a defensive ditch around a fort or temple. Cai would seem to be the personification of just such a fence, for he is several times associated with wood.

In *Culhwch and Olwen*, we learn that he could make himself as tall as a tree in the forest, that he could become fuel for the fire of his companions and that to avoid the murderous embrace he places a log of firewood between himself and the wife of Custennin the Herdsman. He tells the giant Wrnach that it is the latter's scabbard which has damaged his sword: *'Give it to me,'* Cai says, *'and I will take out the wooden side pieces and make new ones.'* With

Bedwyr, Cai makes wooden tweezers and uses these to pluck out Dillus' beard.

Culhwch and Olwen also records Cai's slaying by one Gwyddog son of Menestyr, who is none other than the Irish Fidach of Munster, father of the Crimthainn Mor who is known to have taken land in southwest Britain in the Dark Ages. Fidach means *'wooded, abounding in trees'* as an adjective, but *'trees, timber'* as a noun. The closely related *fedach* means *'boughs, branches'*.

We have an inscription of a god Kagiris from Saint Beat, Haute-Garonne, France. The name is derived from Celtic **kagjo-*, *'fence'*, and *rix*, *'king'*. Kagiris was thus the god who personified or presided over the fence which protected either a settlement or a temenos (temple) or nemeton (sacred grove).

But if Cai is a British version of Gaulish Kagiris, why is he always paired with Bedwyr/Nodens?

The answer to this question lies in the nature of the Nodens temple at Lydney Park. The temple here lies within an Iron Age promontory fort. Late in the Roman period, the original single rampart – which would have been surmounted by a wooden palisade – was heightened and two others were built in front of it. After 364 CE buildings were erected inside the fort and enclosed within a stone wall.

Cai was the personification of the fences on the triple ramparts that protected the temple of Nodens, and he may also have been present in the later stone wall. As already mentioned, the hound was sacred to Nodens. It was doubtless for this reason that Cai's father was named Cynyr/Cunorix the Hound-king. In other words, Cai was the embodiment of the fence that protected the temple of his father Nodens.

Of course, a warrior could be a *'bulwark in battle'* in poetic language, just as a line of warriors could be viewed as a *'battle-fence'*. Such a *'battle-fence'* might well surround a lord or king in a protective sense.

CERIDWEN

Her name means the *'Bent or Crooked Woman'* and she is the quintessential hag or crone, associated in this case with Llyn Tegid or Bala Lake in north-western Wales. The true nature of her magical cauldron will be revealed when we take a closer look at her son, Morfran Afagddu (q.v.).

CREIDDYLAD

She is the Welsh form of the goddess Venus, her name being from two Celtic words that mean literally *'Heart-lust'*. We will meet her again in Chapter 11, in our discussion of the everlasting seasonal battle. The combatants in this battle are Gwynn son of Nudd and Gwythyr, the Romano-British god Vitiris (q.v.). They fight, of course, over the right to possess Creiddylad and share her equally, half a year each.

CULHWCH

The *'Lean Pig'* is a boar god like Mercury Moccus of Gaul. As such, he would doubtless have presided over an everlasting feast in which a boar was cooked and consumed, only to come back to life to be butchered and served again to his Otherworld guests. He would also have been invoked by boar hunters for success in the hunt and avoidance of injury by an animal that can prove to be incredibly dangerous. Ancient hunters prayed to the spirit of the animal they slew for forgiveness and thanks and often performed some ritual of atonement over it that was designed to ensure the eventual rebirth of the animal. This ritual ensured that there would always be more animals to hunt, and assuaged the guilt of the hunters. Hunting was critical to man's survival prior to the domestication of livestock. Culhwch the boar teaches us to truly appreciate whatever bounty we are blessed with and to respect and honour the ultimate source of that bounty. All too often we take for granted that which sustains us – especially in this day and age, when going to the grocery store for farmed, pre-processed, pre-packaged food deprives us of the often ugly, time-consuming work entailed in hunting, killing, slaughtering and preserving of prey animals. So invoke the divine boar whenever sustenance, either physical or spiritual, is needed. This is not the same as calling upon Anu for prosperity. Culhwch instead concerns survival at its most basic level.

DON

She was mother of all the Welsh gods, who has often wrongly been identified with the Irish Danu, *'She who flows'*, a personification of the divine river or of the sources of all fresh-water. Don's name instead is to be seen as similar to Irish *don, 'earth'*. Thus the children of Don in Welsh tradition were the gods born of the Earth Goddess, while the children of Llyr were those born of the Sea God. Ask Don for her blessing in any endeavour which relates to the earth or those living things which dwell within, upon or spring forth from the earth.

DYLAN

'He who moves toward the shore' is the Welsh god of the tides. He is the son of Tonn or *'wave'*. The god of the sea proper was Llyr (q.v.). Being the god of the tides, he is intimately associated with the moon goddess and, indeed, is totally dependent upon her. Anyone who relies upon tidal fluctuations for their livelihood should invoke Dylan. He also symbolizes the ebb and flow of other natural forces, emotional states and substances. As sea water contains salt, so does our blood, and so the flow of our blood to and from our hearts is an action of Dylan. A woman's menstrual flow is also a monthly or lunar event that involves the flowing of blood. He is a reminder that nothing ever remains the same in Nature, but is constantly changing, moving back and forth, in and out, in a constant state of flux. Call

upon him, therefore, for positive change, for a reversal of an unwanted situation. If you cannot walk across the beach because it is submerged, ask Dylan to pull the water back for you. But beware of the tide as it later comes rushing back in!

GILFAETHWY

This *Mabinogion* hero is the violator of the goddess Goewin, the mother of Lleu (q.v.) and Dylan. His name is not *'servant of Maethwy'*, a rendering totally rejected by philologists. Instead it is Gylf-Daethwy, the *'Beak or Bill of Daethwy'*, which over time became simplified to Gilfaethwy. Daethwy is preserved in the place-names Porth-(D) aethwy and Dindaethwy on Anglesey. The *'Bill'* or *'Beak'* in question here belongs to an eagle, the bird of the god Lleu. This eagle may be likened to the one described in *Triad 26* as one of the three offspring born in Arfon to the divine sow Henwen. These include a wolf-cub, a young eagle and a kitten. Lleu himself is found in eagle-form atop an oak at Nantle in Arfon, according to the tale *Math son of Mathonwy*. The eagle in Classical myth was a symbol of the thunder and sky father, Jupiter, bearer of the heavenly lightning. The oak was Jupiter's tree. Welsh *gylf* also came to mean *'knife'*. Before Bedivere, i.e. Bedwyr, took over the role in the French romances, it was Gilfaethwy in the guise of Girflet who tossed the dying King Arthur's sword into the lake. Weapons were found on Anglesey deposited in the bog of Llyn Cerrig Bach. As King Arthur's sword Caledfwlch meant *'hard-lightning'*, it is not surprising that Gilfaethwy in eagle-form would be responsible for carrying it. We will see below that the god Lleu actually wielded Arthur's sword in an early poem. In *Math son of Mathonwy*, Gilfaethwy the eagle is transformed by Math into a hind, sow and wolf-bitch. These three animals, along with the eagle, represented the sun god in the four quarters of the sacred year.

GOEWIN

This virgin foot-holder of Math son of Mathonwy and mother of Lleu and Dylan by Gilfaethwy bears a name that is usually said to be a variant of Welsh goiewin, 'bold, daring'. However, if her name is viewed as a compound, i.e. Go-ewin, then it comes from the British *Woangwina, 'the very clawed one' or 'the scratching one'. She can be compared with the Cath Palug or Clawing Cat of Triad 26, another of the three offspring of the sow Henwen. Because she is the maternal aspect of the triple goddess Goewin-Blodeuwedd-Arianrhod, she is a lunar cat.

GOFANNON

The Welsh smith god; his name literally means 'Smith'. He is identical with the Irish Goibhniu, who finds his way, albeit indirectly, into the Mabinogion as Llassar Llaes Gyfnewid. Gyfnew(id) is known for his magical cauldron, which ends up in the possession of the god Bran (see Chapter 9 below). The Mabinogion presents this cauldron as resurrecting slain warriors - although their 'silence' upon being resurrected is actually a hallmark of the dead. The Irish smith god held the Fled Goibnenn or 'Feast of Goibhniu' in the Otherworld, where the ale conferred immortality on the drinkers. The Irish Luchta and Credne were the other two aspects of Goibhniu, each being responsible for a particular kind of craftsmanship. Anyone who practices a trade, enjoys a craft or embarks on an artistic enterprise or career should adopt Gofannon as their patron deity. He will help guide them in their creative endeavours, inspiring them with ideas and sustaining them through their efforts.

GWALCHMAI

This hero's name was once thought to mean 'Falcon of the Plain'; he became the Gawain of later Arthurian romance. His mother was Gwyar, literally *'blood, gore; field of blood, battle, massacre'*.   We now know, thanks to *Culhwch and Olwen*, where we are told he was *'the best on foot'*, that his name comes from the ancient Wolcomagesos, the *'Wolf of the Plain'*. Wolves walk, trot, lope or gallop. They have long legs and can walk at about four miles per hour. Their usual mode of travel is to trot, which they generally do at between eight to ten miles per hour. They can keep this kind of pace up for hours on end and have been known to cover sixty miles in a single night. Wolves are nocturnal animals and are associated with the moon. They represent the wild side of the dog (see Cai/Cynan above) and, therefore, lack that animal's positive aspects in terms of its relationship with humans, i.e. fidelity, companionship, guardianship. Feared and hated, they were destructive of men's livestock – unlike the domestic dog, whose instinct for hunting had been channelled into the duel tasks of driving and protecting the herd or flock. In Freudian theory, the devouring wolf is the deflowering wolf, and so his name contributed to Gwalchmai's or Gawain's lecherous character in the French romances. Although a pack animal, the wolf was also often perceived as a roving loner, and so was well-suited as a symbol for the wandering warrior, i.e. a knight errant. Gwalchmai's mother, Gwyar or *'Blood'*, was a fairly typical Celtic battle goddess. She was identified with Anna, the sister of Arthur, who as we have seen above was none other than the goddess Anu. One wonders if Gwalchmai should be brought into connection with the wolf-cub born from the sow Henwen. We have seen above that Gilfaethwy the eagle and Goewin the cat are similar to two of Henwen's offspring.

GWAIR

Gwair or *'Gweir'*, as he is called in the early Arthurian poem *The Spoils of Annwn*, is an extremely important personage. The first pagan Grail is described in his story, a bowl that is associated with Rhiannon (q.v.) the *'Divine*

Queen' or Epona the horse goddess because it represents her patera full of grain. But is Gwair a hero or a god? Welsh *gweir*, i.e. *gwair*, is *'hay'* or *'grass'*. Because he is called Gwri Gwallt Eurin or Gwri *'Golden-hair'* (as well as Gwarae Gwalt Eurin) in the *Mabinogion*, some have chosen to interpret his first name as a reference to ripening grass, which turns golden in the Fall. Instead, his name is a loan word from Old Irish, *guaire*, *'hair of an animal, bristles'*. This same Irish word can mean *'folt fionn'* or *'fair/yellow hair'*. In other words, this son of the horse goddess was covered with golden horse hair! The story of his birth, combined with his being placed during the time of the British king Cassivellaunus, allows us to determine his true identity:

> *"As night fell, the mare gave birth to a large, handsome colt... Teyrnon (q.v.)... heard a great commotion, and after the commotion, a great claw came through the window, and grasped the colt by the mane. Teyrnon drew his sword and cut off the arm from the elbow, <u>so that part of the arm and the colt remained inside with him</u>."*
>
> (Pwyll, Prince of Dyfed)

The colt and the arm here are a fanciful rendering of Mandubracius, a chieftain who lived at the time of Cassivellaunus. *Mandu-* is *'pony or little horse'*, and while – *bracius* does not mean *'arm'*, the Welsh may well have interpreted it as being Welsh *braich*, *'arm'*, to which we may compare Old Irish *brac*, Latin *brachium*. The Pryderi (*'Anxiety, Distress'*) name later given to Gwri is a fanciful addition on the part of the story-teller, as is Pwyll (*'Prudence, Wisdom'*), the name of his father. Teyrnon the *'Divine Lord'* and Rhiannon the *'Divine Queen'* are plainly the original parents of Gwri. The mistake crept in when *The Spoils of Annwn* poem was misread. The phrase in the poem *'trwy ebostol pwyll aphryderi'* does not mean *'throughout the epistle [or story/tale] of Pwyll and Pryderi'*, but rather *'throughout the story of wisdom and distress'*. The Welsh later confounded Pryderi with their own Peredur son of Efrawc, or *'Praetor son of York'*.

Chretien de Troyes' *Perceval* has been considered an Old French form of Pryderi or Peredur, although no one has satisfactorily explained what Perceval means and how it was derived from Peredur. The truth is that Perceval has nothing whatsoever to do with either Pryderi or Peredur!

The Old French Percevel is an attempt to render the early Welsh name Brochwel or Brochfael, anciently Brocomaglos, *'Badger-prince'*. Chretien or his source got the name from the Pillar of Eliseg, a Dark Age memorial stone erected a very short distance from Castell Dinas Bran, the Corbenic or Grail Castle of Arthurian romance (see Chapter 9). This particular Brochwel was a son of Eliseg or Elise, and was born c. 705 CE. But he shares the same name with another Brochwel, called *'the Tusked'*, who was King of Powys at the time of Arthur. The Pillar of Eliseg lists several Powys kings, all ancestors of Brochwel son of Elise, and even mentions Vortigern.

Perceval's character of *'country bumpkin'* is a direct development from the name of the kingdom he ruled – Powys. This kingdom name comes from Latin *pagus*, *'country district'*, but also *'country people'*. The word *pagan* comes from *pagus*. In Latin, *paganicus* means *'of or belonging to the country, rural, rustic'*, and in ecclesiastical writings came to be synonymous with *'heathenish'*.

We will see in Chapter 9 that the Grail associated with Perceval or Brochwel at Dinas Bran/Corbenic was a wholly different object from the one found in the Pryderi story.

GWENDDYDD

The name of Myrddin's sister Gwenddydd, called Ganieda in Geoffrey of Monmouth, is thought to mean *'Bright like the Day'*. However, there was an Old Irish feminine name Findad/Findadh/Findath, mother of the 6th century St. Fintan of Clonenagh. Findadh means *'fair, blonde lady'*.

As Geoffrey of Monmouth has her build Merlin's *'house'* or astronomical observatory with its 70 doors and 70 windows, where he can watch Phoebus (Apollo the sun god) and Venus, it has been suggested that she is the goddess Venus herself. Her megalithic house is the prototype for the 'stone' (i.e. the capstone of a cromlech or dolmen) under which the Lady of the Lake entraps Merlin in later romance.

Are there grounds, then, for seeing Gwenddydd as a goddess? As she is presented to us in Geoffrey of Monmouth's *Life of Merlin*, she would appear to be mortal and to function as a priestess. But as we have seen in Chapter 3, the Lady of the Lake or Niviane was none other than the Irish goddess Nemhain, known as Nefain mother of Urien Rheged in Welsh tradition. So if the Lady of the Lake's entrapment of Merlin derives from Gwenddydd's building of a megalithic observatory for her brother, might not we identify her with Nemhain? Could not Gwenddydd be an epithet for the goddess, rather than just a name?

Gwenddydd's building of an astronomical observatory for her brother has often been compared with Merlin's own building of Stonehenge. And, indeed, authorities have interpreted Gwenddydd's building of Merlin's house as a reference to Stonehenge. The problem, of course, is that Stonehenge does not have 140 gaps between its circle of stones – or even 70, if we take the doors and windows to be the same openings duplicated. Furthermore, the context of the *Life of Merlin*, which describes the building of the observatory by Gwenddydd, leaves little doubt that this particular stone circle is somewhere in the Scottish Lowland Caledonian Forest – not on Salisbury Plain in England.

Given that it was Geoffrey who first identified Merlin with the Ambrosius (*'Divine or Immortal One'*) who was said to be Lord of Gwynedd and who can be shown to be not a historical personage, but the god Lleu, and knowing that Lleu and Mabon the youthful sun god were identified in Welsh tradition, the only real possibility for Gwenddydd's stone circle is that of the Lochmaben Stane on the north side of the Solway. The Lochmaben Stane was originally Clach-mabon, *'Stone of Mabon'*. While now only a single standing stone remains, a credible mid-19th century witness claims there was a large stone circle on the site whose stones were cleared to make room for cultivation.

Currently, there is no stone circle in the Scottish Lowlands with 70 stones. This does not mean there never was such a circle, as some have been denuded of many of their stones and others are known to have been completely removed. The closest such circle to the Lowlands would be Cumbria's Long Meg and Her Daughters at Little Salkeld, sometimes called the Maughanby Circle. The earliest form of Maughonby preserves the Old Welsh personal name Merchiawn. There was a famous Dark Age Merchiawn, father of the Cynfarch or *'March'* who left his name at the Mote of Mark hill-fort in southern Dumfriesshire. It was this Cynfarch who was the nephew of Uther, the father of Arthur. Whether the Maughanby Merchiawn was Arthur's uncle is not, alas, something we can establish. But the possibility is intriguing.

One wonders, however, if the 70 doors and 70 windows are to be taken seriously as gaps between the upright stones of a circle. After all, Geoffrey claims Venus is to be watched from the house Gwenddydd builds, and we know this planet's greatest elongations take place approximately 70 days before and after inferior conjunction, i.e. Venus passes from greatest elongation as an evening star to greatest elongation as a morning star in about 140 days.

As mentioned above, Geoffrey of Monmouth calls Gwenddydd *'Ganieda'*. But he also tells us that Mryddin's wife was one Guendoloena, a feminine form of Gwenddolau, the name of Myrddin's lord. As it turns out, Gwenddolau itself is a Cymracized form of another name which is present in several early historical sources. Gwenddolau, who perished c. 573 CE, represents the Pictish king Cindaeladh/Cennalath of the *Irish Annals* (Tigernach and Ulster, respectively), who died c. 580 CE. In the *Pictish Annals*, Cindaeladh/Cennalath is called Galam cennaleph, cennaleph being a byname.

Galam Cennaleph ruled alone 552-3
Galam Cennaleph ruled with Brude son of Maelcon 553-4
Brude son of Maelcon ruled 554-84

Peredur ('*Praetor*', a title for the Roman governor at York) and his brother Gwrgi were present at the Battle of Arfderydd in 573, but according to the *Welsh Annals* they did not die until 580 – exactly the year that saw the death of Cindaeladh/Gwenddolau.

GWENHWYFAR

Who is Guinevere, the wife and queen of King Arthur? Her name first appears as Guennuvar in Caradoc of Llancarfan's *Life of St. Gildas* (c. 1130), a work finished only a few years prior to that of Geoffrey of Monmouth's *History* (c. 1136). Geoffrey calls her Guanhumara. The Welsh form of her name is Gwenhwyfar, '*White Spirit*'.

She has usually been associated with the Irish sovereignty goddess Findabair. This is certainly correct, since Arthur conquers Ireland immediately after marrying Guanhumara. In other words, a king must marry the Goddess of Sovereignty of Ireland before he can rule over the country.

Triad 56 of the *Trioedd Ynys Prydein* (*The Triads of the Island of Britain*) lists the names and patronymics of the '*Three Great Queens*' of Arthur's court. To quote this triad in full:

> "*Three Great Queens of Arthur's Court:*
> *Gwennhwyfar daughter of Cywryd Gwent,*
> *And Gwenhwyfar daughter of Gwythyr son of Greidawl,*
> *And Gwenhwyfar daughter of (G) ogfran the Giant.*"
>
> [Trans. by Rachel Bromwich]

There has been some slight discussion of these three '*great queens*' as a fairly typical Celtic example of a triple goddess, i.e. a goddess split into three aspects. None of the fathers listed in the Welsh triad, however, match the name of the known father of the Irish Findabair, viz. Ailill, '*the elf, fairy , sprite*'.

The three Guineveres can be identified as follows:

1) *Gwenhwyfar daughter of Cywryd*

Given that n and u were often confused by copyists, and u can become w in certain instances, Cywryd is pretty transparently Cenred, King of Wessex. He had a daughter named Cwenburh, whose name was wrongly associated by the Welsh with the name Gwenhwyfar.

2) *Gwenhwyfar daughter of Gwythyr*

Gwythyr is generally considered a translation of the Roman name *'Victor'*. However, we will see below that Gwythyr is Veteres/Vitires, a god found in northern Britain. Two altars dedicated to Veteres were found at Ebchester, the Romano-British period Vindomora. It is quite possible that at an early date the place name Vindomora was wrongly linked with the personal name Gwenhwyfar, Guenhuuara, Guanhumara. Gwenhwyfar was then linked to the god Veteres/Gwythyr, who was worshipped at Vindomora.

3) *Gwenhwyfar daughter of Gogfran (or Ogyrfan, Ogfran)*

This is the most important of the three Guineveres, as she is the actual wife of King Arthur in early Welsh tradition. A diligent search of British records failed to find any trace of a historical or divine personage upon which this Gwenhwyfar was based. An examination of the Irish sources, however, was more revealing.

From the *Rawlinson Genealogies*:

> "Also, Find the Poet sang of the sons of <u>Alb</u> son of Augen the Servant:
> Baeth the yellow, firm little white one
> Of unimpeded talent, the numerous progeny of Alb.
> Achir the furious, belly of red (or 'red spear'?),
> Dondubur the beetle, Gabruan who was begotten upon <u>Findubur</u>.
> That was all of them."

It would seem obvious, then, that Gwenhwyfar daughter of Gogfran = Findubur mother of Gabruan. I have not been able to find a reliable etymology for the name Alb, but if at some point this name had been associated with the English word for elf, there may well have been a perceived connection between this Findabair and Finnabair daughter of Ailill *'the Elf'*.

Gwenhwyfar or Guinevere is the preeminent *'Goddess of Sovereignty'*. As such, she represented the kingdom itself, but also the fertile properties of the earth within the boundaries of the kingdom. To rule over his kingdom, Arthur had to have Gwenhwyfar as his queen. When she forsook Arthur for Lancelot (see Lleu below) or Medrawd (Modred, a rendering of the Latin name Moderatus, the later French Mordred), Arthur lost his kingdom. As every man's home is his castle, Gwenhwyfar should be honoured in the person of one's female life partner. By virtue of the fact that such a female life partner is the human embodiment of the Goddess of Sovereignty, the sacredness of the male-female bond is reinforced in a positive way. Mistreatment or devaluation of the female partner not only harms her directly, but may force her to seek another *'king'* in an attempt to reassert her royal prerogatives. The king and his kingdom are also dependent on the queen for any continuance of the royal line. Without her, there can be no heir to the throne. Thus a kingdom without a queen is no kingdom at all, and the absence of the womb that is the home of us all leads only to a desecration of the soul and to the garden in which that soul lives.

GWYDION

In the Harleian genealogies appended to Nennius' *Historia Brittonum*, the Old Welsh *'Lou Hen map Guidgen'* stands for *'Lleu the Old son of Gwydion'*. This means that Gwydion's name, originally *Gwiddien* from British *Widugenos*, *'Born of Trees'*, was later changed to resemble divine names like Amaethon, Gofannon, Mabon, Modron, Rhiannon, Teyrnon. All of these names show the *–on* suffix, which denotes divinity. Hence Gwiddien became Gwiddion. Always associated with northwestern Wales, Gwydion was born in the druidic groves of Anglesey, mentioned in the writings of Tacitus. Specifically, he was the god of the *'Black Grove'* at the Bryn Celli Ddu passage grave site, which was a major ceremonial complex. Gwydion is always striking other personages and objects with his wand, seasonally transforming them through the cycle of death and rebirth. We may compare him with Mercury Viduces of the Lemovices or *'Elm-fighters'* in Gaul. His wand, given that he resurrects Lleu under an oak tree, is the druidic mistletoe which itself was emblematic of the heavenly lightning that often strikes oak trees. He was not actually the father of Lleu as the Harleian genealogies would suggest (see Math below), but rather the foster-father.

GWYN

Gwyn son of Nudd is the Welsh manifestation of the Irish Fionn son of Cumhail; he is found also in Scottish tradition. We know this identification is correct because Nudd is the same god as the Irish Nuadu, and Fionn son of Cumhail's ancestor was Nuadu, chief druid of Cahir Mor. Cumhail is the Gaulish and British god Mars Camulos. His name, like Irish *cumall*, meant *'Champion'*. Because Fionn's birth-name was *Demne*, *'small deer'*, his mother took the form of a deer, his son Oisin is *'little deer'* and Oscar is *'deer-lover'*, Gwyn of Annwn, who owned the Cwn Annwn or *'Hounds of Annwn'*, was a horned god akin to Herne the Hunter of Windsor Forest (= Cernunnos the *'Horned One'*). It is doubtless because Gwyn was a horned god that he was made the king of Annwn, which in Christian eyes was the equivalent of Hell, ruled over by the horned Devil.

HAFGAN

This god is *'Summer-bright'*, the constellation of Scorpio. Hafgan is the enemy of Arawn or *'Orion'* because the latter is the constellation of winter, while the former is the constellation of summer. They are thus in eternal conflict, with each ruling the underworld of Annwn by turns. In July, Orion is lying just above the eastern horizon at dawn. By late winter, Orion sets in the west just as light appears in the east. The opposite is, of course, true of Hafgan the

Scorpion: he appears in the east at dawn in late winter when Arawn the Hunter drops below the western horizon. He himself is setting in the west at dawn in late summer, when Orion again appears in the east. Hafgan was the native name for the Scorpion constellation. Unfortunately, the Welsh name for the constellation of Orion is unknown.

IMONA

Emain Macha of Ireland, rather than being explained as the 'Twins of Macha', which makes very little sense despite the aetiological tale invented to account for it, should be read as 'the Swift One [Imona] of the Plain'. The horse goddess of this royal site, in other words, was originally named Imona. While Celtic *magos regularly yields 'field, plain', it is now believed there was also a *makaja- which would produce Macha. It may also be that Imona's name is found in that of Imanuentius (see Manawydan below), the father of the Mandubracius known in Welsh tradition as Gwair Golden-hair.

LLEU

Much has been written on the god Lleu, and I do not intend to repeat that here. What is important for an Arthurian druid to recognize is that Lleu was paramount at Carlisle/Luguvalium, the fort that was 'Lugos-strong', which together with neighbouring Stanwix was Arthur's power centre. Medrawd or Modred was said by Geoffrey of Monmouth to be the son of Loth of Lothian, i.e. of Lleuddiniawn, the Place of the Fort of Lleu, but the Welsh corrected this by making him a son of Lleu. Modred is from the Roman name Moderatus, and we know of an important Roman of this name who was active in the Cumbrian region. The later British royalty of the region may well have continued to use the name for their sons and it is thus more likely that Modred was from Luguvalium, the Welsh Caerliwelydd, rather than from Lothian. The Camlann of

Modred and Arthur was the Camboglanna Roman fort, only a short distance to the east of Carlisle. The wise eagle Eliwlod with whom Arthur converses in an early poem is an eponym derived from the –liwelydd portion of the Caerliwelydd place-name. Lleu is also Lleuelys of the *Lludd and Lleuelys* tale, which will be discussed in detail in Chapter 11. Lleuelys or, rather, Lleu(v)elys, is from Welsh *Lleu + melys*. The name means Lleu the *'Delightful, Agreeable, Pleasant, Charming'*. And, finally, there is Lancelot of the Lake to consider. Arthur's greatest knight is the Irish Lugh (= Welsh Lleu) in disguise. In the early Arthurian poem *The Spoils of Annwn*, Arthur is accompanied to the Otherworld on a quest for a magical cauldron by a personage called Lluch Lleawc (or, as other translators would have it, *lluch, 'bright, shining'*, is an adjective meant to be applied to the sword brandished by Lleawc). In the same poem, this Lluch Lleawc (or simply Lleawc) is provided with an epithet, Lleminawc. Some have interpreted this epithet as meaning *'the Leaping One'* (from W. *llam, 'leap'*), but most prefer to see it as a slight corruption of an epithet belonging to the Irish god Lugh, whose name is found in Welsh sources as Llwch or Lloch (a word also meaning loch, i.e. *'lake'*). The epithet in question is Llawwynnawc (variants Llawwynnyawc, Llauynnauc), i.e. Llwch Windy-Hand or Striking-Hand. In Irish tradition, Lugh had epithets such as Lonnbemnech, *'of the fierce blows'*, and Lamhfota, *'of the long hand'*. The Welsh Lleu had a similar epithet, namely Llaw Gyffes or *'Skillful-hand'*.

The same Lugh/Llwch appears elsewhere in Welsh tradition as Llenlleog Gwyddel, Llenlleog the Irishman. In the story *Culhwch and Olwen*, it is Llenlleog who brandishes the sword in the cauldron story, rather than Lluch Lleawc (or Lleawc), who is called Lleminawc.

We may begin with Llwch Llawwynnauc, which is probably a Welsh substitute for the Irish Lugh Lonnbemnech. This became Lluch or Lleawc Lleminauc in *The Spoils of Annwn*. And Lleminauc became *Culhwch and Olwen's* Llenlleawc the Irishman.

1) Lugh Lonnbemnech >

2) Llwch Llawwynnauc >

3) Lluch/Lleawc Lleminauc >

4) (Lluch/Lleawc) Llenlleog

Which leads us to our next question: if Lancelot du Lac = Lugh *'Lancelot'*, with Lancelot being an epithet, what is Lancelot from?

This is pretty obviously an Old French attempt at either Irish Lamhcalad, *'Hard-hand'*, or Welsh Llawcaled with the same meaning. The calad or caled is, of course, the same word we find in the name of Arthur's sword, Caledfwlch. In other words, Lleu's/Lugh's hand is the lightning, a divine weapon symbolized by Arthur's own weapon.

Llenlleoc the Irishman, i.e. Lugh/Llwch the Irishman, is found in Geoffrey of Monmouth as Lucius Hiberus. No known extant written source or inscription records a Lucius Hiberus or Lucius of Iberia in Spain. Roger Sherman Loomis, the great Arthurian scholar, long ago cited Rev. Acton Griscom's observation *"that the best MS. Authority calls Arthur's antagonist Lucius Hiberus, and since n is constantly indicated in MSS. by a dash over the preceding letter, nothing could be easier than for Hibernus to become Hiberus."*

Hibernus, of course, means *'Irishman'* or *'from Ireland'*. We can be relatively confident, therefore, that Lucius Hiberus is actually Llwch Hibernus or the god Lugh of Ireland.

Being able to identify Lancelot of the Lake with Lucius Hibernus/Lugh of Ireland allows us to account for an odd parallel that exists in Geoffrey's story of the end of Arthur's kingdom and in the version of the same story which is found in the French romances. In the first, Arthur is battling Lucius/Lugh in Gaul when Medrawd/Modred/Mordred rebels in Britain and takes over his queen and his kingdom. Arthur returns to battle Medrawd and perish at Camblann (Camlann). In the French sources, Lancelot of the Lake takes Guinevere with him to Gaul. Arthur pursues Lancelot and lays siege to the latter's castle. It is while the siege is in progress that word comes to Arthur of Mordred's betrayal and he must return to Britain for the fatal battle.

Thus, not only the names, but the story motifs featuring Lucius Hibernus/Lugh of Ireland and Lancelot of the Lake, match. The only reasonable conclusion is that Lucius and Lugh are one and the same divine character.

In later Arthurian romance, Perceval the Achiever of the Holy Grail is replaced by Galahad or Galaad, the son of Lancelot by Elaine, daughter of Pelles (= Beli) of Corbenic/Castell Dinas Bran. Elaine is here for the Alyn River, which is from the Celtic *alauna, 'shining'. The Alyn is a tributary of the Dee, which the hill of Dinas Bran overlooks. Welsh tradition records that a Beli son of Benlli the Giant was slain and buried at Y Maes Mawr, 'The Great Plain'. This plain is between Ial and Ystrad ('Strath' or Valley) Alun, near the hill-fort of Moel Benlli. Such a location places it not far to the north of Dinas Bran. While the *Mabinogion* hero Gwalhafad son of Gwyar, brother of Gwalchmai, of whom nothing is known, has been proposed as the prototype for Galahad, the *Vulgate's* claim that Lancelot's birth-name was Galahad suggests a different derivation. According to this source, Lancelot is named 'du Lac' or 'of the Lake' because he was brought up by the Lady of the Lake. As we have seen, this 'Lac' is for *Llwch*, the Welsh spelling of Irish Lugh. But his baptismal name was Galahad in honour of the younger son of Joseph of Arimathea and the first Christian king of Wales.

This Galahad, King of Wales, is a memory of Nennius' Embreis *Guletic*, whom Vortigern makes the lord of 'all the kingdoms of the western part of Britain', i.e. of Gwynedd, but a description easily taken as meaning Wales. Guletic or 'Ruler' is the Latinized form of Welsh *gwledig*, 'lord, king, prince, ruler', from *gwlad*, 'country, fatherland, land, province, district, region; kingdom, realm, domain'.

The *Vulgate* says that Lancelot opens the tomb of Galahad son of Joseph and that monks take the body to Wales. They had foreseen his opening of the tomb in a vision. This is a reference to the fact that Geoffrey of Monmouth has Ambrosius (= Welsh Emrys or 'Embreis') buried at Stonehenge next to Amesbury, but also follows Nennius in placing him at Dinas Emrys in Gwynedd, where the dragons are dug up. The Emrys of Gwynedd was the god Lleu, so Lancelot was Emrys Gwledig or *'Galaad'*.

Lleu was the greatest pan-Celtic sun god. His eagle form atop an oak tree in the Math son of Mathonwy story shows that he had also taken on Jupiter or Sky Father aspects. As the Irish stories of Lugh make plain, this god was indeed skilled at everything. He was even the patron deity of shoemakers! For this reason he is the male counterpart of the goddess Brigantia/Bridget and any man who wishes to be guided by the Light of Lleu will never find himself lost in life.

LLYR

This is merely the Welsh word for *'Sea'* and is the same as the Irish Lir. As such, he is the sea god. Anyone who must travel by sea or who makes their livelihood from the sea should call on him for good fortune. Those who live in coastal regions should also pray to him for protection from those storms and floods that have their origin in the sea. He is also the god of those creatures like salmon who spend part of their time in the sea, but the remainder in rivers and streams.

MABON

The *'Divine Son'* was identified by the Welsh with Lleu. Yet Mabon was very important in his own right, and doubtless had his own independent existence prior to his being identified with Lleu. Mabon had his principal cult centre at the Roman fort of Ladyward in Dumfries. Near this fort is Lochmaben, the Lake of Mabon, and just south is the Clochmabenstane or Stone of Mabon, the lone survivor of what was once an impressive stone circle. These sites are just a little to the northwest of Arthur's ruling centre at Stanwix/Carlisle. The Romans called one or the other of these sites the *'loci Maponi'* or *'place of Maponus'*. The Roman period Maporitum or *'Son's Ford'* may have been a crossing on a stream at Ladyward. The importance to these sites for the region is emphasised in an ancient Welsh poem which refers to Dumfries as *'Gwlad Mabon'*, the *'Country of Mabon'*. The other major shrine of Mabon or Apollo Maponus as he was called in the Roman period was at Corbridge further east on Hadrian's Wall. We have seen in Chapter 4 that Corbridge on the Roman Dere Street was Arthur's Camelot or Campus Alletio. The Romano-British Maponus was identified with Apollo the sun god in his capacity as healer; the Ribchester inscription invokes him for the health of the Emperor and the soldiers garrisoning the fort. An altar found near Corbridge shows that Maponus was also associated with Apollo as Citharoedus or *'Lyre-player'*. In Gaul he was invoked on a curse tablet, and the Welsh *Culhwch and Olwen* depicts him as a mighty hunter and master of a supernatural hound, a role which may be reflected in the Apollo Cunomaglos or *'Hound-lord'* known from Nettleton Shrub in Wiltshire. Mabon is made a prisoner at Caer Gloyw or Gloucester in *Culhwch and Olwen*. Gloyw is from the Romano-British period town-name Glevum, and means in Welsh *'bright'*. As such it is symbolic of the Otherworld Castle. To be a prisoner in the Otherworld is to be dead and awaiting rebirth. At the Abbey of Savigny in France there was anciently a Mabono fonte or *'Well of Mabon'*; this tells us that the young sun also presided over healing springs. Mabon's mother was Modron, the Romano-British Matrona who appears as St. Madrun at the Kirkmadrines to either side of Dunragit. Mabon's father is not known with any certainty, although he is called son of Mellt or *'Lightning'*. This strongly suggests that his father was Taran the Celtic thunder-god, as lightning striking the earth was seen symbolically as the sky-father mating with the earth-mother. Certainly we know that Zeus/Jupiter was father of Apollo, with whom Maponus was identified by the Romans. And, indeed, one of Jupiter's epithets was Fulgor, *'Lightning'*. When we take a look at the god Mogons below, an explanation will be offered as to why in the Arthurian poem *Who is the Porter?* Mabon is called the *'servant of Uther Pendragon'*. Mabon is the god of youth, particularly of male youth. Boys and young men would do well to model themselves upon Mabon. He may also be called upon by parents seeking the wisdom to properly guide their male children, and can help both parents and adolescent boys make the often challenging transition into manhood. Boys should also seek his aid for healing purposes, for contests in music or poetry and for the pursuing of personal goals or physical objects that are not deemed immediately obtainable. He can also help a young person avert frustration or discouragement and instil the confidence necessary for good self-esteem. Because he is the god of Light and all things good and right and true, he can provide the kind of moral compass that does not rely upon threats or fear for its effectiveness. As Mabon had his counterpart in the Irish Mac Og or *'Young Son'*, otherwise known as Aonghus Og, who was both an excellent ball-player and the god of romantic attachment, Mabon may also be invoked for strength, speed, endurance, courage and victory in athletic events as well as success in love. Finally, Mabon should be seen as the shepherd of the young in numinous places like stone circles, henges, holy groves, wells and Otherworld houses. Aonghus Og was the owner of Bruigh na Boinne, the famous chambered tomb of Newgrange in Ireland, where Lugh is placed in the story of Dechtine, mother of Cuchulainn. We have seen how Mabon has his own stone circle in Dumfries, and was rescued from the Otherworld Castle of Caer Gloyw. His counterpart for girls would have to be Brigantia/Bridget, one of whose aspects was the ever-virgin goddess.

MANAWYDAN

The name Manawydan is a strange conflation of two names. He represents a late Welsh attempt at Imanuentius, father of Mandubracius, who was fused with the Irish god, Manannan son of Lir.

Figure 7 - Clackmannan Stone
Large stone said to be sacred to the god Manannan
Clackmannan, Scotland

The result was a *Mabinogion* hero who has a great deal to do with Gwair/Mandubracius and Rhiannon, but nothing whatsoever to do with the sea! Irish Manannan was derived from the place-name Manau, itself from British *man-*, a variant of *mon-*, 'Mountain'. This was used for the Isle of Man by the Irish. He was, quite literally, the hill or mountain that arose from the sea. As such he was also the god of Mona (modern Anglesey) and of the region of Manau Gododdin at the head of the Firth of Forth, where we find Clackmannan, '*Stone of Manau*', and Slamannan, '*Mountain of Manau*'. He is most certainly *not* a sea god like his father Lir, as he has often been presented. Rather, he occupied an important intermediary position between sea and sky and was, therefore, a figure not unlike the Greek Atlas, the earth-mountain who held up the sky and separated the waters above from the waters below. But he was used by seafarers, who on clear days could see him on the horizon from far away. Call upon Manawydan for stability, when you need a firm foundation, when you feel surrounded and powerless, over-burdened or when you need a sign as to which direction to go.

MATH

This god's name means '*the Good One*', which for the ancient Celts was a taboo name for the bear. Goewin, the Clawing Cat moon-mother of Lleu, was his foot-holder, and he transformed Gywdion and Gilfaethwy into different animals who symbolized seasonal transformations. Math may be invoked for the overwhelming strength that resides in the bear, but also for help in withstanding unavoidable states of dormancy, which like a bear's hibernation eventually lead to renewed activity. The bear knows the importance of stocking up on resources for future needs.

MOGONS

The name of this Northern British god does not mean *'Great One'*, as has sometimes been argued. Instead, its root is the same as Old Irish *mug* and means *'lad, youth, young man'*, still seen in Irish *mac* and Welsh *map*, *'son'*. But Old Irish *mug* also means *'servant'*. One of the early Arthurian poems (*Who is the Porter?*) claims that Mabon son of Modron, the *'Divine Son'*, is the servant of Uther Pendragon. This idea may have come about because at some point Mabon and Mogons were associated with each other and hence the former came to be seen as a *'servant'*. The dedications to Mogons are in the same region as those of Maponus or Mabon, i.e. along and to the north and south of Hadrian's Wall. This was within the territory controlled by Arthur and his father.

MORFRAN

The son of the crone Ceridwen of Penllyn, the *'Chief Lake'* that is now known as Lake Tegid or Bala Lake, was named Morfran Afagddu. This name means *'Sea-Raven the Utterly Dark'*. Because he is on Lake Tegid and we have Irish Fiach Mara or *'Sea-Raven'* as a name for the cormorant, this tells us much about Ceridwen's cauldron. Morfran was set at the cauldron to wait for the magical drops to come flying out. Gwiawn Bach, the first incarnation of the poet Taliesin, was set to tend the fire under the cauldron, while a blind man stirred it. Anyone who observes cormorants is aware of their peculiar habit of spreading their wings for several minutes to heat up in the sun before they begin their daily fishing in a lake or the sea. This is what Morfran is doing in front of the cauldron which is symbolic of Penllyn itself. The fire Gwiawn Bach keeps perpetually stoked is the sun, which warms the waters of the lake. The waters of the lake are stirred by the wind, and this accounts for the blind man of the story. Perhaps significantly, the Irish also call the cormorant the Cailleach Dubh, i.e. the *'Black Hag'*. So it is quite possible that the story-teller mistakenly assumed Morfran was a second character, when in reality the cormorant was Ceridwen herself in bird form. Lakes were possessed of great spiritual power for the ancient Celts as they were liminal places, in essence being portals to and from the Otherworld. This is why sacrificial victims were submerged in bogs, and why weapons and other items, often first ritually destroyed, were deposited as votive items. Ceridwen as the goddess of the lake-cauldron should be called upon not only for the brewing of potions, but as the cormorant that can dive into and swim through the watery boundary that exists between our world and the next.

NUDD

Nudd or Lludd means *'He Who Acquires or Catches'*. In the Romano-British period he was known as Mars Nodens and he had his temple at Lydney Park on the Bristol Channel. We have seen above that he was also known to the Welsh through his epithet Bedwyr, the *'Battle-king'*. There will be more to say about him in Chapter 11, as he plays a role in the Everlasting Battle of the Red and White Dragons.

OLWEN

This goddess's name is conventionally thought to be *Ol(g)wen, 'White track'*. The name is explained by the fact that wherever she went, four white trefoils (flowers with three petals) sprang up in her wake. These four white flowers provide us with the numbers 4 x 3, the total number of months and zodiacal signs in a solar year. Each flower, then, represents the sun in three months of the solar year. These three-month seasonal groupings are divided by the two solstices and the two equinoxes. But the trefoils may also represent triskele petroglyphs. A triskele is a conjoined triple spiral decorative motif found in Neolithic/Bronze Age rock carvings. The rings Olwen is said to have left in her washing bowl is an obvious reference to ring marks encircling a cup mark. Such *'cup and ring marks'* are common on stones in Britain, where they are often found in a sepulchral context. Although Olwen's name has been interpreted as a Welsh form of the Irish word *alaind*, *'lovely, fine, splendid'*, her connection with cup and ring marks confirms the *'White Track'* derivation. Why? Because the concentric circles or *'rings'* that often surround the cup marks are often pierced by a channel that radiates out from the cup and continues well outside the outermost circle. This channel is sometimes termed a gutter or duct. I would identify it as the original *'white track'* of the goddess Olwen. The Newgrange barrow tomb in Ireland, which was designed to admit the rays of the sun to its innermost burial chamber only during a handful of days to either side of the Winter Solstice, is covered with sun spirals. Often these spirals are interlocking, and some wind inwards toward the center and then unwind back out. The most famous *'triple spiral'* – to which we may compare Olwen's trefoil - is on a stone in the end recess of the tomb chamber. The three spirals here are connected, and each winds inwards and then back out again. This symbol is struck by the midwinter morning light of the sun. The midwinter sun was the sun of rebirth; at the winter solstice, the days begin to grow longer again. In the same way the sun is reborn on this day, the sacred royal ancesters who had been buried in Newgrange - themselves identified or become one with the sun god - would be reborn. Thus in the *'track'* of Olwen, the *'gutter'* of the cup and ring petroglyphs, we must see the sunlight that issues forth from the sun at midwinter and passes into the Underworld, ending winter, resurrecting the divine dead and bringing the promise of renewed life to earth. The spirals that wind and unwind may even be symbolic of the sun's annual circular journey along the elliptic, the center of such spirals being the solstice, where the sun stops and reverses direction. A spiral is carved on one of the wallstones of the burial chamber of Bryn Celli Ddu or *'Hill of the Black Grove'* in Anglesey. The passage of the chamber at Bryn Celli Ddu was constructed so as to let in the sunlight – Olwen's white track – on the morning of the Summer Solstice. We have seen above how Gwydion was the god of this Black Grove.

RHIANNON

While Rhiannon the Divine Queen has all the characteristics of Epona the horse goddess, she might in reality be the wife of Imanuentius, a human incarnation of Epona rather than Epona herself. All the various Celtic stories which deal with Goddesses of Sovereignty neglect to mention that behind the divine figures are the flesh and blood women who bore the king's royal sons. That the queen would be acknowledged as sacred by virtue of her identification with the goddess is certain. The lines between mortal and immortal would be intentionally blurred. And over the centuries, the human element would naturally be lost. But whether Rhiannon was Epona or a human incarnation of Epona, we will see in Chapter 9 below that the original 'Grail' of the cavalryman Arthur was none other than her own patera, used to hold offerings of grain. Beyond serving this vitally important fertility function, she was chiefly a mother goddess. Mandubracius the king of the Trinovantes was her son. And because the first part of his name meant 'little horse, pony', he was also her foal. She provided mother's milk to the young, and grain to horses and men once they were weaned. Roman soldiers saw in her the archetypical mare, from whom all of their cavalry horses had descended. Hence her image was kept in the stables of the Roman forts to watch over the military mounts. As the story *Pwyll, Prince of Dyfed* makes clear, she was praised for her fleetness; she was, after all, Imona *'the Swift One'*.

TERYNON TWRF LIANT

This is the *'Divine Lord Roar(ing) Sea'*. He is the male complement to the female Rhiannon, *'Divine Queen'*. But he is also Imanuentius, father of Mandubracius/Gwair, referred to as the sea because he was conflated with the Irish

Manannan son of Lir. The Roman Neptune, god of the sea, was the god of horses and horse racing. As such, he was actually referred to as Neptune Equestris. His epithet is the Latin version of the *hippios* or *hippeios* title applied to the Greek sea god Poseidon. So if Manannan son of the *'Sea'* had been viewed as a sea god, and it was known that Neptune god of the sea was the god of horses, then it would be a simple step to confuse Imanuentius – a chieftain named for Imona the horse goddess who was married to an Epona-queen who gave him a son bearing a *Mandu-* or *'Horse'* name – for Manannan and thus create the Divine Lord Roaring Sea. The real Teyrnon was Imanuentius, but he was not a sea god. He was a sacred horse-king of the Trinovantes tribe.

VITIRIS

I have hinted above that this North British god can be equated with the Northern British Gwythyr of the *Mabinogion*. In the past, Gwythyr has been erroneously claimed as a Welsh form of the Roman name Victor. Vitiris, whose name is found also as Veteris, etc., has been linked to the Latin word for *'old'*; this also is not correct. Instead, Vitiris should be compared with the Lithuanian word for *'willow branch'*, and Latin *vitis*, *'wild vine'*. We have a *Witu-* in Gaulish proper names and know that the meaning of *Uito-* is *'willow'* from the equation of the ancient town-names Uitudunum and Salicodunum. So Vitiris was the god of the willow branch. This, in turn, allows us to identify him with the Continental Celtic deity Esus, who in stone carvings is always shown chopping at or chopping down a willow tree. While various derivations for the name Esus have been sought, the best remains something from the Indo-European root *ais-*, *'to respect, worship, be in awe'*. Similar words are found in the languages of ancient Italy, all meaning *'divine, sacred'*, *'sacrifice'*, *'gods'*, *'god'*. So Esus was, essentially, *'the Divine One'* or simply *'the God'*. Esus' willow tree is the Milky Way. We know this is so because his willow is twice associated with Tarvotrigaranus, the *'Bull with Three Cranes'*. In the iconography, the crane or cranes are on the bull's head. As one of the dedications to the Bull with Three Cranes was made by Parisian sailors, the cranes symbolize the Hyades of Taurus' head, the *'Rainy Ones'* whose setting in the fall marked the beginning of the rainy season. Taurus is a Milky Way constellation, and Esus' chopping down of the Milky Way willow is symbolic of seasonal change. In the early morning of the Winter Solstice and the early evening of the Summer Solstice, the Milky Way lies in its fallen position, stretching along the horizon from east to west. Taurus and the Hyades are in the standing Milky Way tree when it stretches North to South on the early morning of the Autumn Equinox and the early evening of the Spring Equinox. So we must presume that it was at one or both of these times that Esus chopped down the Milky Way, causing it to fall.

A more specific identification of Esus in the heavens may be possible: if the end of the Milky Way wherein the Bull and the Three Cranes are situated is considered the base of the cosmic tree, then it is possible Orion with his upraised club, positioned directly under the Bull, is a stellar depiction of Esus. We need only allow for the substitution of an axe for Orion's club.

As we have seen above, the Welsh Otherworld god Arawn is Orion. In Chapter 11 below we will examine the Everlasting Battle of Gwythyr/Vitiris and Gwyn son of Nudd.

CHAPTER SEVEN

ARTHUR AND UTHER

The story of Uther's defeat of Gorlois of Cornwall and the former's taking of the latter's queen, Ygerna, tells us that Ygerna is here, in typically Celtic fashion, being considered the Goddess of Sovereignty, whom the king must possess if he is to have the land. The Ygerna episode informs us that the Terrible Chief-warrior (the usual translation of Uther Pendragon's name, but see below) had conquered the kingdom of Gorlois.

Is Arthur's association with Cornwall correct? Was he indeed born at Tintagel? Or are the Cornish sites merely fictions?

Only in the past few years, excavations carried out at Tintagel by Kevin Brady of Glasgow University have uncovered evidence which provides a very good reason why Arthur was linked to this site. A broken piece of Cornish slate was uncovered bearing the 6th century inscription *'Pater Coliavificit Artognov'*, which Professor Charles Thomas of Exeter University has rendered *'Artognov, father of a descendent of Coll.'* While the name Arthur cannot be identified with that of Artognov, it is quite possible that Geoffrey of Monmouth or his source knew that Tintagel was once owned by someone whose name began with *Arto-*. The mention of Coll in connection with a ruler found residing in Dumnonia is interesting, in that a famous Cole Hen or Coel the Old is placed at the head of genealogies for the British Strathclyde kings. Strathclyde was anciently inhabited by a Dumnonii tribe - a tribe whose name matches exactly that of the Dumnonii who inhabited Cornwall and Devon.

If Arthur was placed at Tintagel because an Artognov ruled from there (although see an alternative possibility below), can we now do anything with the other characters of the play: Uther Pendragon, Ygerna and Gorlois?

UTHER

Ample evidence exists for Uther Pendragon, the *'Terrible Chief-warrior'*, in early Welsh tradition antecedant to Geoffrey of Monmouth's *History of the Kings of Britain*. I have shown in my book *Shadows in the Mist* that he was a brother of Meirchaiun father of Cynfarch (= *'March'*, cousin of Arthur) of the North. Cynfarch is remembered at the Mote of Mark in Dumfries, while Merchiaun may be present at Maughanby (Merganby, *'Merchiaun's By'*) next to the Long Meg and Her Daughters stone circle in Cumbria.

Only recently I have identified Uther's grandson Eliwlod, who assumes the form of a Lleu-eagle, as a slight corruption of the liwelydd portion of the early Welsh city-name Caer Liwelydd. Liwelydd comes from the ancient British name for Carlisle, Luguvalium, meaning the Roman fort that is *'strong as Lugos'*, i.e. strong as Lleu. This city or the neighboring fort at Stanwix was, according to the findings in my book, the Arthurian ruling center.

Gwrwst Ledlwm is intruded into the genealogy of Merchiaun as the latter's father, with the usual Ceneu and Coel (of Kyle in Strathclyde) preceding Gwrwst. Because this Gwrwst is given a son Dyfnarth, he is almost certainly Fergus father of Domangart of Irish Dalriada. Fergus or, as the Dalriadans called him Fergus Mor, died c. 501 CE.

Fergus is also made the father of Eleutherius (later Eliffer) of the Great Warband who belongs at York. My reasoning for placing Eleutherius at York is due to his epithet, which refers to the legion of the legionary fortress of York, as well as the name of his son, Peredur, a Welsh form of the Roman Praetor. The Praetor or Governor of Northern Britain was stationed at York. Peredur fought at the Carrowburgh fort on Hadrian's Wall (the Welsh *'Caer Creu'* or *'Fort of Blood'*) and died in 580 at the Arfderydd battle. An origin for him at York, with a range of battles extending to the central and western areas of the Wall show that this royal family was still operating in the territory once controlled by the Brigantes tribe.

The Roman period Artorius was prefect of the VI Legion at York. While Dr. Linda Malcor has sought to prove that this Roman Artorius was *the* Arthur, chronology and other factors do not support her case. However, it is certainly possible that the name Arthur was remembered in the region and passed down to sons, whose ancestry was Romano-British. York in the Roman period was strongly linked to Stanwix, the fort which acted as the command center for the western end of Hadrian's Wall. Dr. Ken Dark of Reading and other scholars have recently demonstrated that many of the Hadrian Wall forts were refortified during the period under question, suggesting an attempt to replicate or preserve Romano-British culture and military practice in the area.

Another version of Eleutherius' pedigree continues after Fergus of Dalriada with Arthwys (spelled Athrwys in later MSS., which is probably correct) son of Mar (or Mor) son of Ceneu son of Coel. I've written about this family at length in my *Shadows in the Mist*, as well as about the family of Pabo with which it is wrongly brought into connection due to territorial proximity. Both families ruled over kingdoms stretching from York and the river Ribble to the border region of Dumfries and Cumbria. Mar or Mor I placed at the Roman fort at Bowness-on-Solway for a complex linguistic reason I detail in my book. But he could well be simply a late, careless eponym for the –mor- portion of Westmorland or even a vestige of the 'Mor' epithet of Fergus Mor. He sometimes seems to be identified with or substituted for Maeswig Gloff, father of Gwallog son of Lleenog of Elmet in West Yorkshire. In my book, Maeswig was linked with the Roman fort of Burrow Walls in Cumbria, but if 'Mor' designates Westmorland, Maeswig may well belong there, too.

It is probable that Uther Pendragon had an Irish wife. Geoffrey of Monmouth tells us that when Gorlois is threatened by Uther, he waits for the Irish to come to his assistance. This hints at an alliance of some sort between Gorlois and the Irish, and one naturally thinks of one cemented by marriage. It would not be surprising if Igerna were Irish, as Arthur himself was given as wife Gwenhwyfar, the Welsh form of the Irish sovereignty goddess, Findabair.

Having an Irish queen would account for the fact that the Irish-descended dynasties of Dalriada and Dyfed named some of their royal sons after the original Arthur. The real mother of Arthur and her mythological counterpart will be discussed fully in Chapter 8.

There may be an additional cause for the continuation of Arthur's name among these Irish-descended dynasties. Both the Dyfed royal family and that of Dalriada traced their lines to ancestors named Eochaid, 'Horseman'. The Dalriadans, furthermore, occupied the Kintyre peninsula, which had been the home of the Roman period Epidii, the 'People of the Horse', and several of the Dalriadan kings or princes are named Eochaid or Eochu. As Arthur was named for a famous Roman cavalryman and doubtless utilized horse himself in warfare, both factors would have further endeared him to the Dyfed and Dalriadan royal families.

Despite our being justified in viewing Uther as a genuine, historical personage, it is also demonstrable that Geoffrey of Monmouth fleshed out the life of Uther, primarily by making use of episodes in the life of a 10th century Viking.

While this claim may seem outlandish, we need only go to the year entry 915 in the *Anglo-Saxon Chronicle*. There we are told of the Jarls Ohtor and Hroald or Hraold, who come from Brittany to raid the Welsh coast along the Severn Estuary. They concentrate their initial attacks on Archenfield, the Ercing where Aurelius and Uther are first placed when they come to England from Brittany. Hroald is slain by the men of Hereford and Gloucester, but Ohtor goes on to land *'east of Watchet'*. The Willet or *'Guellit'* River, adjacent to Carhampton, the ancient Carrum, is east of Watchet. Both the Willet and Carhampton feature in the tale of Arthur and the terrible dragon (*'serpentem ualidissimum, ingentem, terribilem'*) in the 11th century *Life of St. Carannog or Carantog*. I would propose that this terrible dragon owes its existence to the dragon-ship of Ohtor, i.e. a typical Viking ship with a dragon's head at its prow and a dragon's tail at its stern, and that Geoffrey of Monmouth made use of the terrible dragon's presence at Carrum to associate Uther with Ohtor. After an unpleasant stay on an island (Steepholme or Flatholme), Ohtor and what remains of his host go to Dyfed, where Uther is said to fight Pascent and the Irish king Gillomanius. Ohtor then proceeds to Ireland, where Uther had previously fought Gillomanius over the stones of Uisneach/Mount Killaraus.

We have, then, the following startling correspondences:

Uther is found in Brittany	Ohtor is found in Brittany
Ercing	Archenfield
Carrum (as terrible dragon)	East of Watchet
Menevia in Dyfed	Dyfed
Ireland	Ireland

This Viking jarl is found in the *Welsh Annals* under the year 913, where the concise entry reads *'Otter came'*. This reference to Ottar is also found in the Welsh *Brut t tywysogion* (*Chronicle of the Princes*).

A potentially important family connection of Uther's recorded by the Welsh has gone uninvestigated. In *Culhwch and Olwen*, we are told that Uther was related to the sons of Iaen at Caer Dathal (or that their father was related to Uther; the reading of the passage is rather ambiguous). Iaen is not a real name; it is the Welsh word for *'ice'*. Caer Dathal is situated in Arfon according to the *Mabinogion* tale *Math son of Mathonwy*. Scholars have very plausibly identified it with the Segontium Roman fort at Caernarvon. While I have in the past thought Dathal to be the attested Irish name Dathal, I now think that the identification with Caernarvon is correct and Dathal is from Welsh *dathl*, *'famous, distinguished, renowned, celebrated'*. This would be a fitting designation for the Segontium Roman fort, which was indeed quite famous in Welsh tradition (see the *Mabinogion* story *The Dream of Maxen*).

The problem with Iaen at Segontium is that there is no Iaen place-name at or in the vicinity of this Arfon fort. Arfon means *'opposite or across from Mon'*, i.e. the Isle of Anglesey.

I would read this Iaen as an error for the River Ehen in Cumbria, which derives from iaen and is directly across from the Isle of Man, Welsh *Manau*.

GORLOIS

Geoffrey got his Gorlois from Taliesin's poem XLVIII, *The Death-Song of Uther Ben.* In this poem Uther is referred to as Gorlasar. Noted Celticist John Koch recently pointed out the similarity between Geoffrey's Gorlois and Gorlasar. Hence it appears that Geoffrey of Monmouth took the title gorlassar and converted it into a separate person whose form Uther assumes.

The full stanza containing the name Gorlasar (from *Death Song of Uther Ben*) runs like this:

> "*I was called Gorlasar ['bright blue'],*
> *My belt was a rainbow to [or 'about'] my enemies.*
> *I was a prince in the dark,*
> *[He] who enchanted me placed me in the basket."*

According to the *Geiriadur Prifsygol Cymru*, gorlasar is from *gor* + *glassar*, in Old Irish *forlas(s)ar*, '*fire, conflagration*' or, as an adjective, '*shining, fiery*'. In Welsh the meaning is '*bright blue, having glinting weapons*'. Gorlas (*gor* + *glas*), in OI *forglas*, means '*with a blue face, very blue*' or, as an adjective in Welsh, '*bright or deep blue*'.

Gorlasar may actually be a name the poet Taliesin gave himself. I say this only because of line 4 of the quoted strophe, which has Gorlasar placed in a basket. This sounds suspiciously like what was done to Taliesin, who was placed in a '*coracle or hide-covered basket*' by the goddess Ceridwen. The coracle/basket ends up in a fish-weir. Some obscure lines in Welsh sources hint that the pole upon which Myrddin (as Llallogan) was impaled had a fish-weir attached to it.

Finally, we are reminded of the wicker-work figures filled with humans and animals that Caeser and Strabo claim were sacrificially burned. Scholars of Celtic religion believe these were sacrifices to the thunder god Taranis. We have seen in Chapter 6 that Taranis = Mellt, the consort of Modron, mother of Mabon.

THE PLOUGHMAN AND THE DRAGON

A false tradition, still current today, insists that Arthur's name should be connected with the Welsh word *arth*, 'bear'. In reality, as I showed in my *Shadows in the Mist*, Arthur is without a doubt from the Roman Artorius. Artorius itself is from an Celto-Illyrian word comparable to modern Romanian *artor*, 'ploughman'.

Arthur's celestial correspondence is, therefore, the constellation Bootes, 'the Ploughman'. Greek *bous* is 'cow', with *bootia* being 'arable land or ploughing' and *botteo* being 'plough, to plough'. Ursa Major or the Great Bear, otherwise known as the Big Dipper, is called Arthur's Wain or Wagon in Britain, but the same constellation is also called the Plough. Bootes drives the Plough in a perpetual circle around the Pole Star, thereby causing the rotation of the heavens.

Now that we have covered the possible celestial correspondence of Arthur, what of his father, Uther? Much has been made of Uther's epithet Pendragon. Does this byname have cosmological significance? Modern Welsh scholars do not think so; to them, Pendragon is merely a descriptive title for Uther as the 'Chief-warrior'. In medieval Welsh poetry, 'dragon' indeed came to be a metaphor for a hero whose onslaught in battle was like that of a dragon.

Geoffrey of Monmouth was, apparently, unaware of such a usage of the word 'dragon' in poetry. He concocted a story to account for how Uther acquired his byname:

> "... there appeared a star [comet] of great magnitude and brilliance, with a single beam shining from it. At the end of this beam was a ball of fire, spread out in the shape of a dragon. From the dragon's mouth stretched forth two rays of light [the typical dual tails of a comet], one of which seemed to extend its length beyond the latitude of Gaul, while the second turned towards the Irish Sea and split up into seven smaller shafts of light."

(History of the Kings of Britain, Part 6)

This star appears at the moment of the death of Aurelius Ambrosius, Uther's predecessor as King of the Britons. Merlin explains to Uther that the 'star' and the fiery dragon signifies him, while the beam of light that shines towards Gaul is Arthur and the second ray his daughter Anna and her royal offspring. Geoffrey continues:

> "Mindful of the explanation given by Merlin of the star, Uther ordered two Dragons to be fashioned in gold, in the likeness of the one which he had seen in the ray which shone from that star. As soon as the Dragons had been completed... he made a present of one of them to the congregation of the cathedral church of the see of Winchester. The second one he kept for himself, so that he could carry it round to his wars. From that moment onwards he was called Uther Pendragon, which in the British language means 'a dragon's head'."

What has always puzzled commentators on these passages is 'Why two dragons?' The reason is not hard to find: Geoffrey tells us that Winchester, to whom one of the dragons was given, was originally called Kaerguenit. I suspect the –guenit portion of this name, which represents the Welsh spelling of the earlier Romano-British venta, was wrongly linked by Geoffrey to Welsh guen or gwen, the feminine form of gwyn, 'white'. In other words, the two dragons are actually the white and red dragons of the Dinas Emrys story.

Thanks to the Aneirin poem Gwarchan Maeldderw, we know that Welsh tradition held that the red dragon was still being used as a British war standard by as late as the Battle of Cattraeth (Catterick), which was fought at the end of the 6th century, well after Uther's floruit. The relevant passage of this poem reads:

> "Let them demand the virtue of fame for the great army!
> The champion used to look past a young girl,
> The dazzling one, and the one who required due payment for his lineage;
> In the presence of the spoils of the Pharaoh's red dragon,
> Companions will depart in the breeze."

'Pharaoh' is a designation for Vortigern in Gildas' *Ruin of Britain*, the king to whom Emrys or Ambrosius *'the Immortal/Divine One'* reveals the mystery of the fighting dragons. As we have seen, this particular Emrys is not the historical Aurelius Ambrosius, but is a title for the god Lleu, the Lord of Gwynedd.

Geoffrey further confused matters by identifying Merlin, the Welsh Myrddin, with Emrys of Dinas Emrys. Then to make matters even worse, he has Uther and Aurelius Ambrosius be buried at Stonehenge next to Amesbury, ancient Ambresbyrig, whose name was – like Dinas Emrys – interpreted as meaning the *'Fort of Ambrosius'*.

What exactly were the two dragons of Dinas Emrys? Is there any way we can find out what they originally represented? By the time we get the the ninth century account preserved by Nennius in his *History of the Britons*, the White Dragon is a symbol of the Saxons and the Red Dragon of the Britons. Completely omitted is the well-known fact that Otherworld animals in Welsh belief were unique in that they were always *red and white* in color.

The fort at Dinas Emrys in Gwynedd was begun in the Iron Age, but was also occupied in the Roman and Early Medieval periods. Southwest of the fort is the pool in which the dragons were supposedly discovered, an artificial cistern excavated in either the 5th or 6th century CE to supply the hill-top with water.

According to Nennius' text (*History of the Britons*, 40-42), the objects found when the pool is excavated by Vortigern are:

1. duo vasa, *'two vessels'*,
2. tentorium, *'tent'*,
3. duo vermes, unus albus et alter rufus, *'two worms, one white and the other red'*

The best interpretation of the text has the two worms inside the tent and the tent inside the two vessels, i.e. the vessels are found set together *'mouth to mouth'*. Thus the two vessels have to be separated before the tent can be revealed. The worms are presumably wrapped in the tent.

At Nennius' time (9th century CE), *vermes* in Welsh, as in Old English and Old Norse and Latin, designated creatures as small as earthworms and as large as dragons. Vermis also designated Satan.

But as I have mentioned above, in early Welsh poetry the word *'dragon'* could be used metaphorically for a warrior. It is surely not a coincidence, then, that the *'tent'* or cloth in which the two dragons are found wrapped bears an uncanny resemblance to the cloth used to wrap cremated remains prior to their being placed in a cinerary urn. This practice is recorded as far back as Homer's time. From the *'Funeral of Hector'* in the *Iliad*:

> *"So spake he, and they yoked oxen and mules to wagons, and speedily thereafter gathered together before the city. For nine days' space they brought in measureless store of wood, but when the tenth dawn arose, giving light unto mortals, then bare they forth bold Hector, shedding tears the while, and on the topmost pyre they laid the dead man and cast fire thereon.*
>
> *But soon as early dawn appeared, the rosy-fingered, then gathered the folk about the pyre of glorious Hector. And when they were assembled and met together, first they quenched with flaming wine all the pyre, so far as the fire's might had come upon it, and thereafter his brethren and his comrades gathered the white bones, mourning, and big tears flowed ever down their cheeks.*
>
> *The bones they took and in a golden urn, covering them over with soft purple robes, and quickly laid the urn in a hollow grave, and covered it over with great close-set stones. Then with speed heaped they the mound..."*

Such cloth wrapped about cremated remains has actually been found in an archaeological context in Britain. And so, too, have cremation burials in which two urns were used to hold the remains - two urns that remind us immediately of the two *'vases'* of the Dinas Emrys story. We also cannot help but recall that according to Geoffrey of Monmouth, Uther the *'Pendragon'* and Aurelius Ambrosius, whose death was heralded by the appearance of the dragon-shaped comet, were both buried at Amesbury's Stonehenge.

To learn whether or not the Dinas Emrys vases could have been cremation urns, I turned to several archaeological studies on urn burials.

In some urns discovered in Cambridgeshire, at Muttilow Hill, calcined bones had been collected and *wrapped in cloth before being placed in the urns*. The contents of one of the urns was described as '*burnt human bones enveloped in a cloth, which, on looking into the vessel, gave them the appearance of being viewed through a yellow gauze veil, but which upon being touched dissolved into fine powder.*' The urns were all inverted. A somewhat peculiar feature of urn burial was discovered at Broughton, in Lincolnshire where the urn containing the burnt bones was placed upright on the surface of the ground, and another urn, made to fit the mouth, inverted into it to form a cover. In instances where the ashes of the dead have been collected from the funeral pyre, *and laid in a skin or cloth before interment*, the bone or bronze pins with which the '*bundle*' was fastened still remain, although, of course, the cloth itself has long since perished.

The site is that at Broughton Common near Scunthorpe. The barrow in question is No. 3 in a cemetery of 8 barrows. The vessel is described as a finely decorated tripartite urn, upright, with a smaller urn inverted over it. The cremation urn contained a rough flint flake and a bronze implement, thought at the time to be an arrowhead but considered later to be probably a razor. The urns are described as related to the collared urns from the central and southern Pennines (mountain range) and from north east Yorkshire. The use of smaller vessels as covers in the manner of barrow 3 is also found in the Pennine burials. The razor has also been found with other collared urns related to the Pennines series but also in earlier Bronze Age burials in Wessex and widely on the continent. They are dated roughly to c. 1800 BCE. This tells us that a burial similar to what was found at Dinas Emrys was actually excavated in England. But can we find a case of this kind of burial in Wales itself? Actually, yes, we can.

The burial in question consists of two urns, placed *'mouth to mouth'* so as to give a closed container, in which were the cremated remains of one or more bodies. The site is near Milford Haven, Southwest Wales, and was excavated as part of a project to run a gas pipeline through Wales. The site was excavated by Cotswold Archaeology and the post-excavation work is currently ongoing.

The urns have not been radiocarbon dated yet to confirm a Bronze Age date, but typologically the vessels and site are Bronze Age. Only one vessel was a collared urn with bird bone impression decoration. It is thought there may be the cremated remains of five individuals inside the pot, without accompanying grave goods.

Such urn burials, then, with one vessel as a cover over another do occur ocasionally. These urns are called Collared Urns and belong to the Early Bronze Age, dating usually between 1900-1600 BCE. The recent Milford Haven discovery is one of this type of burial.

In other instances, two urns may be buried side by side with a burial, others may have one or two accessory vessels accompanying or within an urn.

On sixty occasions more than one Collared Urn or Vessel has been interred in the grave. On thirteen, perhaps sixteen, the urn has had a second Collared Vessel placed either within or over it as a cover.

However, it would appear that urns covered with other ceramic vessels were not solely of Bronze Age provenance. Roman cremations were often housed in a large pot with a smaller one on top. In terms of urns that are covered with other inverted urns, there are certainly Roman examples (first and second century CE). However, there are quite a few Bronze Age and Anglo-Saxon examples as well.

Anglo-Saxon cremations don't usually have second inverted pots as a lid, though they do sometimes have pottery lids (e.g. the one from Spong Hill). On the continent there are Iron Age cremations with lids which look like inverted bowls.

Figure 8 - Double Vase Cremation Burial

Vessels included as grave goods rather than functioning as an urn to contain cremated bone are relatively common in most periods of the use of the rite, though they take different forms at different times, including, mostly in the Anglo-Saxon period, two seperate vessels being used to bury the remains of one individual in a single grave. It is probable that most if not all urned burials were originally lidded in some way; most will have used organic materials; flat stones have also been found as covers (esp. Bronze Age). Ceramic covers, either a vessel inserted into the rim of the urn, or more commonly as a dish form of vessel inverted over the rim, are common in the Romano-British period, and in the Iron Age. There is also some evidence - famously the 'Spong Man' - for ceramic covers, sometimes specially designed - in the Anglo-Saxon period.

There is another component of cremation burial which needs to be considered in the context of the Dinas Emrys story, as it relates directly to serpent imagery found as an artistic and religious motif on both Roman and Anglo-Saxon cinerary urns.

A significant number of Roman footed marble vases with strigilated decoration on the body are known today. Strigilated stone vases with entwined snake handles, however, are much rarer. On a vessel in the Marmorpalais in Potsdam the lid and most of the serpents except for their horizontal tails are modern restorations, but the remains of the head of one serpent on the rim makes clear that the handle design was the same. This vase is so similar in size and design to a piece in the Metropolitan Museum of Art that it could come from the same workshop. It is worth mentioning that both vessels bear comparable hard incrustations or burial deposits. The handles of another pertinent marble vase in Venice are somewhat different, as water is seemingly represented flowing beneath the serpents. Both the Berlin and Venice vases have been dated to the 2nd century CE. An earlier funerary urn formerly in the collection of the Waiters Art Gallery in Baltimore combines entwined snake handles with figured decoration carved in relief. The snake handles on the Met urn are presented in a far more dramatic way, with thicker bodies, more intricate knotting, and a greater use of dark and light effects. The bravura carving of the Metropolitan's piece seems appropriate for a work of the late 2nd century CE. Another possible indication of chronology is the treatment of the strigilated surface of the Met vase, with deeply articulated channels similar to those on cylindrical ash urns dated to the Antonine period.

It is difficult to determine whether vases of this type were made as cinerary urns to hold ashes or as purely decorative objects unless their find spot is known, or they preserve a funerary inscription or a panel prepared for a painted funerary inscription. One such cinerary vase, said to come from a tomb in Leptis Magna (on the Libyan coast), has a Latin inscription incised below the rim. The closest parallel to the Met piece, the aforementioned Berlin vessel on loan to Potsdam, was surely intended as a cinerary urn, since it has a blank panel for an inscription. Certainly it is entirely possible that Roman workshops produced these marble vases for both funerary and decorative use. Be that as it may, the motif of entwined serpents is entirely appropriate for a funerary vase. Linked with the earth, snakes were associated with chthonian powers and the Greeks and Romans regarded them as guardians of sacred places, houses and tombs. They appear often in the funerary arts of classical antiquity.

These snakes on Roman urns remind us of the so-called 'wyrm' or serpentine dragon device found on some Anglo-Saxon cremation urns. The suggestion that such decorative schemes on Anglo-Saxon cremation vessels evoke the dragon protecting the treasure mound (cf. *Beowulf*) goes back to the Caistor by Norwich report on incised decoration urn 1539. The analogy is then extended to various S shaped stamps with segmented bodies which are used in decorative schemes on several urns.

In England and Scandinavia the dragon came to be regarded as the guardian of the grave mound, watching over its treasures. It is often implied that the monster should be identified with the dead man who was buried in the mound, and in some of the late legendary sagas we are told that a man indeed becomes a dragon after death. In these accounts the transformed corpse guards the treasure which had been deposited in the barrow with him.

The most famous example of a man who became a dragon - or more accurately, an *orm*, the Old Norse cognate of English *wyrm* and Latin *vermis* - is Fafnir of the *Volsunga Saga*. We must interpret this story as a man being placed in a barrow mound after he dies. His grave goods, which include gold, are deposited with him. Thus Fafnir's transformation into a hoard-guarding dragon represents his continued existence after death within the underworld.

But if the Dinas Emrys 'dragons' were, in fact, actually merely a couple of dead chieftains accidentally unearthed during the Dark Age excavation of a pool, why did they come to be viewed as symbolic of the Britons and the Saxons?

My first clue to answering this question was found in the 5th century CE writings of Sozomen, who records the unusual unearthing of the Old Testament prophet Zechariah.

CHAPTER EIGHT

THE GENIUS OF BRITAIN

> "I shall first speak of the relics of the prophet. Caphar-
> Zechariah is a village of the territory of Eleutheropolis, a city
> of Palestine. The land of this district was cultivated by
> Calemerus, a serf; he was well disposed to the owner, but
> hard, discontented, and unjust towards his neighboring
> peasants. Although he possessed these defects of character,
> the prophet stood by him in a dream, and manifested himself;
> pointing out a particular garden, he said to him, 'Go, dig in
> that garden at the distance of two cubits from the hedge of
> the garden by the road leading to the city of Bitheribis. You
> will there find two coffins, the inner one of wood, the other of
> lead. _Beside the coffins you will see a glass vessel full of_
> _water, and two serpents of moderate size, but tame, and_
> _perfectly innoxious, so that they seem to be used to being_
> _handled._'"

Now none of the hagiographers I contacted could explain
the significance of these two tame snakes, much less the
vessel of water. To me Sozomen's account seemed startingly
similar to the Dinas Emrys burial with its vases (= urns),
pool and two snakes. And it was the tameness of these two
snakes of the Sozomen story that caused me to remember
reading years ago about the concept of the Roman *genius*.

Here is the entry on *'Genius'* by Harry Thurston Peck
from *Harpers Dictionary of Classical Antiquities*, 1898:

> "Genius ('creator, begetter', from gigno). The Italian peoples
> regarded the Genius as a higher power which creates and
> maintains life, assists at the begetting and birth of every
> individual man, determines his character, tries to influence
> his destiny for good, accompanies him through life as his
> tutelary spirit, and lives on in the Lares after his death. As a
> creative principle, the Genius is attached, strictly speaking, to
> the male sex only. In the case of women his place is taken by
> Iuno, the personification of woman's life. Thus, in a house
> inhabited by a man and his wife, a Genius and a Iuno are
> worshipped together. But in common parlance, it was usual

to speak of the Genius of a house, and to this Genius the marriage bed (lectus genialis) was sacred. A man's birthday was naturally the holiday of his attendant Genius, to whom he offered incense, wine, garlands, cakes, everything, in short, but bloody sacrifices, and in whose honour he gave himself up to pleasure and enjoyment; for the Genius wishes a man to have pleasure in the life that he has given him. Hence the Romans spoke of enjoying one's self as indulging one's Genius, and of renunciation as spiting him (Hor. Carm.iii. 17Hor. Carm., 14; Pers.iv. 27). Men swore by their Genius as by their higher self, and by the Genius of persons whom they loved and honoured. The philosophers originated the idea of a man having two Genii, a good and a bad one; but in the popular belief the notion of the Genius was that of a good and beneficent being. Families, societies, cities, and peoples had their Genius as well as individuals. The Genius of the Roman people (Genius Publicus or Genius Populi Romani) stood in the Forum, represented in the form of a bearded/man crowned with a diadem, a cornucopia in his right hand, and a sceptre in his left. An annual sacrifice was offered to him on the 9th of October. Under the Empire the Genius of Augustus, the founder of the Empire, and of the reigning emperor, were publicly worshipped at the same time. Localities also, such as open spaces, streets, baths, and theatres, had their own Genii (Inscr. Orell. 343, 1697). These were usually represented under the form of snakes; and hence the common habit of keeping tame snakes."

It would, therefore, make a great deal of sense to view the tame snakes of the Sozomen story as genii loci, that is, spirit protectors of the place where the prophet had been buried.

In Campanian houses and commercial premises deities are often documented, usually the well-known combination of the Lares Familiares, Genius of the paterfamilias, Genii Loci, and Di Penates. The Lares Familiares protected all inhabitants of a house, including the slaves. As a matter of fact Lar or Lares could even mean *'house'* from the first century BCE onwards. This cult is encountered in relation to the major events in the life of the family (such as births, weddings, deaths, the departure for a journey and returning home), but also in everyday life. Originally there was only one Lar, but in the Imperial period they always form a pair. In Pompeii and Herculaneum the two Lares Familiares are depicted as dancing youths, wreathed, wearing a tunica, holding a rhyton and patera or situla.

In between the Lares Familiares the Genius is usually found sacrificing at an altar. He was a deity under whose protection the paterfamilias resided. A male and a female snake - the male one with comb and beard - have often been painted in the shrines of Campania. These are Genii Loci, protectors of the place.

There is considerable evidence that the snake could be considered a guardian spirit or genius loci. The regular pattern was for a pair of antithetically posed snakes to be painted on the wall beneath the lararium-niche, their heads reared over a religious emblem (an altar, for example) set between them.

The snakes in the paintings at Pompeii and Herculaneum are of some kind of good spirits of the place that may have been called genii loci. They would appear not to be representations of the genius familiaris or other personal genii.

There are clues in the textual and archaeological record that lead us to believe that the genius loci in the Roman world in the 1st century CE was represented as a serpent when an artistic expression was called for. Modern consensus does not hold to the view that the snake was the representation of the genius of a man. This latter view may have arisen as a confusion over a passage in the Aeneid (see below).

Additionally, when we see serpents on the household shrines in Pompeii, those serpents are often shown in the presence of the genius of the head of a household, who is shown as a man - so it seems redundant to interpret the serpent as another expression of the genius of the head of household.

The passage in Virgil's Aeneid alluded to above should be quoted in full:

"Aeneas then advanc'd amidst the train,
By thousands follow'd thro' the flow'ry plain,
To great Anchises' tomb; which when he found,
He pour'd to Bacchus, on the hallow'd ground,
Two bowls of sparkling wine, of milk two more,
And two (from offer'd bulls) of purple gore,
With roses then the sepulcher he strow'd
And thus his father's ghost bespoke aloud:
'Hail, O ye holy manes! hail again,
Paternal ashes, now review'd in vain!
The gods permitted not, that you, with me,
Should reach the promis'd shores of Italy,
Or Tiber's flood, what flood soe'er it be.'
Scarce had he finish'd, when, with speckled pride,
A serpent from the tomb began to glide;
His hugy bulk on sev'n high volumes roll'd;
Blue was his breadth of back, but streak'd with scaly gold:
Thus riding on his curls, he seem'd to pass
A rolling fire along, and singe the grass.
More various colors thro' his body run,
Than Iris when her bow imbibes the sun.
Betwixt the rising altars, and around,
The sacred monster shot along the ground;
With harmless play amidst the bowls he pass'd,
And with his lolling tongue assay'd the taste:
Thus fed with holy food, the wondrous guest
Within the hollow tomb retir'd to rest.
The pious prince, surpris'd at what he view'd,
<u>The fun'ral honors with more zeal renew'd,</u>
<u>Doubtful if this place's genius were,</u>
<u>Or guardian of his father's sepulcher.</u>
Five sheep, according to the rites, he slew;
As many swine, and steers of sable hue;
New gen'rous wine he from the goblets pour'd.
And call'd his father's ghost, from hell restor'd."

(Book V, Virgil's Aeneid, Dryden Translation)

I've highlighted the critical lines, which may also be translated as follows:

"Hoc magis inceptos genitori instaurat honores,
incertus, geniumne loci famulumne parentis"

"All the more he renews the honors that he had begun for his father, uncertain whether he should think that it was the genius of the place or his father's familiar (literally, 'servant')"

Famulus is literally a servant, but here it seems to be used in the technical sense of a *'familiar'* for magical rites, like the black cat of a witch. Honores means *'honours,'* but in this context could be translated *'sacrifices.'* Indeed, one of the Lewis and Short *Latin Dictionary* entry definitions for *'famulus'* is *'a demon attendant'*.

Frequently cited in connection with the two dragons of Dinas Emrys is the ancient Latin document *Notitia Dignitatum*. This work may depict the shield device of the Segontium military garrison stationed in the Roman fort of Caernarvon not far from Dinas Emrys as two crossed snakes. These two crossed snakes of the Seguntienses can possibly be related to the two snakes atop the shield of the infancy story of Hercules. We can make this tentative identification because Hercules at Roman Silchester was called *deo Her(culi) Saegon*. *'Saegon'* is the same component found in Segontium and Seguntienses.

The Hercules serpent story is enlightening. Alcmene placed her twin sons, Hercules and Iphicles, under a lamb coverlet atop a broad bronze shield. At midnight, Hera sent two serpents to the house of Amphitryon, the father of Hercules. They were to destroy Hercules. But the young hero strangled both snakes, one in each hand. However, an alternate version of the tale insists the snakes were harmless and were placed in the cradle by Amphitryon himself.

This second version of the story is doubtless closer to the truth: an iconographic scene of the infant Hercules holding two tame snakes, the genii loci of the House of Amphitryon, was misread at some point as the hero's killing of the said reptiles. The Greeks did have the *agatho-daimôn* or *agathos daimôn*, the *'good spirit'*, and Pindar speaks of a *genethlios daimôn*, which some have interpreted to be exactly the equivalent of the Roman Genius.

We might imagine such guardian serpent spirits being adopted by the Seguntienses, whose tutelary deity was a Celtic deity named Segontios, identified with the Roman Hercules. If the dragon-chieftains of Dinas Emrys had come to be confused with the Herculean genii loci of the Seguntienses, this would have facilitated the evolution of the dragons into the genius of the British people and the genius of the Saxon people.

But whatever the origin of the serpents of Dinas Emrys, it seems fairly clear that the notion the one represented the British people and the other the Saxons was a late development in the story. When we are told in *Lludd and Lleuelys* that the two serpents were placed in a vat and then in a stone chest, which was buried at Dinas Emrys, and that *'As long as they are within that strong place no plague will come to Britain'*, obviously the two serpents are being portrayed as protective spirits of the place, i.e. as genii loci. It is not only difficult, but indeed impossible, to reconcile this notion of two protective serpents of Britain with the later view that one dragon was a good being, while the other stood for a non-native enemy.

We know the Genius of Britain was worshipped during the Roman period, as we have a dedication on an altar by Marcus Cocceius Firmus to *Genio Terrae Britannicae*, found at the Auchendavy fort. This stone is now in the collection of the Hunterian Museum and Art Gallery, University of Glasgow. A Roman such as M. Cocceius Firmus would naturally have envisioned the Genius as taking serpent form.

All of which brings us back, albeit in a very circuitous fashion, to Uther Pendragon, the *'Chief-warrior'*. From what we have discovered regarding the dragons of Dinas Emrys (originally two warriors placed in cremation urns, who were converted into genii loci, one of whom may have been represented by the red dragon standard of Vortigern), it would seem there is no way for us to justify associating them with Uther. Or maybe there is...

Figure 9 - Magister Draconum
Roman Cavalry Standard Bearer with Dragon Standard.

Uther belonged to Stanwix adjacent to Carlisle. The Stanwix fort housed the only 1,000 man strong Roman cavalry unit in Britain. And in the fifth century there was a Roman military rank called the *magister draconum*. Although we are unsure exactly what duties this rank entailed, the *'draconum'* is a reference to the Roman dragon standard. The literal translation of the rank is *'Chief Dragon'*. I have in the past maintained that magister draconum was rendered into Welsh as Pendragon and, so far, I have not received any objection to such an equation of the rank and epithet. Flavinus, a signifier or standard bearer of the Ala Petriana, the cavalry unit attached to the Burgh-By-Sands *'Avalon'* fort, was buried at Corbridge.

Ironically, Geoffrey of Monmouth may have gotten this right! Ultimately, Uther owed his name to a dragon standard. This standard was modeled after that of the Romans, however, and did not owe its existence to the Welsh tradition of Vortigern's red dragon.

Yet another development in the evolution of the dragon story will be discussed below in Chapter 11.

THE MOTHER OF ARTHUR

What can be said about Igerna, the wife first of Gorlois and later of Uther? I've suggested above that a real mother of Arthur would probably have been an Irish woman.

The best MSS. of Geoffrey of Monmouth's *History of the Kings of Britain* have Igerna, Ygerna, Igrina, Ingerna. We can no more pin any etymological speculation on this one product of Geoffrey's imagination than we can on his change of Myrddin to Merlinus. If we want to know the origin of Merlinus, we have to look at the Welsh original Myrddin. If we want to know the origin of Igerna, we have to look at the Welsh original Eigr.

Welsh tradition gives Eigr a father named Anblaud, the *'Very Swift'* or *'Very Fierce'*, who through his sons Gwrfoddw and Llygadrudd Emys (this last being a corruption of the Licat Amr of Nennius' *Marvels*) has been shown to be a king of Ercing. Ercing as a regional name evolved from the Roman name of the town of Ariconium or Achenfield at Weston-Under-Penyard and the region about the town now forms part of Herefordshire.

Why, then, do we find Igerna/Eigr at Tintagel? To begin with, we know that Geoffrey's placement of Arthur's birth at the site was done for political reasons. The man who planned and built the castle of Tintagel was none other than the brother of Reginald Earl of Cornwall, Geoffrey's patron.

His story of Igerna at Tintagel is unconcerned with history. Indeed, he does not even bother to use period proper names when listing the main characters of the drama!

Figure 10 - Tintagel Head
Site of Tintagel Castle, some remains of which are still visible.

According to his account, in order to gain secret access to Tintagel – and thus to Igerna – Merlin transforms himself into Britaelis, Uther into Gorlois and Ulfin of Rhydcaradoc into Jordan *'of Tintagel'*.

Britaelis is a known Norman period name. It means, literally, *'the Breton'*, and its earliest attestation is that of Godwine Brytael, referred to as a minister in Dorset in 1035. The Brytael name (Bretel, Bretellus, Britellus, etc.) came into England with William the Conquerer and is of French origin, so it could not have predated the Conquest. There were Brytaels all over England, including one listed as an owner of Trevelyan in Cornwall during the reign of Edward the Confessor (1043-1066).

Jordan is another Breton name. Geoffrey undoubtedly intended to model this man after Jordan of Trecarrel near Launceston, not far East of Tintagel. In a collection of miracle stories compiled by his son Peter of Cornwall, this Jordan is associated with Earl Reginald of Cornwall, Geoffrey's patron.

Ulfin is for Alwin, and the Rhyddcaradoc or Charford in Hampshire (the *Anglo-Saxon Chronicle's* Ceredicesford) is an error for Crantock in Cornwall, named for St. Carantoc. The *Domesday Book* for Cornwall and other documents list an Alwin who holds Winnianton from Mortain. This is the same Mortain who controlled Crantock, so this Alwin is doubtless our man.

So if Arthur's birth at Tintagel was a fabrication on Geoffrey's part, is there still reason to place Eigr there? Before we can answer this question, we should take a look at the story of the birth of Arthur.

THE CONCEPTION OF ARTHUR

It is well known that the story of Arthur's conception has a clear parallel in that of the Irish Mongan, a 7th century king of the Dal nAraide in Co. Antrim. Instead of Merlin transforming Uther into a semblance of Gorlais so that the king may sleep with Igerna, in the Mongan tale it is the sea god Manannan mac Lir who transforms himself into Fiachna, the husband of Mongan's mother Caintigern.

There are two versions of the story, recorded in the *Ulster Journal of Archaeology* and by Kuno Meyer, and I will supply both here:

> "Fiachna Lurga, the father of Mongan, was sole king of the province. He had a friend in Scotland, to wit, Aedan, the son of Gabran. A message went from him to Aedan. A message went from Aedan asking him to come to his aid. He was in warfare against the Saxons. A terrible warrior was brought by them to accomplish the death of Aedan in the battle. Then Fiachna went across, leaving his queen at home.
> While the hosts were fighting in Scotland, a noble-looking man came to his wife in his stronghold in Rathmore of

Moylinny. At the time he went, there were not many in the stronghold. The stranger asked the woman to arrange a place of meeting. The woman said there were not in the world possessions or treasures, for which she would do anything to disgrace her husband's honor. He asked her whether she would do it to save her husband's life. She said that if she were to see him in danger and difficulty, she would help him with all that lay in her might. He said she should do it then, 'for thy husband is in great danger. A terrible man has been brought against him, and he will die by his hand. If we, thou and I, make love, thou wilt bear a son thereof. That son will be famous; he will be Mongan. I shall go to the battle which will be fought to-morrow at the third hour, so that I shall save Fiachna, and I shall vanquish the warrior before the eyes of the men of Scotland. And I shall tell thy husband our adventures, and that it is thou that hast sent me to his help.'

It was done thus. When army was drawn up against army, the boats saw a noble-looking man before the army of Aedan and Fiachna. He went towards Fiachna in particular, and told him the conversation with his wife the day before, and that he had promised to come to his help at that hour. Thereupon he went before the army towards the other, and vanquished the warriors, so that Aedan and Fiachna won the battle.

And Fiachna returned to his country, and the woman was pregnant and bore a son, even Mongan son of Fiachna. And he thanked his wife for what she had done for him, and she confessed all her adventures. So that this Mongan is a son of Manannan mac Lir, though he is called Mongan son of Fiachna. For when the stranger went from her in the morning he left a quatrain with Mongan's mother, saying:

'I go home,
The pale pure morning draws near:
Manannan son of Lir
Is the name of him who came to thee.'"

Meyer's version goes into more detail and emphasises the shapeshifting aspect of the tale:

"3. Then Fiachna assembled the nobles of Ulster until he had ten equally large battalions, and went and announced battle to the men of Lochlann. And they were three days a-gathering unto the battle. And combat was made by the king of Lochlann on the men of Ireland. And three hundred

warriors fell by Fiachna in the fight. And venomous sheep were let out of the king of Lochlann's tent against them, and on that day three hundred warriors fell by the sheep, and three hundred warriors fell on the second day, and three hundred on the third day. That was grievous to Fiachna, and he said: 'Sad is the journey on which we have come, for the purpose of having our people killed by the sheep. For if they had fallen in battle or in combat by the host of Lochlann, we should not deem their fall a disgrace, for they would avenge themselves. Give me,' saith he, 'my arms and my dress that I may myself go to fight against the sheep.' 'Do not say that, O King,' said they, 'for it is not meet that thou shouldst go to fight against them.' 'By my word,' said Fiachna, 'no more of the men of Ireland shall fall by them, till I myself go to fight against the sheep; and if I am destined to find death there, I shall find it, for it is impossible to avoid fate; and if not, the sheep will fall by me.'

4. As they were thus conversing, they saw a single tall war-like man coming towards them... And the warrior said: 'What reward wouldst thou give to him who would keep the sheep from thee?' 'By my word,' said Fiachna, '[whatever thou ask], provided I have it, I should give it.' 'Thou shalt have it (to give),' said the warrior, 'and I will tell thee the reward.' 'Say the sentence,' said Fiachna. 'I shall say it,' said he; 'give me that ring of gold on thy finger as a token for me, when I go to Ireland to thy wife to sleep with her.' 'By my word,' said Fiachna, 'I would not let one man of the men of Ireland fall on account of that condition.' 'It shall be none the worse for thee; for a glorious child shall be begotten by me there, and from thee he shall be named, even Mongan the Fair (Finn), son of Fiachna the Fair. And I shall go there in thy shape, so that thy wife shall not be defiled by it. And I am Manannan, son of Ler, and thou shalt seize the kingship of Lochlann and of the Saxons and Britons.' Then the warrior took a venomous hound out of his cloak, and a chain upon it, and said: 'By my word, not a single sheep shall carry its head from her to the fortress of the king of Lochlann, and she will kill three hundred of the hosts of Lochlann, and thou shalt have what will come of it.' The warrior went to Ireland, and in the shape of Fiachna himself he slept with Fiachna's wife, and in that night she became pregnant. On that day the sheep and three hundred of the nobles of Lochlann fell by the dog, and

Fiachna seized the kingship of Lochlann and of the Saxons and Britons.

5. ... And then he [Fiachna] went into Ireland and found his wife big-bellied and pregnant, and when her time came, she bore a son. Now Fiachna the Fair had an attendant, whose name was An Damh, and in that (same) night his wife brought forth a son, and they were christened together, and the son of Fiachna was named Mongan."

The most important detail to notice is in the first account of Mongan's conception. This is the mention of the 'terrible warrior' or 'terrible man' sent against Fiachna and Aedan (variously father or grandather of an Arthur). The word used in the Gaelic text is '*h-uathmar*'. The Irish *uath* is cognate with the Welsh root of *Uther*. However, as the whole tale is a heroic version of the Battle of Degasastan, we know from the historical sources that it was Hering son of Hussa who led the English forces against Aedan and his Irish fian.

The name of Fiachna's wife, Caintigern, is given in *The Voyage of Bran (Imram Brain)*:

"49. 'This shape, he on whom thou lookest,
Will come to thy parts;
'Tis mine to journey to her house,
To the woman in Line-Mag.
50. 'For it is Manannan, the son of Lír,
From the chariot in the shape of a man,
Of his progeny will be a very short while
A fair man in a body of white clay.
51. 'Manannan, the descendant of Lír, will be
A vigorous bed-fellow to Caintigern
[Caointigirn in the Gaelic text]:
He shall be called to his son in the beautiful world,
Fiachna will acknowledge him as his son.
52. 'He will delight the company of every fairy-knoll,
He will be the darling of every goodly land,
He will make known secrets-a course of wisdom-
In the world, without being feared.
53. 'He will be in the shape of every beast,
Both on the azure sea and on land,
He will be a dragon before hosts at the onset,
He will be a wolf of every great forest.

54. 'He will be a stag with horns of silver
In the land where chariots are driven,
He will be a speckled salmon in a full pool,
He will be a seal, he will be a fair-white swan.
55. 'He will be throughout long ages
An hundred years in fair kingship,
He will cut down battalions, -a lasting grave-
He will redden fields, a wheel around the track.
56. 'It will be about kings with a champion
That he will be known as a valiant hero,
Into the strongholds of a land on a height
I shall send an appointed end from Islay.
57. 'High shall I place him with princes,
He will be overcome by a son of error;
Manannan, the son of Lír,
Will be his father, his tutor.
58. 'He will be-his time will be short—
Fifty years in this world:
A dragonstone from the sea will kill him
In the fight at Senlabor."*

Not only do we have a *'terrible warrior/terrible man'* present in the conception of Mongan story, but Mongan himself is referred to as a dragon (Gaelic *drauc*) and is killed by a dragon stone (*ail dracoin*)!

'Dragon stone' was a name for a precious stone in Irish. It is derived from Latin *dracontia* (also called *draconite*, *dentrites draconius*, or *obsianus*, *girn-rodor* in Old English), a mystical black gem with special powers that was believed in the Middle Ages to have been found in the heads of dragons. In the Middle Ages, ammonites (a type of horn-shaped fossil) were frequently called *draconites*, but the name *obsianus* seems to imply that it is the volcanic glass obsidian (there were allegedly nine different types of dragon stones, so maybe both of these stones could be dragon stones). It was a jewel that adorned a cup in Fled Bricrend; Cuchulainn is given a cup of red-gold by Ailill and Medb which had embedded on its bottom a decoration of a bird made out of *'dragon stone, the size of his two eyes'*. The stone must have had some sort of special significance to the Irish, because its presence on Cuchulainn's cup helps mark him as the champion deserving of the Champion's Portion. If the dragon stone was obsidian, it was a very hard stone that, when it fractured, had extremely sharp edges, thus making a deadly weapon when used as a sling-stone. Obsidian was used for arrow and spear tips in the Stone Age. Dragon-stones (*dracoin*) are mentioned elsewhere in *Imram Brain* (sect. 12), where they are paired with *glain* or 'crystals':

> "Then if Airchthech (Bountiful Land) is seen,
> On which dragon-stones and crystals drop
> The sea washes the wave against the land
> Hair of crystals [glano] drops from its mane."[1]

Even more important than the presence of the terrible warrior, the dragon and the dragon-stones in the story of Mongan's conception for showing its relationship to Geoffrey's story of Arthur's conception is the identity of the slayer of Mongan, i.e. the warrior who uses the dragon-stone to slay the king. His name is revealed in the Irish *Annals of Tigernach* (Year Entry 625):

> "Mongan mac Fiachna Lurgan, ab <u>Artuir</u> filio Bicoir Britone lapide percussus interit. Unde Bec Boirche dixit:

> "Mongan son of Fiachna Lurgan was struck with a stone by <u>Artuir</u> son of Bicoir the Briton and died..."

> "Is uar in gáeth dar Ile,
> do fuil oca i Cínd Tire,
> do-genat gnim amnus de,
> mairbfit Mongan mac Fiachnae."

> "Cold is the wind over Islay;
> there are warriors in Kintyre,
> they will commit a cruel deed therefore,
> they will kill Mongan, son of Fiachna."

There are thus several reasons why a storyteller such as Geoffrey of Monmouth (or his ultimate source) might have

---

[1] A kenning for the spray of a wave.

borrowed the Mongan conception story and grafted it onto that of Arthur:

1)   There is a terrible warrior who reminds us of Uther Pendragon

2)   Dragons are present, in the form of Mongan and dragon-stones

3)   Mongan is slain by an Arthur with a dragon-stone

I have suggested in my book *Shadows in the Mist* that Bicoir, father of Artuir, is none other than Petuir/Retheoir or *'Petrus'*, father of Arthur of Dyfed. B and P easily substitute for each other and in some MSS., c looks identical to t. Bicoir in Kintyre or *'Land's End'* is duplicated by Petuir in Pembro, also *'Land's End'*.

The real question is still how Igerna fits into this picture. Technically, her role is the same as that as Caintigern. And, indeed, Arthurian scholar John Matthews has very cleverly proposed (private communication) that Igerna may be a truncated form of the name Caintigern. But Caintigern is from Cain, *'beautiful'*, plus tigern, *'lady'*. While it would not be difficult to allow for the dropping of *Cain-* and the retention of *-tigern*, it is all but impossible to account for the subsequent loss of the *t-* of *tigern*. And, as we have already seen, we cannot go by Geoffrey's form of the name of Arthur's mother, but must rely instead on the Welsh form, Eigr.

Eigr's name is a perfectly regular reflex of **akri* (with a Long i), feminine derivative of the familiar **akro-* *'sharp, pointed; point, promontory'*.

Just a little North-NorthEast of Igerna's Tintagel is Hartland Point, which is one of the candidates for the Herakleous akron or *'Promontory of Hercules'* of Ptolemy's *Geography*. According to Ptolemy, writing c. 150 CE in his *Geography* 2.3.3, the cape of Hercules lies between Bridgewater Bay and Land's End on the north coast of the Cornwall Peninsula. An identification with Tintagel Head, which meets the same conditions, would be, according to Ptolemy, quite possible. The coordinates given by him are to be understood as only highly approximate.

The possibility that Tintagel could be the Promontory of Hercules is astonishing, given the story of the conception of Hercules – a story which bears a striking resemblance to that of Arthur's own birth! I quote the account presented in Robert Graves' *The Greek Myths*:

> "Meanwhile, Zeus, taking advantage of Amphitryon's absence [in battle], impersonated him and, assuring Alcmene [Amphitryon's wife] that her brothers were now avenged – since Amphitryon had indeed gained the required victory that very morning – lay with her all one night, to which he gave the length of three... Alcmene, wholly deceived, listened delightedly to Zeus's account of the crushing defeat inflicted on Pteralaus at Oechalia, and sported innocently with her supposed husband for the whole thirty-six hours. On the next day, when Amphitryon returned, eloquent of victory and of his passion for her, Alcmene did not welcome him to the marriage couch so rapturously as he had hoped. Amphitryon... consulted the seer Teiresias, who told him that he had been cuckolded by Zeus..."

Greek *akron* is 'highest or farthest point, mountain top, peak, headland, cape, end, extremity', *akra*, 'headland, foreland', *akraios*, 'dwelling on heights or promontories'. None of the meanings suggest or demand 'sharpness', even though the word would seem ultimately to come from a root meaning pointed or sharp. Thus the round shape of the Tintagel headland could still have been referred to as *akron* or *akra*. Akraios was also an epithet of Hera, mother of Herakles. Hence Hera Akraea or Acraia was Hera 'of the Height or Promontory'.

I would propose, therefore, that Tintagel's promontory is the ancient Herakleous akron and that beneath the Dark Age buildings lurks a shrine to Herakles or to his Celtic equivalent. The folk memory of Hera Akraea is preserved in the name Akri or Eigr, who may later have come to be seen merely as a personification of the headland, rather than as the goddess of the place.

Needless to say, Hera Akraea was not the real mother of Arthur! Although we may never know the real name of

Arthur's mother, we may be able to pinpoint her actual place of origin.

EIGR, ERCING AND THE SONS OF ERC

As mentioned above, the Welsh make Eigr a daughter of the royal house of Ercing, a kingdom of southeastern Wales centered about the Romano-British town of Ariconium.

Certainly, it is possible Eigr was placed in Ercing merely because Arthur and his son were said to be there in Nennius' *Marvels*. But Ercing is an English formation, which we first find in the *Anglo-Saxon Chronicle's* '*Ircingafeld*'. The Anglo-Saxon *–ingas* meant '*people, tribe, descendents, dependents of*' and was often added to proper or place-name elements. Thus Ercingas would have been perceived as the '*descendents of Erc*'.

Fergus Mor, the founder of Scottish Dalriada, was *the son of Erc* and the Dalriadans were all considered to be Erc's descendents. We have seen above how Aedan of Dalriada fought at Degasastan or Dawston in Liddesdale, in what had been Arthur's kingdom just a little north of Carlisle/Stanwix. According to Welsh tradition, Aedan was also present at Arfderydd or Arthuret, even closer to the Arthurian power center. The same Aedan (or his son Conaing, depending on what source is consulted) named his son Arthur after the earlier, more famous chieftain of that name. All of this strongly suggests that Aedan had a *family interest* in the region. Had a Dalriadan princess married Uther, then we can readily account for both Aedan's involvement in the fate of Arthur's kingdom and the later Dalriadan Arthur.

Arthur's real mother, therefore, may have originally hailed from Scottish Dalriada, the kingdom of the sons of Erc, and only later during the development of Arthurian heroic legend was transferred to Ercing in Wales.

EIGR AND THE LIMINAL IN CELTIC RELIGION

For the purposes of Arthurian Druidism, Eigr as a merely *symbolic* designation for Arthur's mother can be employed in an important way.

Celtic religion places a tremendous amount of emphasis on the liminal. Strictly speaking, a limen is *'a threshold'*. For the Celts, numinous power was focused on those thresholds that existed between our physical world and the Otherworld. Hence the doorway to a passage tomb is the liminal zone of a sacred site. The same is true of the point where water meets land at a lake or bog or where the peak of a mountain touches the sky.

The headland or promontory, like that of Hera Akraia or *'Eigr'* at Tintagel Head, was a place of special liminality. Barely joined to the land and nearly wholly surrounded by the sea, it partook of both environments and yet was not entirely one or the other. It was thus the ultimate threshold between worlds. In essence, it occupied a cosmic niche similar to that of the liminal zone between high and low tides.

While we cannot directly associate the Eigr that was Tintagel Head with any other promontory in Britain, it is nonetheless true that the heartland of the Dalriadans, where Arthur's real mother seems to have come from, was the Kintyre Peninsula, the Epidion akron or Headland of the Horse-People of Ptolemy's *Geography*. The modern name for the Kintyre Peninsula is Ard Echde, a Celtic version of the Greek. It would appear to be a coincidence that one of the ancestors of Fergus Mor, the founder of Dalriada, was named Achir, from Irish *aicher*, *'sharp, fierce, keen'* (cf. the **akro-*, *'sharp'*, from which Eigr's name was derived) seen in these two genealogies:

> 1. *Genelach Ríg nAlban:* "... *Fergusa m. hEircc m. Echdach Muinremuir m. Óengusa Fir m. Feideilmid m. Óengusa m. Feideilmid m. Cormaicc m. Croithluithe m. Find Féicce m. Achir...*"

2.   *Poppleton MS: "... filii Fergusa, filii Eirc, filii Echach Muinreuir, filii Oengusaphir, filii Fedilinthe Aislingig, filii Oengusabuiding, filii Fedilinther Uamnaich, filii Sencormaic, filii Cruithinde, filii Find Fece, filii Achir..."*

Eigr *'the Promontory'*, the mythological mother of Arthur, is thus the goddess of liminality in Arthurian Druidism. She is, in effect, the *'threshold'* between worlds. Because such thresholds were found incorporated into many ancient megalithic monuments so as to receive light from seasonal risings or settings of important heavenly bodies, she reminds us of the Roman Janus. Janus was guardian of doors and gates, i.e. thresholds. His dual faces, as betokened by the month name January, looked backwards and forwards into the ritual year. The ending of the old year and beginning of the new was the preeminent liminal time in the solar calendar.

CHAPTER NINE

THE GRAIL OF THE MARE AND THE RAVEN

The quest for Arthur's Holy Grail properly begins with the cauldron of the Irish king Odgar son of Aodh and his steward Diwrnach. This cauldron, which in the Arthurian poem *The Spoils of Annwn* belonged to the Chief of the Underworld, was stolen from Odgar by Arthur and his men in the early Welsh *Mabinogion* tale, *Culhwch and Olwen.*

Odgar's cauldron is taken to the house of Llwydeu son of Cil Coed at Porth Cerddin in Dyfed. Llwydeu is the magician Llwyd son of Cil Coed, the owner of an Otherworld basin in *Manwydan Son of Llyr*. Pryderi or, rather, Mandubracius of the Trinovantes and his mother Rhiannon become stuck fast to this basin, which resides in a typical fairy-mound castle

We have seen in Chapter 6 above that there is good reason for identifying Rhiannon, *'the Great or Divine Queen'*, with the mother of Mandubracius, herself a human incarnation of the Roman period horse goddess Epona Regina or Epona *'the Queen'*. Epona's *'basin'* was actually a patera or offering dish. In her iconography, she is shown feeding foals from such a container. The patera can be depicted over an altar and it is known that libations could be poured from a patera onto an altar.

The importance of the *Culhwch and Olwen* story for the evolution of the Grail legend is obvious, but what has often been overlooked is that it most certainly predates the later French romances that drew upon the story of Bran's cauldron (see below). In the *Culhwch and Olwen* cauldron-stealing episode we have what some have claimed is a rationalization of *The Spoils of Annwn* poem. This poem is indisputably ancient.

Figure 11 - Epona Stone, Maryport
Carving depicting the horse goddess Epona, Maryport, Cumbria.

Here the Otherworld cauldron is said to be warmed by the breath of nine maidens who are, of course, actually goddesses. The number nine is almost always indicative of the presence of the moon, as nine is the premiere sacred number of the moon.

According to *The Spoils of Annwn*, the Otherworld is given several names:

Caer Siddi

'The Fort of the (Fairy) Seat' (A fairy hill like the Irish sidhe. The Arthurian Siege Perilous or Perilous Seat/Chair, supposedly patterned after the chair of Judas Iscariot, actually has its origin in the *'uneasy chair'* of Taliesin, where the poet sits *'above'* Caer Siddi. There have been attempts to identify this chair with all sorts of things, but only because those seeking to do so fundamentally

misunderstand the word Siddi. This word is cognate with Latin sedes, which not only means 'seat, chair, throne, that which is sat upon', but 'the abode of the dead', 'a burial place'. Thus the 'uneasy chair' is itself the fairy mound. There are several Celtic and Norse stories of kings sitting upon burial mounds and having supernatural experiences.)

Caer Pedryfan

'The Four-Cornered Fort' (A Neolithic cist or 'chest' tomb, in which the burial chamber itself is constructed of stone in a square or rectangular shape large enough to hold a body or cremated remains. Or this could refer to any rectangular or square chamber inside a chambered tomb.)

Caer Feddwid

'Fort of Drunkenness' (A description of the Otherworld as a place of endless revelry.)

Caer Rigor

'Fort of Stiffness/Numbness Due to Cold' (From Latin rigor, which among its meanings has 'the stiffness produced by cold, for cold itself'. The dead and the place that housed them was invariably cold.)

Caer Wydr

'Fort of Glass' (Later identified with Glastonbury; the idea of glass as a designation for the Otherworld castle or barrow mound came about when Welsh glas, meaning 'green, grass-coloured, bluish green, verdant; covered with green grass, clothed with verdure or foliage', was mistakenly associated with English glass. Hence the Glass Castle is actually the Grass-covered Castle. This fact is made plain in the Middle English Sir Gawain and the Green Knight, where the Green Chapel is described as a grass-covered barrow mound. The first mention of the Glass Castle in British tradition is found in Chapter 13 of Nennius' History of the Britons. In this tale the son of a warrior of Spain who is on his way with his fleet to conquer Ireland sees a Glass Tower in the sea, with men upon the tower, but when spoken to these men are unable to reply. Such silence is a hallmark of the dead, who indeed dwell silently in the Otherworld. This same silence is exhibited by the slain warriors reanimated by Bran's cauldron, and accounts for the otherwise bizarre inability of Perceval while inside the Otherworld to ask the Grail King the question that will heal, i.e. resurrect, him.)

Caer Goludd

'Fort of Riches or Abundance' (For the treasure often found in barrow mounds, i.e. the burial goods of dead royalty.)

Caer Bandwy

'Fort of the Peak/Mountain/Hill/Summit Goddess' (The fort of the banshee or 'woman of the [fairy] seat'.)

Caer Ochren

'Fort of the Sloping Sides' (An apt description of a barrow mound. This name is derived from Welsh ochr, 'slope, hill or mountain side'.)

Three shiploads of Prydwen went with Arthur to the Otherworld, and only seven individuals returned. These seven are, of course, symbolic of the seven planets that regularly descend into the Underworld and then rise from it again.

The proper identification of Odgar and Diwrnach (variants Dyrnwch, Dyrnfwch, Drynog, Tyrnog) is of considerable importance, in that it would help us gain understanding of this particular cauldron.

Odgar, given that his father is said to be Aodh, i.e Aedh, 'Fire', looks to be the Leinster king Aedh Cerr son of Colman son of Cairbre who died c. 591 or 595. Diwrnach, as has been surmised before, it a Welsh form of the Irish name Tigernach. As Aedh Cerr is recorded as a king of Leinster, and Kildare in Leinster had a 6th century bishop named St. Tigernach (died c. 550), it is probably this saint who is intended as the cauldron-keeper. St. Tigernach is also said to have been bishop of Clones and Clogher in Tyrone. The primary fortress of the kings of Leinster was the Hill of Ailinne, which was only 5 miles East-SouthEast of Kildare. Aedh Cerr would have been resident at the Hill of Ailinne when Arthur arrived to steal the cauldron.

The Cerr epithet of Aedh Cerr means 'crooked, wry, maimed or crippled'. Thus Aedh Cerr would be, like the Welsh Bran/Brons, yet another Maimed King of the prototypical Grail.

Needless to say, any cauldron stolen from St. Tigernach and Aedh Cerr would have been a Christian one. Thus this cauldron, though the author of Culhwch and Olwen attempts to identify it with the cauldron belonging to Llwydeu or Llwyd of Cil Coed, is not a pagan Grail at all.

The cauldron of Diwrnach/Dyrnog/St. Tigernach is taken to Dyfed, where it is left at the house of Llwydeu son of Cil Coed. Llwydeu or Llwyd has been linked to Ludchurch, Welsh Eglwys Llwyd, hard by the stream of Cil Coed in Pembroke. The Otherworld castle of Llwyd of Cil Coed is probably the ancient fort that stands atop the hill overlooking Ludchurch.

The notion that Llwyd may be a Welsh version of the Irish hero Liath son of Celtchair, whose name is preserved in the famous fairy hill in County Longford called Bri Liath, is certainly significant. Bri Leith was for a time the home of the goddess Etain Echraide, that is, Etain 'Horse-rider'. Midir (*Medio-rix, 'King of the Middle', i.e. of Midhe), the god who owned Bri Liath, possessed a magical cauldron, which was stolen from him by Cu Roi. The fortified hill at Ludchurch may well have been thought of as the Welsh counterpart of Bri Liath in Ireland and, hence, became the respository of the horse goddess's patera. This is especially true since the Dark Age ruling dynasty of Dyfed was of Irish Dessi origin.

It has very plausibly been suggested that the St. Medan of Galloway who is paired with St. Madrun (a Christianized version of the pagan mother goddess Matrona, the Modron of Welsh myth) is none other than Mo-Etain, a Christian manifestation of Etain Echraide of Ireland. The Kirkmaiden or Church of Mo-Etain sites are on the Rhinns and the

Machars. This is the location of the Penrhyn Rhionedd of the *Welsh Triads*, over which Arthur is said to be the ruler.

It seems appropriate that Arthur, a cavalryman, should be portrayed as making off with a magical cauldron that was identified, even if unintentionally, with the patera of the horse goddesses Etain and Rhiannon.

Robert de Boron, the first writer of an Arthurian Grail romance, properly hints that the Grail was conveyed to the *'vales of Avaron'*, i.e. to Avalon. While by this time Glastonbury was meant, we know that the real Avalon was at Burgh-By-Sands in the North. Subsequent Grail romances soon altered Robert's story, having the precious object housed instead in the Castle of Corbenic. From Corbenic the Grail or actual cup of Christ is returned to the Holy Land, the land of *'Sarras'* or the Saracens from which it originally came. Once in Sarras it ascends into heaven and is never seen again by mortal men. Even earlier versions of the story, like that of the Manessier *Continuation* of Chretien's *Conte Du Graal*, inform us that the Christian Grail was taken up to heaven. Yet modern-day questors continue to look for Christ's cup!

Of Corbenic itself, I am in total agreement with the very old theory that this word derives from the French word *corbin*, *'raven'* or *'crow'*. Long ago it was suggested that Castell Dinas Bran in northern Wales might be meant, the Castle of the Fort of the Raven, this place being associated by the romance writers with the pagan Bran of cauldron fame. I am now able to prove conclusively by analysis of place-names found in the romances that Corbenic is, in fact, Dinas Bran.

Corbenic is in Listenois or Listinois, which itself is either in or the same as La Terre Foraine, the *'Land Beyond'*. In the Land Beyond is a city called *'Malta'*. Corbenic has a church of *'Notre Dame'*, i. e. of *'Our Lady'* St. Mary.

'Malta' was the clue to unraveling this mystery. This is Mold in Flintshire, Wales. As Corbenic is founded for Alan son of Bron or Brons (= the Welsh Bran), it is surely not a coincidence that Mold is encircled on three sides by the Afon Alun or Alyn (from Celtic **alauna*). Le Terre Foraine or the

'*Land Beyond*' is this part of Wales to the west of the March of Wales, or Marchia Wallia, as it was called. For most of the period when the March of Wales (the boundary between England and Wales) existed, the fringe of Flintshire was '*beyond*' it to the west, in Pura Wallia. Listinois is a slightly corrupt form of the Welsh *Dinas*, preceded by the Old French definite article. Hence the '*isle of Listinois*' (isle being, in the French medieval sense, '*valley*') is the valley of the *dinas*. The *dinas* or '*fort*' in question is Dinas Bran.

Notre Dame is a reference to Valle Crucis Abbey hard by Castell Dinas Bran. In 1200 Madog ap Gruffydd, Lord of Powys Fadog, established Valle Crucis Abbey. It was this same Madog or his son Gruffydd Maelor II who built the medieval castle of Dinas Bran.

Originally the Church at Chirk was regarded as a chapel attached to the Llangollen Church. The benefice was said to be under the control of the abbey by Bishop Anian II when he visited Oswestry in 1275.

In the Taxation of Pope Nicholas in 1291 the Church at Chirk is reported as Eglwys y waen ('*Church of the Moor*') and with the appropriation of the Church by Valle Crucis Abbey it was re-dedicated to St. Mary.

Lastly, in Chapter 6 I showed that the name Perceval derived from Welsh Brochwel or Brochfael, whose name is found on the Eliseg Pillar near Dinas Bran.

The Fisher King himself, the object of Perceval's quest, has remained an enigmatic figure, although some have identified him with the Celtic god Bran, the Bron or Brons (Christianized form, Hebron) of later Grail romance. Such an identification makes a great deal of sense, given the presence of the decapitated head in *Peredur son of Efrawg's* Grail procession and the god's laming in *Branwen daughter of Llyr* – or emasculation, if the Morddwyd Tyllion/'*Pierced Thigh*' is, as seems probable, a designation for Bran. Chretien's Fisher King had been '*struck by a javelin through both thighs*' during the course of a battle. A magical cauldron plays a major role in Bran's story.

Unfortunately, no source presents Bran as a fisherman. How, then, do we account for Chretien's Fisher King? I believe Chretien or his source took the name Bran to be the Welsh word *brenin*, 'king', equivalent to Old French *Roi*. Bran's title *Bendigeid, 'Blessed, Holy'*, may have been given an opposite meaning at some point by substituting Old French *pecheur, 'sinner'*. Bran was a pagan figure and hence '*sinful*'. Pecheur itself would later have been replaced – perhaps as a pun – by the very similar Old French *pescheur, 'fisherman'*. Bendigeid Vran/Bran thus became '*Roi Pescheur*'.

Bendigeid (*'blessed'*) Bran
Pecheur (*'sinner'*) Brenin/Roi
Pescheur (*'fisherman'*) Roi

A less convoluted explanation for Chretien's '*Fisher King*' would be to propose that the Welsh Bran, owner of the magical cauldron, was mistakenly conflated at some point with the Irish Bran son of Febal. This latter Bran is the hero of the *Imram Brain*, the *Voyage of Bran*. The central theme of the *Voyage of Bran* is an Otherworld boat journey by Bran and his companions. Sea imagery is utilized through the story; salmon, for instance, are referred to as calves or lambs that leap from the womb of the sea. The Otherworld itself is an island in the sea – none other than Emhain Ablach, the Apple Island of the goddess Imona. Bran son of Febal in his coracle may well be the origin of the designation '*Fisher King*'.

Bran's cauldron, according to Welsh tradition, had been obtained from the King of Ireland, who himself had come into possession of it through a personage known as Llassar Llaes Gyfnewid. Llassar had brought the cauldron of rebirth from out of the Lake of the Cauldron (Welsh '*pair*', Irish '*coire*'). Of course, we have seen in Chapter 6 above that Ceridwen's cauldron symbolized the lake of Penllyn.

Llassar is a Welsh substitution for the Irish name Laisre, a diminutive of Laisren. St. Laisren, called Mo-Laise (a term of endearment which accounts for the Llaes of Llassar Llaes Gyfnewid's name), was of the 6th century. He succeeded St. Gobban as abbot of Leighlin. Gobban or '*Smith*', in turn, is a Christianized version of the smith god

Goibhniu. His name is preserved in the Gyfnewid epithet applied to Llassar/Laisre.

The saints Laisren or Mo-Laise and Gobban were in County Carlow, Old Irish Ceatherloch or *'Quadruple Lake'*. As the *–th-* of Ceatherloch was not pronounced, the Welsh may have wrongly interpreted Carlow as being Coireloch, i.e. the Lake of the Cauldron.

The Irish king had tried to kill Llassar in a fiery house of iron, and this story derives from the Irish tale *The Destruction of Dind Rig*. Dind Rig is an ancient citadel on the west bank of the Barrow River near St. Laisren's Leighlin in County Carlow.

The real cauldron of Llassar Llaes Gyfnewid was, of course, the cauldron of the smith god Goibhniu. This cauldron was used during the Otherworld Fled Goibnend or Feast of Goibhniu, an event which gave the gods eternal life.

The French romancers borrowed the story of Bran's cauldron (Brons the *'Fisher King'* or *'Maimed King'*) and linked it improperly to Arthur. As we have seen, Arthur's cauldron was initially a conflation of the pateras of the horse goddesses Etain and Rhiannon. Neither have anything to do with Bran's cauldron.

A great deal of mystery has surrounded the nature of the Christian object called the Holy Grail. The authors of the various Grail romances doubtless intended to convey such mystery and they have, to a remarkable extent, been successful. Is there any way to make the Grail a little less slippery for modern questors?

I believe so. What follows is a brief comparative analysis of the so-called *'procession scenes'* found in the Grail romances. I have tried to avoid allowing mystical or religious feeling from interfering with what aims to be a straightforward, logical attempt to interpret the nature of Grail symbology. I am here concerned neither with the theological nor psychological applications of the Grail. Yet at the same time I have tried to remain true to what the objects themselves may have represented to a people who were prescientific in their outlook.

A. Chretien's Procession

- white lance dripping blood
- candelabra
- grail made of gold
- silver carving platter

The white lance dripping blood is, as is evidenced by similar weapons in Celtic mythology, a typical lightning-weapon. The blood symbolizes rays of sunlight (see below under the discussion of Manessier's *Continuation*), which *'bleed'* from the sun. The flames of the candles on the candelabra represent the stars. The golden Grail is the sun. The silver carving dish is the moon. Chretien tells us that the grail so brightly illumined the hall *"that the candles lost their brilliance like stars and the moon when the sun rises."* In other words, he tells us in no uncertain terms that three of the objects present – the candles, the grail and the carving dish - represent the stars, sun and moon, respectively. Gold is known to be the color and metal of the sun, while silver is sacred to the moon.

The word grail, or rather, gradale, is well attested in the medieval period, being applied to a serving dish or platter. The Fisher King's Grail contains a single Holy Wafer (= the body of Christ) and this wafer alone sustains the Fisher King. Chretien may be punning when he says that the Grail does not hold a pike, salmon or lamprey: Christ's symbol was the fish, and since Christ's body is contained in the Grail, in essence there is a fish there after all.

B. Peredur Son of Efrawg

- huge spear dripping blood
- platter bearing a bloody head

The spear is the same lightning-spear of Chretien's account, the platter the lunar vessel and the bloody head a distinctly Welsh substitute for the solar Grail. The Welsh author was probably thinking of the god Bran's head, also a solar symbol. This symbolism might seem overtly pagan, but the Christians had their own counterpart to Bran's head on a lunar platter: that of St. John the Baptist on a dish.

C. ROBERT DE BORON

Robert first made Chretien's solar Grail into the cup of the Last Supper, used by Joseph of Arimathea to catch the blood that fell from the Crucified Christ. This cup has been recognized as the prototype of the Mass chalice. Because the chalice holds Christ's blood, it is symbolic of Christ's solar body.

D. PSEUDO-WAUCHIER CONTINUATION OF CHRETIEN

- bier covered with silk cloth, bearing a body and a broken sword

The bier is much like that upon which an image of the dead Christ is conveyed at Easter time in the Greek Church. The body in this context is that of the dead/lame/emasculated solar king. The broken sword here replaces the lightning-lance, which is elsewhere in the romance referred to as the lance of Longinus. The Roman Longinus used this lance to pierce Christ's side during the Crucifixion. Thus Christ the Fisher of Souls is identified with the solar Fisher King.

The silk cloth may represent the cloud which veils or hides the sun and moon (for the cloud as the Holy Spirit, see the discussion of Wolfram Von Eschenbach's *Parzival* below).

E. MANESSIER'S CONTINUATION

- lance of Longinus
- Grail used to catch Christ's blood (see above under Robert de Boron)
- silver dish or trencher used to cover the Grail to prevent exposure of the Holy Blood

- broken sword (broken when the sacred solar king is killed/lamed/emasculated)

Holy Grail (sun), trencher (moon) and lance (lightning) accompany Perceval's soul to heaven. Because the lunar trencher is used here to *'cover'* the solar Grail and prevent the Holy Blood from being exposed, we can be fairly certain that the Holy Blood is indeed a symbol for the sun's light. In a solar eclipse, the sun is indeed covered by the moon and its light shielded from our view.

F. QUESTE DEL SAINT GRAAL

- silver table
- Grail (set atop table)
- candles
- cloth of red samite
- bleeding lance

Here the silver table is a lunar object, the Grail the sun, the candles the stars, the cloth of red samite the cloud, the bleeding lance the lightning-weapon.

G. HEINRICH VON DEM TURLIN

- lights (stars)
- spear (lightning)
- plate of gold containing blood (sun and light, respectively)
- box containing bread (bread = Host/sun/Christ's body, box – see below for the ark)

H. DIDOT-PERCEVAL

- bleeding lance (lightning)
- two silver plates and cloths (moon – waxing and waning? – and clouds)
- Grail containing Christ's blood (sun and light)

I. Perlesvaus

- chalice (sun)
- child (Christ the solar king at the beginning of his life/reign)
- Crucifixion (Christ the solar king at the end of his life/reign)

J. Grand St. Graal

A very long, tiresome list of 'hallows' which I will not attempt to identify. Besides the holy dish of blood, there are the nails of the Crucifixion, the Cross, the vinegar sponge, a scourge, a separate vessel of gold, a man's head, bloody swords, tapers, Christ himself, angels, holy water and a watering pot, a bloody lance head, white cloths and a red samite cloth, basins, towels, gold censors, and a man all in red.

A nice touch is the wooden ark which is built to hold the holy dish. This object was borrowed from the Bible's Ark of the Covenant, the latter being essentially a portable throne for Yahweh.

K. Wolfram Von Eschenbach

Wolfram's Grail is the strangest of them all: it is called the lapsit exillis or 'small stone'. Supposedly the Grail-stone's power is derived from a Holy Wafer (the solar Body of Christ) that is brought down from heaven every year on Good Friday. The Host is at this time placed on the stone by a dove.

What is this dove? Origen, in his *Homilies on Exodus* (5.1, 5) says that *"What the Jews... believe to be a cloud, Paul says is the Holy Spirit..."* In the *Old Testament* the angel or spirit of Yahweh is the cloud. A comparison of the Baptism and Transfiguration from the *Gospel of Matthew* is enlightening in this regard:

"As soon as Jesus was baptized he came up from the water, and suddenly the heavens opened and he saw the Spirit of God descending like a dove and coming down on him. And a voice spoke from heaven, 'This is my Son...'"²
"He was still speaking when suddenly a bright cloud covered them with shadow, and from the cloud there came a voice which said, 'This is my Son...'"³

During the first few centuries of Christianity, hosts for the sick were kept in receptacles that took the form of a dove and which were hung from the ciborium or altar canopy.

So if the dove is the cloud, the Host or Body of Christ the sun, then what is the Grail-stone? One clue may help us find what the lapsit exillis really is: Wolfram tells us that *"By the power of that stone [lapsit exillis] the phoenix burns to ashes..."*

Guillaume le Clerc, in his 13th century *Bestiare*, says of the phoenix:

"There is a bird named the phoenix, which dwells in India and is never found elsewhere. This bird is always alone and without companion, for its like cannot be found, and there is no other bird which resembles it in habits or appearance. At the end of five hundred years it feels that it has grown old, and loads itself with many rare and precious spices, and flies from the desert away to the city of Leopolis [properly Heliopolis, the Egyptian City of the Sun, as is made clear by other accounts]. There, by some sign or other, the coming of the bird is announced to a priest of that city, who causes fagots to be gathered and placed upon a beautiful altar, erected for the bird. And so, as I have said, the bird, laden with spices, comes to the altar, and smiting upon the hard stone with its beak, it causes the flame to leap forth and set fire to the wood and the spices. When the fire is burning brightly, the phoenix lays itself upon the altar and is burned to dust and ashes."

We see in this medieval account of the phoenix that the bird strikes the stone altar with its beak to start the fire. Throughout the Middle Ages church altars were made of

---

² Matthew 3:16.
³ Matthew 17:5.

stone. They were usually quite monumental in composition. However, it was also common practice to make available *portable altars, made of stone and often quite small.* They could be several inches on a side and only an inch or so thick. These portable altars had to be consecrated by a bishop and were granted only by a special license issued by the Pope.

Other versions of the phoenix story more perfectly match Wolfram's account of the dove setting the Host upon the little stone. To quote from *The First Epistle of Clement*, from the early Church Father Clement:

> *"Then, when it has acquired strength, it takes up that nest in which are the bones of its parent, and bearing these it passes from the land of Arabia into Egypt, to the city called Heliopolis. And, in open day, flying in the sight of all men, it places them on the altar of the sun."*

Thus the comparison is perfect: the dove sets the Host onto the little stone, the Phoenix sets the remains of its parent onto the altar of the sun. The lapsit exillis or *'small stone'* is a portable altar.

CHAPTER 10

THE LIGHTNING AND THE STONE

Much in the past has been made of the fact that the early Welsh name for Arthur's sword, Caledfwlch, appears to be cognate with that of the famous sword of the Irish hero Fergus mac Roich, Caladbolg. Various etymologies have been proposed for both swords, but given the qualities ascribed to them, the most reasonable derives the name from *calad/caled*, *'hard'*, and *-bolg*, *'lightning'*, cognate with L. *fulg-*. Derivations which take *-bolg* to mean *'gap/cleft'* (cf. W. *bwlch*) create a sword name that is nonsensical, i.e. a gap or cleft cannot be hard, nor can a sword be a gap or cleft. A later form of the name of Fergus' sword, Caladcholg or *'Hard-sword'* (Early Irish *cholg* = *'sword'*), is thought to be a clerical alteration of the original.

As a mythological lightning weapon, Caladbolg /Caledbwlch, *'Hard-lightning'*, performed marvels in Fergus' hands. To quote from the Celt Electronic Text Edition of the *Tain Bo Cuailnge*:

> "Then said Medb to Fergus: 'It were indeed fitting for you to give us your aid unstintingly in fighting today, for you were banished from your territory and your land and with us you got territory and land and estate and much kindness was shown to you'. 'If I had my sword today' said Fergus, 'I would cut them down so that the trunks of men would be piled high on the trunks of men and arms of men piled high on arms of men and the crowns of men's heads piled on the crowns of men's heads and men's heads piled on the edges of shields, and all the limbs of the Ulstermen scattered by me to the east and to the west would be as numerous as hailstones between two dry fields (?) along which a king's horses drive, if only I had my sword'. Then said Ailill to his own charioteer, Fer Loga: 'Bring me quickly the sword that wounds men's flesh, O fellow. I pledge my word that if its

condition and preservation be worse with you today than on the day when I gave it to you on the hillside at Crúachna Aí, even if the men of Ireland and of Alba are protecting you against me today, not all of them will save you'. Fer Loga came forward and brought the sword in all the beauty of its fair preservation, shining bright as a torch, and the sword was given into Ailill's hand. And Ailill gave the sword to Fergus and Fergus welcomed the sword: 'Welcome to you, O Caladbolg, the sword of Leite' said he. 'Weary are the champions of the war-goddess. On whom shall I ply this sword?' asked Fergus. 'On the hosts that surround you on all sides' said Medb. 'Let none receive mercy or quarter from you today except a true friend'.

And Fergus grasped the Caladbolg in both hands and swung it back behind him so that its point touched the ground, and his intent was to strike three terrible and warlike blows on the Ulstermen so that their dead might outnumber their living. Cormac Cond Longas, the son of Conchobor, saw him and he rushed towards Fergus and clasped his two arms about him. 'Ready; yet not ready (?), my master Fergus. Hostile and not friendly is that, my master Fergus. Ungentle but not heedful (?) is that, my master Fergus. Do not slay and destroy the Ulsterman with your mighty blows, but take thought for their honour on this day of battle today'. 'Begone from me, lad' said Fregus 'for I shall not live if I strike not my three mighty, warlike blows upon the Ulstermen today so that their living outnumber their dead'.

"'Turn your hand level' said Cormac Cond Longas, 'and strike off the tops of the hills over the heads of the hosts and that will appease your anger'. 'Tell Conchobor to come then into his battle-position'. Conchobor came to his place in the battle. Now that sword, the sword of Fergus, was the sword of Leite from the elf-mounds [sidib]. When one wished to strike with it, it was as big as a rainbow in the air.—Then Fergus turned his hand level above the heads of the hosts and cut off the tops of the three hills which are still there in the marshy plain as evidence. Those are the three Máela of Meath.

Now as for Cú Chulainn, when he heard the Óchain Conchobuir being struck by Fergus mac Róig, he said: 'Come now, my friend Láeg, who will dare thus to smite the Óchain of Conchobor my master while I am alive?' 'This huge sword, as big as a rainbow, sheds blood, increase of slaughter' said Láeg. 'It is the hero Fergus mac Róig. The chariot sword was *hidden in the fairy mounds [assidib]. The horsemen (?) of my master Conchobor have reached the battlefield'."*

Cruachan is the diminuative of cruach, a rick, i.e. a stack or pile, as of turf, but is also applied to hills or mountains. This is to be related to British *croucio-, later *croco-, 'mount, tumulus', cf. Welsh crug, Irish cruach – 'hill, hillock, mound, heap, stack, tumulus, barrow, cairn'.

The Cruachan Ai or Little Tumulus of Ai was on Mag Ai, the great plain in County Roscommon that extends from Ballymore to Elphin, and from Bellanagare to Strokestown. The most important tumulus at Cruachan is now called Rathcroghan Mound, a site now firmly established as a ceremonial center associated with pre-Christian ritual.

Rathcroghan Mound is 88m in diameter on average at its base, and is about 4m in height on its northern side. There has been much speculation over the years as to its function, but recent research by NUI Galway indicates that it was used for ceremonial purposes, and possibly contains a passage tomb. Through techniques such as ground probing radar and magnetic susceptibility, the Archaeogeophysics Imaging Project of NUI Galway, under Professor John Waddell have discovered a massive enclosure surrounding the mound, approx. 380m in diameter, the largest of its type in the country. It also encloses a number of other archaeological features near the mound.

Uamh Cruachan or the *'Cave of the Little Tumulus'* was an Otherworld entrance in this same location. This is now called Oweynagat, *'Cave of the Cats'*, and is an ancient souterrain.

It is interesting that the Welsh *Spoils of Annwn* poem has the god Lugh (Llwch) raise Arthur's sword to a magical cauldron in Caer Siddi, the *'Fairy Fort'*, while Caladbolg in Irish tradition is said to come from the elf or fairy mounds. Caer Siddi is also called Caer Wydr or *'Glass Fort'*, a name later connected with Glastonbury. For this reason, Glastonbury came to be identified with Geoffrey of Monmouth's Avalon, where the sword Caliburn or, rather, Caledbwlch had been forged.

The King Arthur Cross

The leaden plate in the form of a Cross found in King Arthur's grave at Glastonbury Abbey in the reign of King Henry II.

The inscription reads: Hic jacet sepultus inclytus Rex Arthurus in Insula Avalonia (" Here lies interred in the Isle of Avalon the renowned King Arthur.")

Figure 12 - King Arthur Cross, Glastonbury

Anyone reading these Irish and Welsh accounts cannot possibly see Caladbolg/Caledbwlch as a mere mortal sword. Rather, it is a divine lightning weapon, used by a sacred hero.

So how came such a weapon to be in Arthur's hands?

To begin, it is important to remember that the first author to tell of the *'Sword in the Stone'* does not, in fact, place the weapon in the stone. Instead, in his romance *Merlin*, Robert de Boron states that the sword was in an anvil, and the anvil was atop a stone.

A possible Continental origin for the Arthurian *'Sword in the Stone'* motif has been proposed by some scholars. In 1180, the medieval Italian knight Galgano Guidotti plunged his sword into a rock when he renounced war and worldly goods to become a hermit. The abbey at Montesiepi near Siena preserves the sword in its chapel. There the hilt and some of the blade protrude from the rock in the shape of a cross. For many years the sword was thought to be a fake, but recent metal testing has determined that the alloys and style of the sword are consistent with a genuine 12th century weapon. In addition, ground penetrating radar has shown that beneath the sword is a six and a half foot by three foot room, which is quite possibly St. Galgano's tomb.

If St. Galgano really dates to the 12th century, this would place a *'Sword in the Stone'* story just prior to Robert de Boron's Arthurian version, which is dated c. 1200 CE. What remains to be determined is what may have influenced Robert to import such a tale into his *Merlin* romance. And an important detail is missing from the St. Galgano legend: the Italian knight's sword does not bear an inscription, which is true of the Arthurian *'Sword in the Stone'*.

I have a solution to this problem. As I have already mentioned, Geoffrey of Monmouth said Caliburnus was forged on the Isle of Avalon. Medieval tradition identified Avalon with Glastonbury. Robert de Boron claims that the *'Sword in the Stone'* is in a churchyard. Arthur's grave was supposedly discovered in the yard of St. Dunstan's church at Glastonbury. It is the inscribed lead cross of this grave that accounts for the inscription on the sword. From the account of the exhumation of Arthur at Glastonbury, by Gerald of Wales, c. 1193 (144):

> *"Unde et crux plumbea lapide supposito, non superius ut [nostris] solet diebus, [sed] inferiori potius ex parte infixa, quam nos quoque vidimus, namque tractavimus litteras has insculptas et non eminentes et exstantes, sed magis interius ad lapidem versas, continebat"*

> *"Whence also a lead cross with a stone placed beneath, not further above, as is customary in [our] days, [but] rather infixed [the antecedent is feminine, so 'cross', not 'stone'] from*

the lower part, which we also have seen, for we have passed hands over these letters, ensculpted and not raised and outstanding, but rather turned inward toward the stone, it contained ..."

There is no way one could construe this as implying that the cross was under the stone. Instead, we are to envisage an inscribed lead cross whose lower portion is infixed, i.e. thrust into, a stone.

We thus have, in St. Dunstan's churchyard at Glastonbury/'*Avalon*', where according to Geoffrey of Monmouth the sword Caliburnus was forged, an inscribed cross driven into/piercing a stone - a stone which was found above the supposed tomb of King Arthur. To this we may compare the Italian St. Galgano cruciform hilted sword, driven into the rock above an interior chamber which may well be the grave of the knight-turned-saint.

Robert de Boron, perhaps utilizing the St. Galgano example, merely transformed the inscribed cross thrust into the stone at Glastonbury into an inscribed sword thrust into the anvil-stone.

If we cannot rely on his having known the St. Galgano story, the fashioning of his own tale may have been facilitated by a more purely local or British example of this literary motif. I am referring to an incident referred to in the *Vita Sancti Edwardi*, where Bishop Wulfstan of Worcester, in order to prove his legitimacy, thrusts his staff into the gravestone of the late King Edward. This action was in response to the claim by Lanfranc, Archbishop of Canterbury, that Wulfstan was not worthy of his position. Other holy men try to pull Wulfstan's staff from the stone, but all fail. Wulfstan himself them approaches and easily extracts his staff from the stone.

Does this mean that we must settle for the entire story of Arthur's Sword in the Stone having been stolen or adapted from other tales exhibiting a similar motif?

Fortunately, no, we don't. The true '*Sword in the Stone*' did not belong in Britain or in Italy. It has its proper place, as does the name of the sword itself, in Ireland.

Going now to the LL text of the Irish *Tain Bo Cuailnge* or 'Cattle Raid of Cooley', headed *Do fhallsigud Tana Bo Cualnge* ('*How the Tain Bo Cuailnge was Found Again*'), we find the following pertinent episode:

> "Emine, Ninene's grandson, set out for the east with Senchan's son Muirgen. It happened that the grave of Fergus mac Roich was on their way. They came upon the gravestone at Enloch ['liic oc Enloch', see Oir leac, 'gravestone'] in Connacht. Muirgen sat down at Fergus's grave stone, and the others left him for a while and went looking for a house for the night. Muirgen chanted a poem to the gravestone as though it were Fergus himself. He said to it:
> 'If this your royal rock
> Were your own self mac Roich
> Halted here with sages
> Searching for a roof
> 'Cuailnge' we'd recover
> Plain and perfect Fergus.'
> A great mist suddenly formed around him - for the space of three days and nights he could not be found. And the figure of Fergus approached him in fierce majesty, with a head of brown hair, in a green cloak and a red-embroidered hooded tunic, with a gold-hilted sword and bronze blunt sandals. Fergus recited him the whole Tain, how everything happened, from start to finish."

What seems remarkable about this account is that a sword bearing the same name as that of King Arthur's is placed at a stone or rock at a lake. The stone in question, as made plain by reference to a *'roof'*, was a chambered tomb, an Otherworld castle like those mentioned in the *Spoils of Annwn* poem. But even more startling, we find at this stone a personage bearing the name Muirgen, a name cognate with the Welsh Morgen or Morgan, as in Morgan le Fay. Morgan le Fay ends up being one of the Ladies of the Lake.

Enloch is a disguised version of Loch (na) nEn, which is now represented by Loughnaneane tl., p./b. Roscommon. Loch na nEn means *'Lake of the Birds'*. According to the megalithic survey there is no monument in or near Loughnaneane and no standing stones are recorded in or around there in the Roscommon Record of Monuments and Places of the Duchas (the Heritage Service). The likelihood is that, with the town so close, any such monument would have been dismantled and used as building stone.

The real 'Sword in the Stone', after which Arthur named his own weapon, was that of the legendary Iron Age Irish hero, Fergus ma Roich. And the 'stone' itself was the now vanished chambered tomb in which Fergus was buried.

As far as ritual purposes go, a replica of Arthur's Caledbwlch or 'Hard-lightning' would serve many purposes for the Arthurian druid. Arthur's actual historical sword would have been patterned after a late-period Roman spatha or cavalry sword. The ceremony of dubbing with a sword, part of the conferring of knighthood on a squire, was an invention of the High Middle Ages, long after Arthur's time. Yet the concept is so inextricably bound up with the notion of Arthurian knighthood that, in my opinion, it should be allowed to stand. A knighthood ceremony could be used as part of the induction of new members into a druidic circle. More ancient qualities of the king's sword include the same phallic symbolism that Wiccans now ascribe to their athame. This phallic symbolism extends to the king's sword as the heavenly lightning which blesses the fields at planting time, thus impregnating the earth with the sky-father's seed. And, of course, the martial properties of such a weapon cannot be forgotten: nothing in Nature can withstand the divine lightning. It shatters great treess and rocks with equal efficiency, and all too often kills those humans who are struck by it. Those who survive a lightning strike must be seen as particularly holy individuals, who have been touched by the divine power, yet spared its usual catastrophic effects.

The Sword of Arthur, when used as a ritual object, should be kept inside a stone cist that represents the Stone of Enloch. Needless to say, such a structure – even if on a diminuative scale – must be constructed outside. The location of the sword, therefore, must be kept secret. Precautions must also be taken to cover it with a wrapping or case that will prevent it from being exposed to dampness.

It should only be withdrawn from the cist for ritual purposes, after which it should be cleaned, if necessary. Proper protocol must be observed when handling the sword. While pagans should always be wary of placing too much privilege in the hands of a head druid, the care and keeping of the sword should be restricted to someone whose office it is to be Sword-Bearer. Such an office should be an elected position that can rotate among the members of an Arthurian druid group.

CHAPTER 11

THE EVERLASTING BATTLE AND AVALON

THE RED AND WHITE DRAGONS

In Chapter 7 I discussed the nature of the Red and White Dragons of Dinas Emrys. These creatures were shown to have originally been the cremated remains of warriors placed in a double-urn. Over time they came to be identified as Roman genii, which took serpent form. Such genii could be specific to a place or to a people and so the Red Dragon evolved into the genius of the Britons, while the White Dragon became the genius of the Saxons.

By the time we get to the much later Welsh story of *Lludd and Lleuelys*, we are told the *'back story'* on how the two dragons came to be imprisoned at Dinas Emrys. It turns out that the god Lleuelys (see the listing for Lleu in Chapter 6) dug a pit at the center of the island, here situated at Oxford. In the pit he placed a vat filled with mead and covered with a silk sheet. The dragons, as was their habit, began fighting on May Eve as monstrous animals – probably oxen, given the Oxford location. The scream of the red dragon during its fight with the white dragon was heard over every hearth in the island of Britain. The hearth in this context points to Roman household deities like the genius, which could be portrayed above or next to the hearth.

The monstrous animals or oxen then flew into the air as dragons. When they wearied of the battle, they sank into the vat as pigs, dragging the sheet to the bottom. There they drank the mead and fell asleep. Lleuelys wrapped them in the sheet and locked them in a stone chest, which he then took and buried at Dinas Emrys.

The first question that must be asked about this account of the origin of the dragons is simply, *'Why Oxford as the centre of Britain?'*

Because within Oxfordshire is found Ambrosden, in Old English, Ambresdone, supposedly *'Ambre's Hill'*. This place-name is a substitute for Amesbury, Anglo-Saxon Ambresbyrig. Indeed, the Welsh storyteller of *Lludd and Lleuelys* could not have helped but find more of a parallel in Dinas Emrys and Ambrosden than was obvious with Dinas Emrys and Amesbury. Thus the naval or *'omphalos'* of Britain at Amesbury's Stonehenge was relocated to Oxfordshire.

Another new element introduced into the dragon story by the *Lludd and Lleuelys* author is the precise dating of the conflict of the two monsters: May Eve. This was, of course, the pagan Beltane, the festival that celebrated the beginning of Spring and what had come to be seen as the summer half of the year. For the Romans, May 1st was the festival of the goddess Bona Dea, whose temple contained sacred snakes.

As Oxford or rather Ambrosden in Oxfordshire was a substitute for Amesbury next to Stonehenge, we can be certain that May Eve as the time of the dragon fight was adapted from Geoffrey of Monmouth. In his *History of the Kings of Britain*, Geoffrey tells us that during the reign of Vortigern, the Saxons (= the White Dragon) slew the Britons (= the Red Dragon) during a truce on May Eve at the future site of Stonehenge.

This slaying of the Britons at Stonehenge reads like a mass human sacrifice. They are killed by having their throats slashed with knives, which is the usual form of execution meted out to sacrificial victims. On another level, this episode could be read as an imaginary capture of the sacred British omphalos by the Saxons.

Geoffrey furthermore tells us that about 460 members of the British nobility were slain at what was to become Stonehenge. Why *'about 460'*? Plainly this number has some special significance. I could find no astronomical cycle that employs the number 460, although Mercury transits (when the planet appears from our vantage point on earth to pass in front of the sun) can occur every 46 years close to 7 May. Now it is true that the god Lugos or Lleu, who plays the role of *'Emrys'* in the story of the red and white dragons, was identified by the Romans with their own god Mercury. Mercury was not only distinguished by the double-serpent caduceus or wand, but was often placed in or near the same household shrines or lararia in which the snakes or genius loci were depicted. According to Hyginus (*Astronomica* 2.7), Mercury's/Hermes' staff originated thusly:

> "At Apollo's request he [Hermes] gave him permission to claim the invention of the lyre, and received from him a certain staff as reward. When Mercury [Hermes], holding it in his hand, was journeying to Arcadia and saw two snakes with bodies intertwined, apparently fighting, he put down the staff between them. They separated then, and so he said that the staff had been appointed to bring peace. Some, in making caducei, put two snakes intertwined on the rod, because this seemed to Mercury a bringer of peace. Following his example, they use the staff in athletic contests and other contests of this kind."

This motif of fighting serpents reminds us immediately of the fighting of the red and white dragons.

In addition to the snake as genius loci, snake jewelery hoards are found in Roman Britain. Snake rings and snake bracelets of the Romano-British hoards have been associated with Asclepius, the Genius Paterfamilias and Lares, Mercury, Sabazius, Mithras and Glycon (who may have had affinities with both Asclepius and Sarapis). There may also be a link between such snakes and Mother Goddess cults, such as those belonging to Ceres/Demeter, Minerva and Fortuna.

Snakes regularly slough off their skin and so were associated with death and rebirth. For this reason, snake symbolism often features in funerary monuments. The tombstone of Longinus at Colchester includes snakes grasped between the paws of lions, and a stone pine cone encircled by a snake may have formed an independent gravestone at Carlisle. The association of snakes with re-birth also led to snakes being found in cult images and decorations asscoiated with mystery religions that looked to saviour gods.

But to return to the Britons said to have been slain at Stonehenge. Geoffrey of Monmouth's number of slain Britons – 460 - is also found in Wace. But Lawman has 405, Nennius 300, while Alfred of Beverley, the Anglo-Norman *Brut*, Robert of Brunne and the Welsh copies have 360. 360 *could* be a reference the number of days in an ancient year.

However, it may be that the Anglo-Saxon dates for Vortigern supply us with a clue as to what 460 actually represents. The advent of the Saxons, who were invited in by Vortigern, is said to have occurred in 449 CE. He is also said to have fought a battle with the Saxons in 455. Could it be that Geoffrey's '460' is either code or an error for 460 CE?

I used NASA's eclipse tables to determine that while no solar eclipse visible from Britain had taken place 'about 460' on or close to May 1, there was a total lunar eclipse on May 3, 459. During a lunar eclipse, the moon, which is ordinarily white, can become blood-red in color. The *Anglo-Saxon Chronicle* records such an event under the year entry for 734:

> "In this year the moon was as if it were suffused with blood..."

The possibility that Geoffrey's 'about 460' was referring to a total lunar eclipse in 459 immediately after Beltane has tremendous ramifications for the nature of the red and white dragons. These ramifications may reveal that the genii of the Britons and the Saxons were at some point subjected to a further mythological interpretation.

Let us begin by viewing the White Dragon as the moon. The White Dragon becomes the Red Dragon during a lunar eclipse. When the eclipse is over, the Red Dragon is gone and the White Dragon has returned. Such a cosmic drama may have been considered a battle between opposing dragons.

The sun is never white, and can only be reddish at sunrise or sunset or when viewed through smoke. Hence it is very unlikely that the two dragons are solar monsters who divide the year between themselves, one ruling the period from Beltane to Samhain and the other the period from Samhain to Beltane. It is true that the division of the year into two solar halves was observed anciently by the Celts, as is proven by the Coligny Calendar (see the Appendix below). We will see that prior to the *'slipping'* of the calendar, Beltane, now May 1st, fell on midsummer, and Samhain, now November 1st, belonged at midwinter. And neolithic monuments such as the Newgrange and Bryn Celli Ddu passage graves and various stone circles and alignments indisputably marked the summer and winter solstices. But although it is tempting to relate this divided solar year to the two dragons, there is a considerable amount of evidence that prohibits us from doing so.

For example, when we go back to the account of the dragons in Lludd and Lleuelys, we recall that it was the horrifying scream of the Red Dragon on May Eve that caused men to lose their color and strength, women to suffer miscarriages, children to lose their senses and animals and trees and soil and water to become barren. As is well known, the moon was closely associated with the nine month term of pregnancy (as the term *'month'* comes from the word moon), and with madness, called lunacy in honour of the lunar body.

It has long been known that a snake's shedding of its skin was associated by the ancients with the moon going from old to new. The sun, on the other hand, does not go through phases of cyclic death and rebirth that could be symbolized by the sloughing of skin.

Figure 13 - Bryn Celli Ddu
Chambered tomb on Anglesey, Wales

If the Red and White Dragons did come to be perceived as lunar monsters, Lleuelys' entrapment of them in the vat, his wrapping them in the sheet and locking them in the chest that was buried on Dinas Emrys may be metaphorical language for the setting of the moon into the earth during a total lunar eclipse.

It would have been poetic genius to describe the dragon of the Britons as being like the eclipsed moon, as the Britons themselves, confronted with the onslaught of the Saxons, were in truth being *eclipsed* by their enemy.

In passing, it is interesting that two British snake species actually exhibit white and red color patterns, although these are sexual distinctions. The male viper has a grey, creamy white or steely grey background color, while the female ranges from brown and yellow to brick red. In the smooth snake, the female is usually a uniform silver grey, while the male tends towards brown and red. Since we now know that the Otherworld white cattle with red ears that appear in Celtic mythological tradition had their counterpart in the real world, could it be that the white and red lunar dragons had their earthly counterparts in one of these two species of native British snakes?

An alternate version of the creation of Mercury's /Hermes' caduceus, found recorded in several ancient sources (Phlegon, *Mirabilia 4*; Tzetzes, *Scholiast on Lycophron 683*; Eustathius on *Hom. Od. 10.492*, p. 1665; *Scholiast on Hom. Od. x.494*; *Ant. Lib. 17*; Ov. *Met. 3.316ff.*; Hyginus, *Fab. 75*; Lactantius Placidus on *Statius, Theb. ii.95*; Fulgentius, *Mytholog. ii.8*; *Scriptores rerum mythicarum Latini*, ed. Bode, i. pp. 5, 104, 169; *First Vatican Mythographer 16*; *Second Vatican Mythographer 84*; *Third Vatican Mythographer iv.8*), presents one of the serpents as male and the other as female. Instead of fighting, the snakes are described as copulating.

GWYN AND GWYTHYR

According to *Culhwch and Olwen*, the gods Gwyn and Gwythyr fight each other every May Eve until Judgment Day for the right to possess the goddess Creiddylad. We have seen in Chapter 6 that Gwyn, the *'White, Fair or Holy One'*, is a Horned God. Gwythyr is the Northern British god Vitiris or *'He of the Willow Branch'*, whom I identified with the Continental Celtic god Esus.

As these two gods fight each other on the same day as the Red and White Dragons, could there be a relationship between the two sets of divine entities?

Gwyn, being white, would accord very well with the White Dragon. We know that dedications to Vitiris are accompanied by animals, including a serpent and a boar. We have seen in the *Lludd and Lleuelys* story that the dragons transformed into pigs.

Cernunnos the *'Horned One'* is shown in iconography holding a sun-torc in one hand and a ram-horned snake, i.e. the crescent moon, in the other. In another representation, this one found at Cirencester, the Horned God's legs curve upward to form two horned serpents. The same god is also depicted on a coin from Petersfield, Hampshire, with the solar wheel between his upraised antlers. Clearly this sky-father had both solar and lunar attributes. This means that as well as symbolizing the sky, he could manifest himself in either the sun or the moon.

Gwythyr, a god who seasonally chopped down the cosmic willow tree that is the Milky Way, would thus appear to have had a lunar aspect. British and Continental traditions affirm that the willow had strong lunar affinities.

A universal motif in ancient European and Near Eastern religion is the serpent or dragon at the tree. Often this serpent has as its heavenly counterpart an eagle or comparable bird that perches at the top of the tree. Whether we are talking about the 'Snake that knows no charm' and the Imdugud-bird of the Mesopotamian Gilgamesh Epic, the Biblical serpent and Tree of the Knowledge of Good and Evil, the dragon Ladon and the apple tree of the Hesperides, the dragon and oak of the solar ram's Golden Fleece, the serpent Nidhogg (a name which in Old Norse means literally 'Waning-moon striker') and eagle of the Ash Yggdrasill or the serpent-footed monster and Sky-rider of the Gaulish Jupiter columns – all seem to preserve a similar symbology featuring a lunar serpent, a solar deity and a sky tree. In most instances the serpent and bird or Sky-rider are in opposition to each other, something which accurately reflects the relationship of bird of prey and snake in Nature.

In the Mabinogion tale Math son of Mathonwy, the god Lleu sits in eagle form atop an oak. Every day a sow finds her way to the tree to consume the rotten flesh and maggots which fall from Lleu. I make this sow out to be a lunar pig; her eating of that which falls from Lleu is a poetic way of acknowledging that the moon shines only because it receives the sun's light. The sow is thus Goewin, Arianrhod and Blodeuedd.

Apollo the sun god had slain the lunar Python inside Gaia, i.e. inside the earth. Beowulf slays the lunar dragon (which can fly across the sky in fiery fashion only from sunset to sunrise, i.e. during the night) guarding its golden sun-hoard within the earth-barrow. Likewise Sigurd the Dragon-slayer slays the dragon Fafnir, who was sitting on his solar gold inside another barrow. The Norse Glam (a poetic word for 'moon') became a draug in death, and came forth from his barrow to haunt the countryside until he was destroyed by Grettir the Strong.

At least in the Germanic sources, then, the dead man in the barrow, guarding his grave-goods, became identified with the moon. It may be significant that in Norse belief the moon is male, while the sun is female.

I have alluded to other 'everlasting battles' in previous chapters: Hafgan (the summer constellation Scorpio) is in endless conflict with Arawn (the winter constellation Orion), while Lleu is slain at Midwinter by Goronwy, only to return the favor by killing his opponent on Midsummer. There are hints in other sources of similar seasonal contests.

For example, in Nennius' de Mirabilius Brittanniae, we are told of the 'Two Kings of the Severn':

> "When the sea floods into the Severn estuary in the Bore, two heaped-up wave crests are built up separately, and fight each other like rams. One goes against the other, and they clash in turn, and then one withdraws from the other, and they go forth again at each tide. This they have done, from the beginning of the world to the present day."

Yet another Everlasting Battle is mentioned in the Myrddin poem Yr Afallennau or 'The Apple Trees', in which Myrddin says (in Strophe 4):

> "Sweet apple that grows beyond Rhun;
> I have contended at its base in order to please a maiden..."

The apple tree for the ancient British (and the Irish) was the tree of the happy Otherworld, where summer reigned without end. In the same poem, we are told of this particular tree that it is in the Celyddon Wood, but that its virtue lay in the fact that it could not be found and that no one would succeed in getting its fruit. Myrddin, when 'calm in his mind', i.e. not in the death-state that was metaphorically described as madness (see Chapter 4 above), 'used to be at its base with a fair, playful maiden', presumably the same one for whom he contended. This is generally believed to be Gwenddydd. 'Rhun', beyond which lay the Celyddon Wood and its apple tree, is probably a region in northwestern England or southwestern Scotland over which Rhun son of Urien of Rheged ruled.

This poem betrays some confusion on the part of the poet. Myrddin as the *'elf-man'*, the warrior-bard who perished at Arfderydd, went in spirit form to reside at the Otherworld apple tree. Prior to his death, this Otherworld apple - a sky-tree like Lleu's oak - would have been inaccesible to him, exactly as is said to be the case for the still-living followers of Rhydderch of Strathclyde (Strophe 5):

> *"Sweet apple tree that grows in a clearing,*
> *Its virtue hides it from Rhydderch's lords,*
> *A crowd around its base, a host around it."*

In other words, even when Rhydderch's men are surrounding the tree, which stands out in the open, they cannot see it.

Myrddin's contention for the maiden led to his death. He was fighting for the goddess. When he died, his spirit was able to easily find the hidden apple tree of the Otherworld, where the goddess was waiting for him. The corollary of this story, if Myrddin is in this instance being treated as a human incarnation of the god, is to allow for his rebirth.

Geoffrey of Monmouth got close to the truth of this in his *Life of Merlin*. In lines 1387-1456, we learn of a madman named Maeldin (= the Irish Mail Duin, who along with his crew subsists on an apple branch for 40 days during a voyage to Otherworld islands). He had accidentally consumed a poisoned apple intended for Merlin. The poisoner was a certain woman whom Myrddin had supposedly *'discarded'*, an alias for the goddess. No sooner had Maeldin eaten the apple than he went mad. Or, to be less poetic, the apple killed him, allowing his spirit to join the goddess at the Otherworld apple tree. Maeldin may have forsaken the goddess in life, but she would possess him in death.

THE SPIRITUAL AVALON

In Chapter 1, we explored the physical Avalon that was the Roman fort of Burgh-By-Sands in Cumbria. Here I wish to touch more upon the spiritual aspects of the apple tree Otherworld.

We human beings are obsessed with the effects of both linear and cyclic time. The latter is experienced every year of our lives as we watch the endless march of the hands of a clock, the ceaseless turning of the pages of a calendar, the alternating of the seasons. Birthdays and anniversaries are celebrated to mark what are judged to be important intervals of time. But we all know that for everything in the universe, cyclic existence does end with death or dissolution. As if to compensate for this, we invent scientific theories or religious systems that seek to give time itself a definitive beginning and end. Time thus becomes linear, passing distinctly from point A to point B. Yet we grapple so poorly with the concept of an ultimate and irrevocable extinction of being or consciousness that we ingeniously tag on a point C – an imagined afterlife that is eternal in nature and free from the ravages of cyclic time. In this afterlife we do not age and existence is inevitably paradisical.

The pagan Celts also acknowledged the role of time in the cosmos, and they were not immune to the same impulses that led to the formation of religious concepts designed to facilitate the intellectual and emotional acceptance of seasonal fluctuations and death. There is no evidence that the druids were in dread of an eventual 'end of the world'. Indeed, Strabo tells us that not only did they deem souls to be eternal, but the universe itself was 'indestructible'. Classical writers claim that the druids subscribed both to a belief in reincarnation and to that of an afterlife in the *'infernal regions'* – statements which would appear to contradict one another.

The only evidence for reincarnation that I've found in the Celtic sources pertains not to human beings, but to deities. For example, the goddess Etain Echraide is reborn. Lleu is also *'reborn'* by being transformed from the death-eagle back into his *'human'* form. This is the normal seasonal transformation of the goddess and the god.

To some extent the Classical authorities may have been confused by the Celtic philosophy expressed beautifully in the *Cad Godeu* of Taliesin, the Irish *Song of Amairgen* and the *Voyage of Bran* son of Febal:

> *"I was a slender, enchanted sword – I believe that is was done.*
> *I was rain-drops in the air, I was stars' beam;*
> *I was a word in letters, I was a book in origin;*
> *I was lanterns of light for a year and a half;*
> *I was a bridge that stretched over sixty estuaries;*
> *I was a path, I was an eagle, I was a coracle in seas;*
> *I was a bubble in beer, I was a drop in a shower;*
> *I was a sword in hand, I was a shield in battle.*
> *I was a string in a harp enchanted nine years, in the water as foam;*
> *I was a spark in fire, I was wood in a bonfire..."*

(From the Cad Godeu)

> *I am Wind on Sea,*
> *I am Ocean-wave,*
> *I am Roar of Sea,*
> *I am Bull of Seven Fights,*
> *I am Vulture on Cliff,*
> *I am Dewdrop,*
> *I am Fairest of Flowers,*
> *I am Boar for Boldness,*
> *I am Salmon in Pool,*
> *I am Lake on Plain,*
> *I am a Mountain in a Man,*
> *I am a Word of Skill,*
> *I am the Point of a Weapon (that poureth forth combat),*
> *I am God who fashioneth Fire for a Head.*

Who smootheth the ruggedness of a mountain?
Who is He who announceth the ages of the Moon?
And who, the place where falleth the sunset?
Who calleth the cattle from the House of Tethys?
On whom do the cattle of Tethys smile?
Who is the troop, who the god who fashioneth edges
in a fortress of gangrene?
Enchantments about a spear? Enchantments of Wind?
(From the Song of Amairgen)

He [Mongan] will be in the shape of every beast,
Both on the azure sea and on land,
He will be a dragon before hosts at the onset,
He will be a wolf in every great forest.
He will be a stag with horns of silver
In the land where chariots are driven,
He will be a speckled salmon in a full pool,
He will be a seal, he will be a fair-white swan.
(From the Voyage of Bran son of Febal)

In these beautiful passages, the poets claim to have been all manner of things other than themselves – even God! In other words, everything in the cosmos is One and Dualism is an illusion. This is not the same as reincarnation, of course.

As was the case with Lleu in his oak, when Myrddin is said in the early Welsh poetry to be at his apple tree we are being told he is in the sky. Before the sun can enter the earth, it must cross the sky. Irish and British myth and folklore is full of instances in which a hero must obtain or be given an apple or apple branch before he can enter the Otherworld. This is why the Norse *Eddas* place the sky-tree in front of the door of Valholl, the Viking paradise that was located within the earth.

To understand the function of the great barrow mounds is of paramount importance in determining what exactly the ancient Celts believed happened after death. Although erected as early as the Neolithic and so often predating the Celts, an understanding of and reverence for the mounds is evident in Celtic literature and folk beliefs.

These great chambereds tombs were communal in nature. While it may be that only royalty were deposited in them, it is possible commoners were as well, or that commoners had their own less grand Otherworld portals. In any case, the more important monuments have their entrance passages so aligned that the rays of the rising or setting sun can only pass down the passage and strike the bodies or cremated remains of persons deposited within the central chamber on or about the winter or summer solstices.

The idea was simple. When the dead person was touched by the rays of the sun, which itself was in the process of dying and being reborn, his spirit became one with the sun. Probably the spirit traveled up the light beams or, perhaps, the light beams plucked up the soul and conveyed it to the source. By becoming part of the sun at this instant, a dead person was reborn as the sun and partook of the god's immortality.

Christians would be very uncomfortable with such a concept, but only because they continue to deny that their own Christ was early on 'solarized', and that by participating in Communion, where they consume the blood (light) and body (sun) of their god, they are likewise seeking to share in his immortality by becoming one with him.

We may imagine the pagan Celtic conception of the afterlife as something like this: a person dies and is taken to the tribal barrow mound. This 'journey' to the mound was symbolically likened to the setting of the seasonally-slain sun god into the earth. Once deposited with all due ritual in the barrow, his spirit remains bound to his body until midwinter or midsummer, when it joins with the sun to be reborn.

Similar practices appear to have been engaged in at henge monuments, as archaeology has provided us with indisputable proof that burial took place within banked enclosures and stone circles. We even have examples of chambered tombs or cairns being enclosed by circles, even if the two phases of construction did not coincide with one another. As stone circles can have alignments for celestial objects other than the sun – the moon, other planets, even stars – it is probable that souls could join with any number of deities. A person's birth-date, declared divine patron, cause of death, circumstances surrounding that death and death-date may all have been contributing factors that helped druids presiding at a person's funeral determine to which heavenly body the spirit should go.

In the Appendix, which concerns itself with the ancient Irish tree alphabet called the ogam, I will demonstrate that the current Celtic festivals of Imbolc (February 1), Beltane (May 1), Lughnasadh (August 1) and Samhain (November 1) were originally solstice and equinox festivals. The scholar Garrett Olmsted's work on the Gaulish Coligny calendar has proven that Beltane was once the Summer Solstice (around June 21), Lughnasadh was the Autumn Equinox (around September 21), Samhain was the Winter Solstice (around December 21) and Imbolc was the Spring Equinox (around March 21).

These four vitally important days of the solar year, that of the longest day (Summer Solstice), the day ending summer when night and day are of even length (Autumn Equinox), the shortest day of the year (Winter Solstice) and the day ending winter when night and day are of even length (Spring Equinox), were those most charged with supernatural power.

The old view of the spirits of the dead as revellers inside the fairy hill must be abandoned as a quaint fancy. Celtic feelings towards the Otherworld have always been ambivalent; fear of the dark, cold grave resides side by side with poetic visions of beautiful maidens, endless food and drink, and sprightly song. Instead, dying was a much more profound experience. It was all about becoming the god or goddess. The Otherworld, the earth, the barrow mound, although a home to the celestial deities, was merely a stopping point for human spirits on their way from mortal life to immortal life. When we worship Lleu the sun, we also worship those spirits who have become Lleu.

The myths hint at similar identifications of women with goddesses. The various Sovereignty Goddesses who marry kings in the Irish and Welsh sources show that such identifications could be made. As the Egyptian Pharoah could be a divine human incarnation of the sun god, so could his queen be an incarnation of Isis the moon goddess. Again, divinity of this nature may have been the prerogative of the ruling elite. But it is possible that in more egalitarian societies, the promise of joining the god in immortality was not restricted to royalty or even to nobility.

Avalon is not so much a place – although it could be localized in the human landscape – as it is a state of divine existence. It is not an Otherworld of the souls of the dead, but rather the home of those gods and goddesses with whom the spirits have become joined with as One.

Avalon is also a time or, more correctly, a season. For the apple tree not only stood for the sky, but as my re-interpretation of the ogam alphabet will show, it was the sky-tree of Summer. There were other trees that governed Summer as well, and trees corresponding to the other seasons.

When Arthur was taken to Avalon after his fall in battle at Camlan, he was buried at the place of the apple tree. His journey to the Otherworld was the earthly reflection of the journey of the summer sun across the sky. Once he had 'set' into the earth, he waited for the annual rebirth of the god. When that time came, his spirit and the deity became one. Arthur became immortal, never to experience anything other than eternal Summer.

For it is only from our mortal perspective that Summer ends. The sun is *always* attended by Summer. When the god moves south in Winter, he takes Summer with him to the southern hemisphere. When he comes back to the northern hemisphere, Summer returns. This is the story of the Holy Grail, whose disappearance brings on the Waste Land, i.e. the dead land of Winter. Only by achieving the Quest of the Grail and bringing the precious object back to the North can the Waste Land be healed by the onset of Summer.

And so for the god – and for the spirits who have become One with him – the sky is always the apple tree.

Arthur is indeed the Summer King.

APPENDICES

THE TREES OF AVALON:

A NEW INTERPRETATION OF THE OGAM ALPHABET

Much has been made of the ogam tree alphabet. But though there have been those who claim to have deciphered the mystery of the ogam, most scholars believe that either the mystery remains unsolved or that it actually exists only in the imagination of writers such as Robert Graves and those who adhere to his system of thought.

The truth is that an answer to the ogam mystery may further explain the significance of Arthur's presence in the Otherworld Avalon. A proper interpretation of the ogam may also tell us more about Myrddin, who is himself in ancient Welsh poetry placed at an Otherworld apple tree with the goddess.

What follows is my brief investigation on the ogam and its possible correspondences with the ancient Celtic calendar.

The ogam alphabet is composed of a series of marks representing letters, originally carved on stone and wood and bone. There are 20 such letters, gathered into four groups of five. According to the Irish, Ogma Sun-Face invented the ogam alphabet. Ogma is known on the Continent as Ogmios. This god or culture hero (he is identified in Gaul with Hercules) created the Celtic alphabet by raising four pillars of equal length. He then carved the sacred letters of the pillars.

The proper arrangement of the letters, which run from left to right and from bottom to top, are as follows:

Figure 14 - The Capon Tree
The oldest oak tree in Scotland.

N	Q	R	I
S	C	Z	E
F	T	Ng	U
L	D	G	O
B	H	M	A

The meanings assigned to the letters vary in the earliest extant tradition, and it has been shown that they underwent a considerable evolution of definitions. Many of the letters did not originally represent trees and some had very uncertain, even utterly unknown meanings (see the works of Damian McManus on the subject). At the end of this process, we ended up with the following versions of the ogam alphabet, all found in *The Scholar's Primer.*

B – birch
L – rowan or elm
F – alder
S – willow

N – maw of the spear (ash was used to make spears) or nettles
H – test-tree or whitethorn
D – oak
T – holly or elderberry
C – hazel
Q- holly or quicken tree or aspen
M – vine
G – cornfield
Ng – broom
Z – willowbrake
R - ?
A - ?
O – furze or ash
U – thorn
E – yew
I – service tree

B – birch
L – quicken tree
F – alder
S – willow
N – ash
H – thorn
D – oak
C – hazel
Q – apple-tree
M – vine
G – ivy
Ng – broom
Z – sloe
E – elderberry
A – fir
O – furze
U – heath
E – aspen
I – yew

B – birch

L – elm (put for quicken tree)
F – elder
S – willow
N – ash
H – no tree listed
D – oak
T – holly
C – hazel
Q – apple-tree
M – no tree listed
G – ivy
Z – sloe
R – elder
A – no tree listed
O – no tree listed
U – heather
E – aspen

Eventually, these different versions coalesced into a single, conventional form of the alphabet. What follows is this conventional form, complete with the three known kennings used for the letters/trees as these last are found in *Briatharogam Morainn mic Moin*, *Briatharogam Maic ind Oc* and *Briatharogam Con Culainn*, respectively.

B – birch (withered of foot with fine hair, greyest of skin, beauty of the eyebrow)
L – rowan or mountain ash (lustre of the eye, friend of cattle, sustenance of cattle)
F- alder (vanguard of hunting/warrior bands, milk container, protection of the heart)
S – willow (pallor of the lifeless one, sustenance of bees, beginning of honey)
N – ash (establishing of peace, boast of women, boast of beauty)
H – whitethorn (assembly of packs of hounds, blanching of faces, most difficult at night)
D – oak (most exalted tree, handicraft of an artificer, most carved of craftmanship)

T – holly (one of three parts of a wheel, marrow of charcoal, one of three parts of a weapon)

C – hazel (fairest tree, friend of nutshells, sweetest tree)

Q – apple (shelter of a lunatic, substance of an insignificant person, dregs of clothing)

M – vine (strongest in exertion, proverb of slaughter, path of the voice)

G – ivy (sweetest grass, suitable place of cows, sating of multitudes)

Ng – broom (sustenance of the leech, raiment of physicians, beginning of slaying)

Z – blackthorn (strongest reddening/dye, increase of secrets, seeking of clouds)

R – elder (most intense blushing, reddening of faces, glow of anger)

A – fir (loudest groan, beginning of an answer, beginning of calling)

O – furze (wounder of horses, smoothest of craftmanship, sustaining equipment of hunting/warrior bands)

U – heath (in cold dwellings, propagation of plants, shroud of a lifeless one)

E – aspen (discerning tree, exchange of friends, brother of birch)

I – yew (oldest tree, fairest of the ancients, energy of an infirm person)

The original meanings of the letter names, as determined by Damian McManus' linguistic analysis of the letter names themselves, coupled with the analysis of the associated kennings, are as follows:

B – birch (although one theory has this as coming from Latin beta)

L – flame, blaze, radiance or plant, herb, vegetable

F – alder

S – willow

N – lofty, forked, a part of a weaver's loom, or better, a forked branch that establishes peace, i.e. the olive branch, the shaking of which in Irish tradition caused men to cease from fighting. Nin never means ash, which in Irish was onn (see O below). The equation of Nin or 'N' with nettles was done simply because nettles in Middle Irish was nenntog, in Early Irish nenaid.

H – fear, horror. Huath is h-uath, the normal early Irish way of writing uath.

D – oak

T – bar, rod of metal, ingot, mass of molten metal

C – hazel

Q – tree or bush (cf. Welsh perth, 'hedge')

M – upper part of the back, neck or a wile, ruse, trick, i.e. fate, treachery, or love, affection, esteem

G – field (cf. Welsh garth, 'enclosure, garden')

Ng – act of wounding

Z – sulphur

R – red

A – Unknown, but I think this could be a borrowing of English 'elm' (cf. Latin ulmus, Old Norse almn). Another theory derives this simply from Latin alpha (as beithe or 'birch' is sometimes seen as a substitute for beta).

O – Onn was the earliest name for the ash tree.

U – earth, clay, soil

E – Originally perhaps either yew (eo) or salmon (eo/e). Edad appears to be an artificial creation, part of the pair Edad and Idad (see below).

I – Old Irish eo, 'yew', derives from *iwas, and hence this letter could have been from an earlier form of the word for yew than the later, more normal ibar.

Given the above as the original meanings of the ogam letters, clearly the divinatory method that has been employed in the past – the one based on Robert Graves' analeptically derived system – must be considerably revised.

In order to bring the letters into better accord with the various trees and plants, I would simplify the original meanings for the ogam letters thusly:

B – birch

L – flame: this is given in *The Scholar's Primer* as rowan, quicken tree or elm. But we shall see that rowan actually belongs at E, and elm belongs at A. The quicken or quickbeam /quickenbeam is the rowan tree, and the name quicken was probably first used for an aspen or some tree with quaking or quivering leaves. As the aspen was wrongly associated with E, I take L's original tree to have been the aspen, *'brother of birch'*, the B letter than immediately proceeds L.

N – olive

S – willow

F – alder

H – horror: the white or blanched face of someone terrified has been here linked with the white flowers of the whitethorn or hawthorn. The tree is also frightening because of its substantial thorns.

D – oak

T – In a Norse myth, the thunder hammer of Thor is replaced by a red-hot, glowing iron bar. This bar is clearly symbolic of the lightning, as is the mistletoe thrown at the god Balder. I would say that a holly spear may have had the same ritual significance.

C – hazel

Q – bush: the crabapple, whch was a shrub-like tree that could form hedges. In the Irish story of the madman Suibhne, we are told that in his Glen Bolcain, where the madmen congregated,

> *"Tis great folly*
> *for me to come out of Glen Bolcain,*
> *there are many apple-trees in Glen Bolcain..."*

M – neck, love: the grapevine hangs from its trellis like one's arms draped around a lover's neck. This is rightly the vine.

G – field: a field of grass is *'ever-green'*, and McManus thinks this notion may have been related to ivy, which is evergreen. However, I think it is more likely we are talking about common European Ground Ivy, which frequently invades fields and lawns. In other words, ivy is the plant of the field.

Ng – wound: In addition to broom, the reed, fern/bracken and even the bog myrtle are identified with this letter. Of these plants, the only one that has anything whatsoever to do with wounds is the bog myrtle. It has been traditionally used in poultices to treat wounds. However, reeds are known to have been used for arrows, and the kennings for this letter seem to point to the act of wounding, not to the act of healing a wound. In Northern England, the broom's twigs and branches were substituted *for reeds* in making fences of screens. Hence, this is properly the letter of the reed.

Z – sulphur: associated with the blackthorn or sloe, because of the red dye that could be obtained from this tree's berries. When sulphur's temperature is raised to a certain level, it takes on a dark red color.

R – red: elder or elderberry, whose berries are red. Here redness is associated with the redness of shame, embarrassment or anger infusing a person's face.

A- elm

O – ash

U – earth: as earth covers the corpse, so does the heather cover the earth. Hence, heather is like the earth and is, perhaps, the primary plant of the earth. Futhermore, heather grows extremely well on peaty soils. If the kenning *'in cold dwellings'* is not a poetic reference to the grave, it may be that heather is here being thought of as the *'marker'* of peat. Peat is *'earth'*, but it can also be brought into cold dwellings and burned to provide heat for the occupants. Heather and peat were both used as fuel for heat and cooking, and huts could be made of heather cemented together with peat mud, with straw and dried grasses added.

E – salmon: one of the alphabet lists in *The Scholar's Primer* has *'service tree'* for I, while two lists there have aspen for E. Aspen makes no sense in the context of the name deriving from salmon. Instead, I take his as a reference to the service tree. The service tree was a type of rowan and had berries. There was a magical well in Ossory that was the mythical fountain-head of the Shannon River. This well was surrounded by rowan trees. The bright red berries of the rowans fell into the water, where they fed the Salmon of Knowledge. Whoever ate the red-spotted salmon became gifted with divine knowledge. The goddess Shannon tried to eat the salmon, despite the injunction against women eating the fish's flesh. As punishment, she became the river. This story is paralleled by the tale of the hazel-tree well of the Boyne, whose salmon imparted its wisdom to Fionn mac Cumhail. So, this letter belongs properly to the rowan or service tree (see L above).

I – yew

But are these letters, as Robert Graves claims, truly symbolic of months or of special days in the months? The problem with his system is that one is forced to both drop out letters and combine others in order to make things work. The method employed is random and cannot be checked against an independent source. Scholars such as Peter Beresford Ellis have gone so far as to demonstrate convincingly that Graves relied on untrustworthy sources to conjure up his explanation of the ogam calendar.

So must we abandon the notion of an ogam calendar entirely?

No, I do not think we need to go this extreme. Rather, we need to re-examine the ogam and its possible relationship to ancient Celtic calendrics.

The best place for us to start is with the Gaulish calender, found at Coligny, France. Although this calendar is fragmentary, great progress has been made in recent years in reconstructing and deciphering it. Several theories have been put forward to explain how this early calendar worked. The best, although it was initially quite controversial, is that devised by Garret Olmsted. Olmsted was able to prove that the months Samonios and Giamonios, because they marked the start of the waxing year and the start of the waning year, respectively, must represent months of the Winter Solstice and the Summer

Solstice. Critics of Olmsted's theory (chiefly Dival and Pinault) have been forced to abandon the commonly held view that Samonios, because its name corresponds with the modern Samhain, starts on November 1st.

The months of the Coligny Calendar can, therefore, be equated with our modern calendar in the following manner. Note that the months highlighted with an asterisk are my own interpretations of the Gaulish names; the rest belong to Olmsted or to his sources.

Samonios – Summer Month, December-January. Begins on the 21 December Winter Solstice, the original Samhain, which after roughly 1500 years of operation the Irish calendar had shifted to 1 November. This occurred at the time of the adoption of Christianity and the Julian calendar. In the ancient system, Samhain = Winter Solstice, Imbolc = Spring Equinox, Beltane = Summer Solstice and Lughnasadh = Autumn Equinox. Samonios was thus the beginning of the waxing solar year, i.e. the true summer half-year, when the sun increases in size and strength as it moves steadily north from the winter solstice to the summer solstice.

Dumannos – Dark Month, January-February.

Rivros – Frost Month, February-March.

Anagantios* - Unnatural Month, March-April. Begins with the March 21 Spring Equinox, the original date of Imbolc. Cf. the Gaulish to Old Irish *anaicenta, anaigeanta*, 'extraordinary, unusual', used in terms of natural phenomena, i.e. extreme weather. From Part 64 of the *Annals of the Four Masters* (815 CE, from Christmas to Shrovetide):

> *Aighreadh anaigeanta & sneachta mor,*
> '*unusual ice and great snow*'

From Part 392 of the *Annals of Ulster* (882 CE):

Aigh anaicenta,
'extraordinary ice'

Year 986 of AFM:
> *Gaoth mhor anacnata,*
> *'great and unusual wind'*

Part 487 of AU (917 CE):
> *Sneachta & h-uacht dimhar & aig anaicenta,*
> *'snow and extreme cold and unnatural ice'*

Ogronnios – Growing Month, April-May.

Cutios – Bright Month, May-June. Cutios is from **kwei-tio, 'bright, white'*.

Giamonios – Winter Month, June-July. Begins on the 21 June Summer Solstice, the original Beltane. Start of the waning solar year, i.e. the beginning of the true winter half-year, when the sun began growing smaller and weaker as it moved steadily south from the Summer Solstice to the Winter Solstice.

Simiuisonna – Half-summer Month, July-August. Called such because it lies exactly halfway between the Summer Solstice and the Autumn Equinox, i.e. at the midpoint of the summer season.

Equos – Horse Month, August-September. Time of the summer horse fairs. Gaulish for horse was epo-, e.g. Epona, the *'Divine Horse'*. But Archaic Gaulish used qu for p.

Elembivios – Deer Month, September-October. Begins with the 22 September Autumn Equinox, the original Lughnasadh. Named for the onset of the deer rutting season. The European red deer rut began in September, that of the fallow deer in October. Deer are easily hunted during the mating season.

Edrinios – Fire Month, October-November. Fires are lit as the weather grows colder.

Cantlos – Song Month, November-December. Cf. with the Carmentalia of the Roman month of January, the month of the goddess Carmenta/Carmentis. L. *carmen* means '*a tune, song; poem, verse; an oracular response, prophecy; a form of incantation*'.

Intercalary months were used in the Coligny calendar to bring the lunar and solar calculations into accordance with each other. The five year calendar begins with Quimonios (before Samonios of Year 1). Quimonios is perhaps '*The Ordering Month*', in the sense that as an intercalary month it brought into order the solar and lunar calendars, and/or brought order to the five year sequence. However, I think it is more likely the '*Guardian Month*' (cf. Old Irish *coimetaid*, '*guardian*', from *coimet*, '*guard*', *coim*, '*protection*'). Standing as it does in front of the five year sequence, it symbolically fulfills a function similar to that of the Roman Janus as guardian of the beginning of the sacred year. Two and a half years into the five year cycle, we find the second intercalary month Rantaranos/Santaranos (before Giamonios of Year 3). It is unknown whether this month name begins with an r or an s. Rantaranos could be related to Old Irish *rand*, *ranntar*, words which mean '*division*', Santaranos to Proto-Celtic *samtero-, Welsh *hanner*, '*half*'. So, this is the '*Dividing or Halving Month*'.

The five year cycle itself repeated five times, making for a larger cycle of 25years.

We have seen above that, discounting the five late forfheda letters (a late invention involving a scribal need to conform to certain demands of the Classical alphabets), there were 20 ogam letters:

N	Q	R	I
S	C	Z	E
F	T	Ng	U
L	D	G	O
B	H	M	A

According to P.W. Joyce, the earliest recorded Irish calendar was composed of Errach or Spring (1 February to 1 May), Samrad or Summer (1 May to 1 August), Fogmar of Autumn (1 August to 1 November) and Gemred or Winter (1 November to 1 February). It will be noted that each season began and ended on one of the four great Celtic festivals, i.e. Imbolc, Beltane, Lughnasadh and Samhain. But we also know that this structure was artificial, and that the original calendar – like that of Coligny – was arranged according to the equinoxes and solstices. Hence the restored ogam calendar would look like this:

	Dec 21 – Mar 20	Mar 21 – Jun 20	Jun 21 – Sep 20	Sep 21 – Dec 20
Year 5	N	Q	R	I
Year 4	S	C	Z	E
Year 3	F	T	Ng	U
Year 2	L	D	G	O
Year 1	B	H	M	A

Professor Damian McManus tells us that the letter Q was originally *cert*, cognate with Welsh *perth*, 'bush, hedge', and also cognate with Latin *quercus*, 'oak'. One of the kennings for the letter Q is 'sanctuary of the lunatic', which reminds us of the madman Myrddin, who took refuge in an apple tree. I have already suggested that the cert or 'bush' in question is the crabapple, *Malus sylvetris*, a small, thorny deciduous tree common in oak woods and hedges, and native to the British Isles.

If we take Q to be the crabapple, then it represented the tree that governed the period from March 21-June 20. This is the second half of the Celtic waxing half year, our own season of Summer. The tree of Avalon is thus the summer-tree. And it is, of course, the tree of Arthur.

We have clear evidence for the magical and divinatory use of the ogam alphabet from the insular literature of medieval Ireland. In the Irish tale *Tochmarc Etaine*, for example, a Druid named Dalan used a method of ogam divination to find where the God Midir had taken Etain. He cut four wands of yew on which he inscribed three ogams, and used them to find the *'eochra ecsi'* (*'keys of divination'*), which enabled him to discover that the goddess had been taken to the fairy mound of Breg Leith, where Midir dwelt. Other Irish sources refer to the use of four ogam-inscribed yew wands or a single wand with four sides being used in divination. The number four is surely significant, as the ogam were divided into four groups.

The ogam letters, their trees and the matching divinatory meanings can be set out as follows:

B – birch, the promise of transformation from old age to youth, as this occurs when one goes from the middle of Winter to the beginning of Spring; also birth, beginnings

L – aspen, flame/blaze/radiance, passion, both of the heart and spirit; the light of the Divine and of the soul

F – alder, defense, physical and psychic; also, anything that contains nourishment that will bolster or replenish the natural defenses of body or soul

S – willow, life from lifelessness, as the old moon passing to the new moon

N – olive, cessation of hostility, bringing of peace, internally or externally

H – hawthorn, fear/horror, hauntings, nightmares, the dread of being pursued by enemies or hostile forces, anxiety

D – oak, kingship, pre-eminence in any sphere of endeavor, especially art and craftmanship, durability, strength

T – holly, symbolic of the heavenly lightning, the weapon of the sky and thunder god; over-powering force, that which nothing can withstand, starting a fire (including metaphorically)

C – hazel, the secret knowledge of and pertaining to men and the god, as embodied in Fionn, who ate the Salmon of Wisdom, who in turn had eaten the hazelnuts

Q – crabapple, the Spirit of Summer, the time and place of eternal life, the tree of Arthur, Myrddin, prophecy and poetry; the tree of potentiality and of manifesting one's destiny

M – vine, love and physical/emotional closeness, sexual power and its expenditure, the power inherent in a lover's voice

G – ivy, as the plant of fields represents the satisfying of physical hunger or mental/emotional needs

Ng – reed, wounding or being wounded, physically or psychically

Z – blackthorn, matters pertaining to blood, i.e. to blood relatives and ancestors, or to diseases or conditions of the blood; family secrets that are often kept to hide or obscure the truth for good or ill

R – elder, shame, embarrassment, anger, either experienced by oneself or brought about in another

A – elm, physical or emotional pain, often accompanied by a barely audible cry for help, or by a less obvious cry for help, sometimes manifested subconsciously (as someone committing a crime as an indicator of an underlying problem that requires professional help to resolve, or harming oneself as a means of gaining attention)

O – ash, the symbol of warfare and hostility in general. To be viewed as the opposte of N, the olive tree of peace.

U – heather, the providing of shelter and warmth, domestic happiness, prosperity

E – rowan, the secret knowledge of and pertaining to women and the goddess, as embodied in the Irish river-goddess Shannon; this is the counterpart of the male knowledge embodied by Fionn in letter C

I – yew, the opposite of birth; the process of aging, of going from youth to old age, as in going from Fall to Midwinter; also death or an ending

The exact method of divination that was employed was unfortunately not recorded. This precaution was doubtless taken to preserve the magical secret. We do know how the pagan Germanic peoples, whose religion was very similar to that of the Celts, divined with their own runic letters. An account of how this was done can be found in Tacitus' *Germania.* He describes how the Germans would:

> *"... cut off a branch of a nut-bearing tree and slice it into strips; these they mark with different signs and throw them completely at random onto a white cloth. Then the priest of the state, if the consultation is a public one, or the father of the family if it is private, offers a prayer to the gods, and looking up at the sky picks up three strips, one at a time, and reads their meanings from the signs previously scored on them. If the lots forbid the enterprise, there is no deliberation that day on the matter in question; if they allow it, confirmation by the taking of auspices is required."*

One interesting point jumps out at the reader of this passage; it bears an uncanny resemblance to Pliny's account of the harvesting of mistletoe by the druids:

> *"Anything growing on those trees [oaks] they regard as sent from heaven and a sign that this tree has been chosen by God himself. It [the mistletoe] is however very rarely found, and when found it is gathered with great ceremony and especially on the sixth day of the moon... They prepare a ritual sacrifice and feast under the tree, and lead up two white bulls whose horns are bound for the first time on this occasion. A priest attired in a white vestment ascends the tree and with a golden pruning-hook cuts it [the mistletoe] which is caught in a white cloth. Then next they sacrifice the victims praying that God will make his gift propitious to those to whom he has given it."*

The parallels between this passage and that of Tacitus can be listed thusly:

1) We begin with a nut-bearing tree in one, with the acorn-bearing oak in another

2) The strips of the tree and the mistletoe are placed on a white cloth

3) Auspices must be taken with a positive result of rune-reading, and sacrifices are made after the mistletoe is placed on the cloth

I have suggested above that the mistletoe, especially given its association with the oak, a tree often struck by lightning, is itself symbolic of the sky-father's weapon. Could it be that the forked and many-tined lightning, which could assume many different shapes, was considered the heavenly pattern for both runes and ogam letters? The antlers of the Horned God, that strike with such deadly efficiency and whose sound can be heard for long distances, were perceived as the lightning of the sky-god.

The Norse runes were said to have been obtained by Odin while he hung upon the sky-tree Yggdrasill:

> *"I know that I hung on a windy tree*
> *nine long nights,*
> *wounded with a spear, dedicated to Odin,*
> *myself to myself,*
> *on that tree of which no man knows*
> *from where its roots run.*
> *No bread did they give me nor a drink from a horn,*
> *Downwards I peered;*
> *I took up the runes, <u>screaming I took them</u>,*
> *Then I fell back from there."*
>   (Sayings of the High One, Stanzas 138-9)

The screaming of the sky-father is poetic language for a thunder-clap, something which attends a lightning-strike. Surely it is not a coincidence that Odin took up the runes the moment thunder screamed from the sky?

Elsewhere Odin is said to have *'interpreted them [the runes], cut them, thought them out, from the liquid which had leaked from the skull of Heiddraupnir, and from Hoddrofmir's horn.'* The skull of Heiddraupnir is probably another name for the skull of the primeval giant Ymir, who was slain by Odin and whose skull was made into the sky. As the brains of Ymir were made into the clouds, I take it that the liquid from which the runes were taken are these same clouds. Lightning, of course, comes from the clouds.

If I am right about Pliny's account of the cutting of the mistletoe from the oak being a Celtic version of the runic divination ritual recorded by Tacitus, and both runes and ogam letters were thought of as symbols for the heavenly lightning, then it is possible both were employed in a similar fashion.

A METHOD FOR OGAM DIVINATION

The standard claim that the three Germanic runes drawn in the Tacitus account represent past, present and future, as embodied in the Norse fate goddesses Urd, Verdandi and Skuld, is plainly wrong and must be abandoned. The three runes were drawn to determine whether a future enterprise might prove propitious. Quite probably the hoped-for result would be the drawing of three *'favourable'* runes, or at the very least two *'favourable'* runes, with a third neutral or unfavorable rune. If only one unfavorable rune were drawn out of three, this would act as a qualifier of the two favorable runes. Two or more unfavorable runes would indicate that a future proposed action should not be undertaken, or should not be undertaken at the time proposed for such an action. One is reminded of our tradition of coin-tossing, in which heads stands for the affirmative or a course of action, while tails stands for the negative or a second course of action. Often we reach a decision with the coin-toss by resorting to *'best two-out-of-three'*. Two heads means *'yes'*, while two tails means *'no'*, etc.

Ogam divination must have employed the tree-alphabet letters to determine the answer to specific questions. One example has already been cited above, in which the ogam was used to discern the unknown whereabouts of Etain. Interpreting an ogam drawing would also have been a highly intuitive process, embarked upon only by someone who had shown a natural propensity for divination and who, as a novitiate, had received extensive training in the reading of ogam lot drawings by an acknowledged master.

The three ogams Dalan carved on the four yew wands would seem to suggest that Irish ogam lot drawing followed the Germanic practice of taking up three runes. However, we know that there were five tree-letters per 'wand', not three. Three times four equals twelve, and this points towards zodiacal and solar year symbolism. The account of Dalan's divining Etain's location is thus immediately suspect, and we can detect here the hand of antiquarian creative license.

One other aspect of the Dalan ogam episode should be briefly examined: the use of yew wood for all four wands. The yew was the tree of death and endings, and traditionally yew trees are found in cemeteries. Bri Leith, where Etain was residing, was an ancient sepulcher mound and thus we might well expect for it to be associated with the yew. If based on genuine tradition, Dalan's choice of yew for his ogam wands points to his knowing *in advance* that wherever Etain was, she most probably would be found in one of the portals to *'fairyland'*, the Celtic Otherworld and the place of death.

The implication is that ogam wands could be carved of a wood whose tree-alphabet quality predisposed them for use in answering only one question or one type of question. If so, it would be necessary for an ogam-master to have access to all the woods of the tree-alphabet, and to either carve the letters on the appropriate wood each time something was divined, or to possess multiple sets of wands carved from all the various woods.

I myself do not think this is a requirement of ogam lot casting, and it is hardly practical. The power of each tree-letter comes from the ritual meaning of the letter itself, not from the wood it is carved on. My own set of ogam letters are inscribed on sawn sections of a deer's tibia. Their potency does not derive from the bone itself, but from their symbolic significance. This is true despite my having used the deer bone because of its sacred properties; I dedicated the bone to the horned stag god Belatucadros. Yet I did so with full knowledge of the fact that Belatucadros was not the god who invented the ogam. Instead, I desired an ogam set that was of a more permanent nature than wood, and that was associated with my particular patron deity.

Ogam letters can also not be divorced of their season-year correspondences. In other words, when a drawing is made they must always be assigned to the designated time periods to which they belong. This is not a consideration when reading the Germanic runes, as the latter do not seem to have represented stages in a sacred calendar. Thus the symbolic meaning and application of a drawn ogam letter is restricted to either the present or a future season and year.

Lastly, the ogam system is not a fortune-telling game. You cannot ask of the ogam *'What will happen six months from now?'* It is not designed to reveal the future to us; the gods quite wisely keep that dangerous and ultimately destructive knowledge from us. Instead, the ogam is a tool meant to assist us in properly preparing ourselves to deal with the future, whatever that may be. What you can ask the ogam is *'If I take a certain course of action to achieve X, will I obtain favourable results?'* or *'Should I decide to pursue goal A or goal B?'* or *'Should I take path A or path B in order to reach my desired destination?'*

Taking all of this into account, then, the method for ogam lot casting and drawing is as follows:

One should begin by asking Ogma to guide one's hand to the right letters, and for the wisdom to read them aright. All the ogam letters as separate pieces are then placed in either a drawstring bag or non-transparent receptacle that has an opening large enough to admit one's hand. At this point one should empty one's mind and enter a state of meditative calmness. When the moment seems right, the question may be asked. As soon as a surge of productive energy is felt, three ogam letters may be drawn from the bag and placed on white cloth which itself has been spread atop a flat surface such as a table top.

The three ogam letters represent three potentialities. We know from Norse religion that Odin obtained the runes when he hung upon the ash tree. This is explicitly termed a *self-sacrifice*. He is also said to have been pierced with a spear and we know from an account of the sacrificial rituals performed at Uppsala in Sweden in the pagan period that hanging was accompanied by drowning. This fact brings us to the famous Lindow Man, a human sacrifice found in a bog in the English Midlands in 1984.

Lindow Man, as a human incarnation of the god Lleu, was subjected to a triple death: he was simultaneously garrotted and stabbed, struck three times in the head (probably with a hammer) and submerged in a sacred pool, i.e. sent to the Otherworld. Anne Ross has very plausibly theorized that the garrotting (cf. hanging) and stabbing was in honor of Esus (who in Gaulish iconography is found in close proximity to the willow tree, and in Classical literature is linked to wicker effigies, doubtless made of willow), the three blows were in honor of Taranis the Thundergod and the drowning was in honor of Teutates. These three gods are, in reality, triple aspects of the same deity.

Ogmios or Ogma, the inventor of the ogam alphabet, was identified with the club-bearing Hercules by Classical authorities. Hercules, both because of his character and his club, was associated with thunder gods. It is permissable, therefore, to implicitly view Ogma as Taranis.

The first ogam drawn is thus sacred to Taranis. It stands for Realization, as when one is suddenly 'thunder-struck' with an idea or awareness. Revelation or epiphany is also manifest in this letter. To be equated with the conception of the ogam by Ogma.

The second ogam drawn is sacred to Esus. It stands for Sacrifice, and is that which one must do in order to achieve a purpose or a goal. To be equated with the winning of the ogam through struggle and suffering by Esus.

The third ogam drawn is for Teutates. It stands for Arrival (as the god *arrives* in the Otherworld after his self-sacrifice), and is the achievement of a purpose or goal, along with the attendant consequences. To be equated with the actual use of the ogam by Teutates.

And as for the rest, well, I leave that up to the intuitive powers of the ogam master and his students.

THE THIRTEEN TREASURES OF THE ISLAND OF BRITAIN AND THEIR RITUAL USES

According to fairly late Welsh tradition, *'the Thirteen Treasures of the Island of Britain... were brought together by Myrddin in Avalon.'* Avalon is identified with the House of Glass or Ty-Gwydr, localized in Bardsey, an island off Anglesey famous for its saints. Ty-Gwydr is an echo of Caer Wydr, the Fort of Glass, or rather the Fort of Green Grass, the Fairy Mound/chambered tomb conceived as the symbolic Otherworld or the portal to the Otherworld. Caer Wydr itself was linked via specious etymology with Glastonbury as Avalon. We have seen above that the real Avalon is the fort at Burgh-By-Sands in Cumbria. Myrddin does not belong to Bardsey or Glastonbury, but to Lowland Scotland.

The Thirteen Treasures are magical items that represent aspects or elemental forces of Nature that can be harnessed by a druidic adept. I will list below the items themselves, how they are described by the Welsh texts, their revealed forms and to what use they may be put in a ritual context.

Gwen, the Cloak of Arthur (= the Cloak of Caswallon of the Catuvellauni): whoever went under it would see everybody, and nobody would see him wherever he went.

Gwen is the feminine form of Welsh gwyn and means *'white, fair, blessed'*. This cloak is emblematic of the cloud, which hides the sun, the moon, the stars, the day or night sky, a mountain top or even earthly landscapes in the case of fog. A king or druidic priest who dons such a cloak is identifying himself with one or the other of the objects a cloud can obscure. The ritual use of a cloud-cloak is obvious: to be hidden from one's enemy or from negative energies projected at oneself is to provide oneself with a certain measure of protection. What cannot be seen cannot be found, and what cannot be found cannot be harmed.

Another treasure imparting invisibility was imported to the list from later Arthurian romance. This is *'the Stone and Ring of Eluned the Blessed: which she gave to extricate Owein son of Urien, who was between the portcullis and the gate, contending with the Black Knight of the Fountain. That ring has a stone in it and if the stone were concealed, the one who concealed it would not be seen at all.'* We see in this object the operation of a typical sympathetic magic effect, in which the wearer identifies himself with the ring's stone.

Dyrnwyn, the Sword of Rhydderch of Strathclyde: whoever drew it from its scabbard, it would go into a flame of fire about his head from its hilt to its tip, except for the person that owned it; and he would refuse nobody the loan of it, and when its properties were known it was given back to the person who owned it. And because of that he was called Rhydderch the Generous.

This sword-name means, literally, *'White Fist'*. However, Welsh *dyrn*, *'fist'*, may originally have had the meaning of *'stone the size of a fist'*. Scottish *Dornock, Dornoch* are from a Celtic **durnaco-*, *'site covered with fist-sized pebbles'*. For this reason Dyrnwyn, a flaming sword, should be equated with the Roman Jupiter Lapis, a stone representing the heavenly lightning once it had fallen to earth. The Romans swore oaths on this lightning-stone. Some have theorized that the stone of Jupiter was actually a fragment of a meteorite, but as Jupiter was the god of thunder and lightning, it is more likely his stone was a fire-striking material like flint. A sword named Dyrnwyn could thus be used during rituals for the swearing of oaths or, alternately, a shard of flint could be substituted. A fire struck from a *'Dyrnwyn flint'* would be purifying in nature, and such a fire could be lit during the taking of sacred oaths.

The Hamper of Gwyddno Long-shank of the Setantii: food for one man would be put into it and food for a hundred men would be found in it when it was opened.

The hamper is here an error or substitute for the fishing weir of Gwyddno, which was noted not only for catching salmon – an animal in Celtic religion strongly associated with divine knowledge – but for ensnaring the prophet-poet Taliesin, who in the *Cad Godeu* poem assumes the form of a salmon. The hamper or weir of Gwyddno is thus the receptacle of the holy salmon of wisdom. Participants in a feast of the salmon of wisdom partake of the god's immortality, this being the immortality of the soul, not of the physical body. Christians adopted this symbology when they partook of Christ's solar body in the form of a fish.

The Horn of Bran the Hardy, son of Ymellyrn. Ymellyrn = Y Maelor in North Wales, where is found Castell Dinas Bran or Corbenic the Grail Castle. Kynwyd, father of Ymellyrn = Cynwyd and the Cynwyd Forest just west of Dinas Bran. *'The drink which was asked for would be found in it when wished for.'*

We have seen in the chapter that discusses that Grail and its evolution from pagan prototypes that Bran's original cauldron represented a sacred lake, which for the ancient Celts was viewed as an entrance to the Otherworld. Bran's cauldron was associated with that of the smith god Goibhniu. As Goibhniu was linked with the fire within the earth, and thus probably with volcanoes – as was true of his Greek and Roman counterpart, Hephaistos/Vulcan – we must consider that his cauldron may originally have been patterned after lakes that form in the craters of extinct or dormant volcanoes. Such lakes may boil, vent gases and even explode. For ritual purposes, a cauldron of water kept simmering over a fire (perhaps one started with a Dyrnwyn flint) can symbolize the smith god's lake. Sacrificial meals or drinks may be prepared in this cauldron, or items requiring purification may be immersed in the water.

In some versions of the list of Thirteen treasures are found the dish of Agwneren the Cleric or the pot and dish of Rhagenydd the Cleric: *'the food wished for in it would be found.'* These items are described as horns of plenty, and would seem to complement the liquid-containing cauldron of Bran the Hardy. However, I discount them as Christian intrusions. Both Agwneren and Rhagenydd are said to be clerics, i.e. Christian priests. Their *'dish'* was unlikely to have been a patera or shallow bowl for offering libations, as that was a pagan custom. Instead, it may have been the paten, a small plate used to hold the Eucharistic Host that is to be consecrated. Rhagenydd's pot may have been a fire pot or censer.

The Chariot of Morgan the Wealthy of Strathclyde: whoever went into it and wished to be where he desired, he would be there.

This is, of course, not an actual physical vehicle. Rather, Morgan's chariot stands for the attainment of a transcendental or shamanistic state of being. The chariot is, as it were, a veritable mandala for transportive meditation. It thus assists in the movement among spiritual realms.

The Knife of Llawfrodedd [= *llawfrydedd, 'sorrow, misery, dejectedness, wretchedness, melancholy']* the Bearded [of ?]: which would serve twenty-four men at once from table to table when there might be need.

The meaning of the name of the personage who supposedly owns this *'knife'* provides us with the clue to understanding its utility. It is used to *'cut away'* sadness or grief or, indeed, any negative, draining emotion which is inhibiting the development of a person into a fully-realized, multi-faceted being. Excessive or prolonged sadness or grief can lie at the root of chronic conditions like depression. A ritual performed with the Knife of Llawfrodedd can thus help clear the psyche of emotional impediments.

The Halter of Clydno of Din Eiddyn: which was below the foot of his bed. Whatever horse he wished for would be in it when he wished.

The *'horse'* alluded to here is whatever person Clydno needed in order to get him where he wanted to go. In other words, the *'halter'* is a species of binding spell. Not a binding spell in the sense of enslavement, mind you, but of the application of positive direction. We all know people in our lives who would somehow benefit us if only they could be steered clear of error and transgression. Such people, when they take a wrong turn on the path, can, directly or indirectly, adversely affect our own lives. On the other hand, when properly guided – not against their will, but with their own freely granted understanding and approval – the very same individuals can vastly improve their own lot. And with everyone headed on parallel tracks towards their own unparalleled destinations, the world of man is brought ever closer to an existence that does not require binding of any sort.

The Cauldron of Tyrnoc the Giant of Ireland: if flesh for a coward were put into it, it would never boil, and if put in for a brave man, it would quickly boil enough; and then the distinction would be made between a brave man and a coward.

We have discussed above Tyrnoc as St. Tigernach, and how the cauldron of Midir at Bri Leith has here become fused with the symbolism implicit in the Christian chalice. But why did this particular cauldron (or chalice) come to be recognized as a test for courage and cowardliness? The answer is easier to come by than one might expect: in the Irish sagas, the warriors of a chieftain would frequently engage in personal combats for the so-called *'champion's portion'* of a cauldron-boiled boar. Those who refused to participate in such contests were doubtless thought of as cowards, while only the bravest, the strongest and the most skilled stood to win the best cut of cooked meat. Obviously, no sensible, modern druid would propose that all members of a circle fight each other for the champion's portion of a sacrificial feast! Instead, the food prepared for such a feast should be blessed in a way that confers upon that food the quality of the bestowing of bravery upon whoever consumes it. This way, rather than acting as a highly divisive element in ritual performance, the cauldron of Tyrnoc further unifies a circle by increasing each member's level of personal courage.

The Coat of Padarn Red-tunic of the Votadini: for a nobleman it would fit well, and for a churl it would not fit.

Class distinctions were for the ancient and medieval periods, and have no place in modern, democratic druidic ritual. So while it is important to adhere to tradition, it sometimes becomes necessary to alter previous practice and belief. In the case of Padarn's tunic, we know that the Welshman who recorded this tradition took grave liberties with it to begin with! The tunic in question actually belonged to St. Padarn, and the story of it is told in the *Life of St. Padarn* thusly:

> *"When Padarn was in his church resting after so much labour at sea, a certain tyrant, Arthur by name, was traversing the regions on either side, who one day came to the cell of saint Padarn the bishop. And while he was addressing Padarn, he looked at the tunic, which he, being pierced with the zeal of avarice, sought for his own. The saint answering said, 'This tunic is not fitting for the habit of any malign person, but for the habit of the clerical office.' He went out of the monastery in a rage. And again he returns in wrath, that he might take away the tunic against the counsels of his own companions. One of the disciples of Padarn seeing him returning in fury, ran to saint Padarn and said, 'The tyrant, who went from here before, is returning. Reviling, stamping, he levels the ground with his feet'. Padarn answers 'Nay rather, may the earth swallow him.' With the word straightway the earth opens the hollow of its depth, and swallows Arthur up to his chin. He immediately acknowledging his guilt begins to praise both God and Padarn, until, while he begs forgiveness, the earth delivered him up. From that place on bent knees he begged the saint for indulgence, whom the saint forgave. And he took Padarn as his continual patron, and so departed."*

So, in reality, the tunic of Padarn does not distinguish between high-born and low-born men. It instead symbolizes the raimant worn by a person pure of spirit, in contrast to that worn by a person whose soul is consumed with the need to conquer and possess everything it sees around it. Arthur here, as he does in several saints' *Lives*, appears as just such an evil tyrant for didactic purposes. In ritual, a Padarn's tunic could be donned by any member of a druidic circle for the express purpose of aiding in the quelling of avarice or lust or other base desires which, if exercised, can have damaging or disastrous consequences.

The Whetstone of Tudwal People-Defender of Strathclyde: it would sharpen the weapon of a brave man, and blunt the weapon of a coward, and if it was used to sharpen the sword of a brave man then anyone wounded with the sword would be sure to die. If the sword belonged to a coward, the man struck with it would be none the worse.

The lesson of this treasure is simple: no matter what weapon a coward has, it will eventually fail him in battle. And this realization leads to an important question. Can any weapon given to someone who is suffering from cowardice in a specific situation or set of circumstances or who has a naturally meek or submissive personality contribute to the development of genuine strength of character? Or can one's inherent spiritual weapon be honed to the point where it exhibits the sharp edge of a brave warrior's sword?

Both Tudwal's name and epithet are important in this context. Tudwal means *'People-ruler'*. The implication is that a chieftain-like figure who possesses the ability to rule and the ability to defend does so primarily out of personal bravery. This bravery arises out of a profound sense of confidence. However, while ruling and defending by virtue of this peculiar brand of courage, the chieftain instills in his people a *shared* bravery, a true communal courage. The potentiality for this communal courage resides with the whetstone. Any weapon, whether psychic or physical, that is exposed to its power contributes to the combined courage of the members of the circle. This treasure, then, is the natural complement of Tyrnoc's cauldron, wherein resides personal bravery.

The Chess Board of Gwenddolau son of Ceidio of the Selgovae: if the men were placed on it they would play by themselves; the men were gold and the board was silver.

This chess set (actually *'gwyddbwyll'*, cf. Irish *fidchell* or *fid-ciall*, *'wood-intelligence'*) resembles that played by Arthur and Owain son of Urien in the Welsh tale *The Dream of Rhonabwy*. In this story, the moving of pieces on the board manifests itself as actual battles being fought simultaneously between armies. The game could thusly be used as a means of instructing would-be commanders in the practical application of strategy and tactics in warfare. It could be said that Arthur and Owain – or the Northern chieftain Gwenddolau – were controlling and manipulating the fates of their own soldiers. On the surface, the exertion of this kind of control may seem morally reprehensible, perhaps even blatantly evil. We have seen in our modern world, however, that military force is often necessary to defend the homeland or to protect the peace either here or abroad. This kind of control over the very life of men and women, a control that frequently leads to maiming or death, is not something to be undertaken lightly. Only a truly wise leader, who through careful deliberation has determined that no other option is available, will send his people forth to do battle with an enemy.

In a ritual sense, the significance of this treasure lies in its ability to *peacefully* resolve conflicts within the druidic circle. Such a claim may seem ironic in the extreme, but for a conflict to be allowed, and for its results to be sanctioned, it must lie within the purview of the divine powers. If a disagreement arises within a druidic circle that cannot otherwise be settled by majority or super-majority vote, two members of the opposing sides, of as close to equal ability as possible, shall be chosen to play gwyddbwyll. The victor's position will then be accepted by all members of the circle, either as policy or sacred law, depending on the nature of the point of disagreement. If, after an agreed upon term the position put into practice by the victor has proven unsatisfactory, the group may either revert to the position held prior to the victory or a new gwyddbwyll game can be played to establish yet another position as the prevailing one.

The Coulter of Rhun the Giant [or of Tringer the Warlike son of Nudd the Famous/Notable]: when this was put in a plough, it ploughed until it was asked to stop.

The coulter was a technical innovation introduced to Britain by the Romans. Its function was to make a vertical cut in advance of the plough-share, which then undercut the furrow made by the coulter. This made it easier to cultivate heavy soils. Roman coulters were therefore stout knife-like iron blades with a heavy shaft by which they were secured to the plough's wooden beam.

A coulter or a similar iron object symbolizing a coulter may be used during the opening of any fertility ritual, whether the ritual has to do with human fertility, that of a garden, field, orchard or greenhouse, or of a druidic circle in general. And fertility rituals need not be restricted to the biological sphere. Those seeking a fertile imagination, a fertile mind or a fertile heart may also avail themselves of the coulter of Tringer. It is likely that Tringer, which means *'warlike'*, was originally the name of the coulter itself, which being made a iron and resembling a knife, could be poetically invested with warlike qualities. If so, then the *'Tringer coulter'* was probably part of the plough of the plough god Amaethon, brother of Nudd.

The Mantle of Tegau Gold-breast, wife of Caradog Stout-arm: it would serve suitably for Tegau and it would come for her down to the ground, but for Gwenhwyvar it would not come down to her buttocks, nor for one who broke her marriage nor for a maiden whose virginity was broken.

As presented to us, this treasure is obviously an object meant to test one's faithfulness as a spouse, or one's chastity. We have seen above that Gwenhwyvar is the Welsh version of the Irish goddess Findabair. Her supposed illicit affair with Lancelot is a medieval Christian misunderstanding or besmirching of the union of a Sovereignty Goddess with the god Lugh. Tegau would appear to derive from Welsh *teg*, *'beautiful'*, and was a British version of such Roman goddesses as Pudicitia, Diana and Venus Verticordia, all of whom concerned themselves with sexual modesty, fidelity and chasteness.

So how does the mantle of Tegau fit into druidic practice? A woman – or man – who wishes to publicly declare Tegau as her or his divine patron within the confines of the realm of human sexuality may don the mantle during group meetings and ritual performances. Donning the mantle must represent a genuine commitment. By wearing the mantle, an individual not only makes known his or her own intention, but because of the power manifested by such a proclamation of a sacred vow, he or she contributes additional energy to any magical endeavor undertaken. The mantle should not be worn during fertility rites, but only during those times when a decrease in the promotion of sexual energy is required for group events.

ZODIACAL CORRESPONDENCES OF ARTHUR'S BATTLES

For my identifications of the Arthurian battle sites, I refer the reader to my book *Shadows in the Mist: The Life and Death of King Arthur* and the updated essay at the Vortigern Studies Website. In this Appendix I mean to restrict myself solely to the possible zodiacal correspondences of these battles. The Arthurian battles have a *'canonical'* order, established in the *Historia Brittonum* of Nennius. They remind us of the Twelve Labors of the Greek hero Herakles – labors well known to have occurred in the signs of the Zodiac.

1) The mouth of the river Glein (= the Northumberland Glen)

2) Battles 2-5 at the Dubglas River in the Linnuis region (= the Devil's Water at Linnels near the Corbridge Roman fort)

3) The River Bassas (= a stream at Bassington near Alnwick)

4) The Celyddon Wood (= the ancient wood surrounding the Eildon Hills)

5) Fort Guinnion (= the Binchester Roman fort)

6) City of the Legion (= York, not only a legionary fortress, but the Roman period capital and judicial center of Northern Britain)

7) A shore called Tribruit, the *'Pierced-Through'* (= Broken Hook on the River Avon west of Edinburgh)

8) Mount Breguoin or Agned (Breguoin = the High Rochester Roman fort, while Agned is a reference to the Roman fort at Catterick)

Figure 15 - St Anne's Well, Buxton
Site of King Arthur's famous Battle of Badon Hill.

9) Mount Badon (= Buxton Roman spa town in the Peak
District)

[10] Camlann (= Castlesteads Roman fort at the western
end of Hadrian's Wall)]

As we are told by Nennius that Arthur carried the image
of the Virgin Mary on his shield during the Guinnion battle,
it would seem safe to assign this battle – in its seasonal
aspect – to Virgo. This being so, the Twelve Battles of Arthur
can be arranged as follows on the Zodiac:

Mouth of the Glein – Aquarius. Glein means *'pure'* or *'clear'*, and is a descriptive of the nature of this river's water, or perhaps an indication the river was considered holy. 1 February, the pagan Imbolc, falls in this sign.

Dubglas – Pisces.

Dubglas – Aries (in which falls the Spring Equinox or March 21).

Dubglas – Taurus (in which falls Beltane or May 1).

Dubglas – Gemini (in which falls the Summer Solstice or June 21). Dubglas is British for 'Black Water'. All four of the battles here were fought close to Arthur's *'Camelot'* fort, i.e. the Corbridge Roman fort. Alletios, as we have seen, was the pre-eminent god of the Otherworld. This grouping begins not long after Imbolc and extends to midsummer. It thus corresponds to our Spring season.

Bassas – Cancer.

Celyddon – Leo. The proper place for the lion is the wood. Again, the Welsh word for the god Lleu could be confused with their word for lion, llew, and Lleu's Eildon Hills lie at the center of the Lowland Scottish Caledonian Wood. The *'lion'* within Merlin's Chapel atop Eildon Mid Hill is actually the god Lleu. Lughnasadh or 1 August falls in this sign.

Guinnion – Virgo. Autumn Equinox or September 21.

City of the Legion – Libra. The Scales of Justice are appropriately placed at the Roman judicial center of North Britain.

Tribruit – Scorpio. The *'pierced-through'* meaning of the shore was transferred to images of pierced shields in the early Arthurian poetry. Needless to say, the Scorpion's tail is a piercing weapon. November 1 or Samhain falls in this sign.

Breguion/Agned – Sagittarius. The Winter Solstice or December 21.

Badon – Capricorn.

And what of Camlann, the Camboglanna Roman fort at Castlesteads where Arthur and Medraut (or Mordred) perished? Where does this tragic event belong on the Zodiac?

It would be tempting to place Arthur's death somewhere in the Zodiac wherein we find either Beltane or Samhain (or, perhaps, the more ancient summer and winter solstices). But although the 12 signs of the Zodiac are sacred to the sun, Arthur's astronomical symbol, as we have seen, is Bootes the Ploughman.

We have only one potential clue to the seasonal date of the Battle of Camlann in 537 CE: Geoffrey of Monmouth tells us it happened in the summer. Now, we have explored above Bootes the Ploughman as the celestial aspect of Arthur. The very bright star Arcturus (not related to Arthur's name!) is in Bootes, and archaeo-astronomers have determined that some stone circles had alignments designed to calculate one or more of the four important dates of Arcturus risings and settings.

Using the CyberSky planetarium program set to Carlisle as the *'observatory'*, I was able to come up with the following dates for the year 537:

February 24, 5:40 p.m. Acronical rising
Sun sets
Arcturus rises

July 4, 3:40 a.m. Heliacal setting
Sun rises
Arcturus sets

September 1, 5:20 a.m. Heliacal rising
Sun rises
Arcturus rises

December 26, 4:09 p.m. Acronical setting
Sun sets
Arcturus sets

If Arthur did fall at Camlann in the summer, as Geoffrey contends, then his *'celestial death'* can be reckoned as occurring when Arcturus set at sunrise on 4 July, 537 CE. This date fell in the sign of Cancer.

BIBLIOGRAPHY

Alcock, Leslie. *Arthur's Britain*. New York: Penguin Books, 1989

Austen, Paul. *Recent Excavations on Hadrian's Wall at Burgh-by-Sands*. Cumberland and Westmorland Antiquarian and Archaeological Society, Vol. XCIV, 1994

Bakker, J. T. *Living and Working with the Gods: Studies of Evidence for Private Religion and its Material Environment in the City of Ostia*. Amsterdam, Dutch Monographs on Ancient History and Archaeology Vol XII, 1994

Barber, Richard. *The Figure of Arthur*. New Jersey, Rowman and Littlefield, 1973

Bartrum, Peter C. *A Classical Welsh Dictionary*. Cardiff, The National Library of Wales, 1993

_____. *Welsh Genealogies* (Eight Volumes). Cardiff, University of Wales Press, 1974

Bergstrom, Theo. *Hadrian's Wall: Handbook to the Roman Wall with the Cumbrian Coast and Outpost Forts*. New York, Jupiter Books Inc., 1984

Bidwell, Paul, (ed). *Hadrian's Wall 1989-1999*. Cumberland and Westmorland Antiquarian and Archaeological Society, 1999

Boyce, G.K. '*Significance of the Serpents on Pompeian House Shrines*'. American Journal of Archaeology 46, 1942, 13-22

Breeze, David J. *J. Collingwood Bruce's Handbook to the Roman Wall*. Fourteenth Edition. Society of Antiquaries of Newcastle Upon Tyne, 2006

Bromwich, Rachel (ed., tr.). *The Triads of the Island of Britain*. 3rd Edition. Cardiff, University of Wales Press, 2006

Brook, Daphne. *Saints and Goddesses: The Interface with Celtic Paganism*. The Seventh Whithorn Lecture, Friends of the Whithorn Trust, 1999

Chambers, E.K. *Arthur of Britain*. New York, October House, Inc., 1967

Clarke, Basil (tr.). *Life of Merlin*. Cardiff, University of Wales Press, 1973

Collingwood, R.G. *Explorations of the Roman Fort of Burgh-by-Sands*. Cumberland and Westmorland Antiquarian and Archaeological Society, Vol. XXIII, 1933

Collins, Roger, and Judith McClure (ed., tr.). *The Ecclesiastical History of the English People*. New York, Oxford University Press, 1994

Connor, Peter. *Lararium – Household Religion*. Chapter Four from Descoeudres, J.P., *Pompeii Revisited: The Life and Death of a Roman Town*. Sydney, Meditarch, 1994

Cool, H.E.M. *The Significance of Snake Jewellery Hoards*. Britannia Vol, 31, 2000, 29-40

Cowief, Trevor, and Brendan O'Connor. 'A group of bronze socketed axes from Eildon Mid Hill, near Melrose, Roxburghshire'. Proceedings of the Society of Antiquaries of Scotland, Vol. 115, 1985, 151-158

Davidson, H. R. Ellis. *Gods and Myths of North Europe*. New York, Pelican Books, 1964

Dutton, Marsha L. 'The Staff in the Stone: Finding Arthur's Sword in the Vita Sancti Edwardi of Aelred of Rievaulx'. Arthuriana, Vol. 17, Number 3, Fall 2007

Ellis, Peter Beresford. 'The Fabrication of 'Celtic' Astrology'. The Astrological Journal, Vol. 39, No. 4, 1997

Flanagan, Deirdre and Laurence.*Irish Place-Names*. Dublin, Gill and MacMillan, 1994

Ford, Patrick K. (tr.). *The Mabinogi*. Berkeley and Los Angeles, University of California Press, 1977

Froelich, Thomas. *Lararien - und Fassadenbilder in den vesuvstadten Untersuchungen zur 'volkstumlichen' pompejanischen Malerei*. Mainz, Zabern, 1991

Gantz, Jeffrey (tr.). *The Mabinogion*. New York, Penguin Books, 1976

Giraldus Cambrensis. *De Instructione Principum*. London, S. & J. Bentley, Wilson & Flev, 1846

Goodrich, Peter. *The Romance of Merlin*. New York, Garland Publishing, Inc., 1990

Grabhoff, Gerd, and Alfred Stuckelberger (eds.). *Ptolemaios, Handbuch der Geographie, Griechisch-Deutsch.* 2 Volumes. Basel, Schabe Verlag, 2006

Graves, Robert. *The Greek Myths: Complete Edition.* New York, Penguin, 1993

Hunt, August. *Shadows in the Mist: The Life and Death of King Arthur.* Kirkby Stephen, Hayloft Plublishing, Ltd., 2006

Jewitt, Llewellynn, F.S.A. *A Manual of Archaeology, as exemplified in the burials of the Celtic, the Roman-British, and the Anglo-Saxon Periods.* London, Groombridge and Sons, 1870 (see *'Internments by Cremation'*)

Joyce, P.W. *A Social History of Ancient Ireland.* 2 Volumes. Irish Genealogical Foundation, 1997

Kinsella, Thomas (tr.). *The Tain.* New York, Oxford University Press, 1969

Koch, John Thomas (ed.). *Celtic Culture: A Historical Encyclopedia.* Five Volumes. ABC-CLIO, 2005

Larrington, Carolyne (trans.). *The Poetic Edda, A New Translation.* Oxford, Oxford University Press, 1996

Leach, J. *'The Smith God in Roman Britain'.* Archaeologia Aeliana, 40, 1962, 171-184

Lewis, Roger Sherman. *Celtic Myth and Arthurian Romance.* London, Constable, 1993

_____. *The Grail: From Celtic Myth to Christian Symbol.* New Jersey, Princeton University Press, 1991

Longworth, I.H. *Collared Urns of the Bronze Age in Great Britain and Ireland.* Cambridge, Cambridge University Press, 1984

Mattingly, H. (trans). *Tacitus on Britain and Germany.* Harmondsworth, Middlesex, and Baltimore, Penguin Books, 1954

May, Jeffrey. *Prehistoric Lincolnshire.* Lincoln, History of Lincolnshire Committee, 1976

McManus, Damian. *A Guide to Ogam.* An Sagart, Maynooth Monographs 4, 1997

_____. *'Irish Letter Names and Their Kennings'.* Eriu 39, 1988, 127-168

Meyer, Kuno (trans.). *The Voyage of Bran Son of Febal to the Land of the Living*. London, David Nutt, 1895

Murphy, G. Ronald. *Gemstone of Paradise: The Holy Grail in Wolfram's Parzival*. Oxford, Oxford University Press, 2006

Myres, J.N.L. *Corpus of Anglo-Saxon Pottery of the Pagan Period*. 2 Volumes. New York, Cambridge University Press, 1977

Olmsted, Garret. *The Gaulish Calendar*. Bonn, 1992

_____. *A Definitive Reconstructed Text of the Coligny Calendar*. Columbia, University of Missouri Press, 2001

Owen, D.D.R. (tr.). *Guillaume de Clerc's Fergus of Galloway: Knight of King Arthur*. Vermont, J.M. Dent and Sons, Ltd., 1991

Picon, Carlos A. 'The Metropolitan Museum of Art: Two Roman Sculptures, New Acquisitions'. London, Apollo Magazine, May 2007

Richards, Julian D. *The Significance of Form and Decoration of Anglo-Saxon Cremation Urns*. Oxford, BAR British S J N series 166, 1987

Rivet, A.L.F., and Colin Smith. *The Place-Names of Roman Britain*. London, B.T. Batsford, Ltd., 1982

Robins, Don, and Anne Ross. *The Life and Death of a Druid Prince*. New York, Simon and Schuster, 1989

Ross, Anne. *Pagan Celtic Britain*. Chicago, Academy Chicago Publishers, 1996

Thorpe, Lewis (tr.). *Geoffrey of Monmouth's History of the Kings of Britain*. New York, Penguin Books, 1966

Tolstoy, Nikolai. *The Quest for Merlin*. Boston, Little, Brown and Co., 1985

Trollope, A. 'Account of the Examination of Tumuli at Broughton, Lincolnshire'. Archaeological Journal 8, 1851, 341-51

Various. *Ulster Journal of Archaology*. Vol II. No I, October 1895.

Electronic Texts

Cruachan Ai Visitor Center

(www.cruachanai.com/frameset.html)

Electronic Dictionary of the Irish Language or eDIL (www.dil.ie)

James, A.G., and Taylor, S., Index of Celtic and Other Elements in W.J. Watson's The History of the Celtic Place-Names of Scotland (www.spns.org.uk/watsIndex2.html)

The Annals of Tigernach (www.ucc.ie/celt/published/G100002/index.html)

The Cattle Raid of Cooley (www.ucc.ie/celt/published/T301035/text040.html)

The Natural History of Pliny (http://www.perseus.tufts.edu/hopper/text?doc=Plin.+Nat.+toc&redirect=true)

The Story of Canobie Dick (http://myths.e2bn.org/mythsandlegends/)

The Tale of Mongan (www.ancienttexts.org/library/celtic/ctexts/mongan.html)

The Tale of Mongan, Version B (www.maryjones.us/ctexts/mongan2.html)

The Voyage of Bran (www.maryjones.us/ctexts/branvoyage.html)

Vermaat, Robert, Vortigern Studies Website (www.vortigernstudies.org.uk/vortigernhomepage.htm)

_____, Faces of Arthur Website (www.facesofarthur.org.uk/articles/articles.htm)

INDEX

A

Aballach, 27
Aballava: Cumbria, 24, 27, 28, 29, 37, 65
Achren, 38, 68, 69
Aedan, 134, 135, 137, 142
Aeneid, 126, 127
Afallach, 70, 73
Agwneren, 211
Ailill, 55, 89, 90, 138, 160
Alder, 69, 189, 190, 191, 192, 194, 201
Alderley Edge: Cheshire, 48
Alletios, 56, 57, 58, 221
Alyn: River, 96, 150
Amaethon, 69, 70, 91, 217
Ambrosius, 40, 50, 57, 59, 60, 61, 87, 96, 115, 116, 117
Amesbury: Wiltshire, 39, 60, 61, 97, 116, 117, 170
Anglo-Saxon Chronicle, 111, 134, 142, 172
Annals of Tigernach, 139
Annan: River, 38, 70
Annwn, 34, 69, 71, 92, 94
Anu, 31, 38, 70, 72, 73, 81, 84
Aodh, 145, 148
Aonghus Og, 32, 99
Apollo, 71, 73, 87, 98, 171, 176
Apple, 27, 28, 49, 70, 176, 177, 178, 179, 181, 184, 188, 190, 191, 192, 194, 200
Appledore: Devon, 28, 29
Aquarius, 74, 221
Arawn, 69, 71, 92, 107, 177
Arcturus, 222
Arfderydd: Battle of, 39, 40, 46, 51, 52, 53, 54, 56, 89, 109, 142, 178

Arianrhod, 70, 71, 75, 83, 176
Aries, 221
Arnemetia, 72, 73
Arran: Island, 27
Arthur: King, 15, 18, 20, 22, 23, 25, 26, 27, 28, 31, 32, 38, 40, 42, 48, 49, 54, 59, 62, 63, 64, 65, 70, 72, 76, 77, 82, 84, 86, 88, 89, 90, 91, 93, 94, 95, 96, 97, 98, 102, 105, 108, 109, 110, 111, 114, 115, 132, 134, 137, 139, 140, 141, 142, 143, 144, 145, 148, 149, 150, 153, 160, 162, 163, 164, 165, 166, 167, 184, 188, 201, 202, 209, 214, 215, 216, 219, 220, 221, 222
Arthur's Wain, 114
Arthuret: Cumbria, 40, 46, 56, 142
Artognov, 108
Artorius, 110, 114
Asclepius, 171
Ash, 48, 121, 190, 191, 193, 195, 202, 207
Aspen, 190, 191, 192, 194, 195, 201
Athena, 77
Atlas, 101
Autumn Equinox, 107, 183, 197, 198, 221
Avalon, 18, 23, 25, 26, 27, 28, 29, 30, 31, 32, 35, 39, 62, 63, 64, 70, 76, 131, 150, 162, 164, 165, 169, 179, 184, 188, 201, 209

B

Badb, 36, 70, 76
Baldock: Hertfordshire, 33
Bassas: Battle of, 219, 221
Battle of Godeu, 68, 69
Bedwyr, 74, 78, 79, 82, 103

Belatucadros, 64, 65, 66, 67, 206

Belenos, 73

Beli Mawr, 70, 73

Beltane, 73, 75, 170, 172, 173, 183, 197, 198, 200, 221, 222

Beowulf, 122, 176

Bertholais, 61, 62

Bertilak, 61

Bestiare, 158

Birch, 189, 190, 191, 192, 193, 194, 201

Black Book of Carmarthen, 51

Black Mountains, 58

Blackthorn, 192, 195, 202

Blodeuwedd, 74, 75, 83

Bootes, 114, 222

Bran, 32, 69, 75, 83, 145, 148, 149, 150, 151, 152, 153, 154, 181, 211

Bran the Hardy, 211

Breccan, 35

Bregans, 76

Breguion: Battle of, 221

Bri Liath, 149

Bridget, 76, 77, 97, 99

Brigantes: Tribe, 45, 63, 76, 109

Brigantia, 57, 63, 76, 77, 97, 99

Broceliande, 37, 38

Broom, 190, 192, 195

Brougham: Cumbria, 64

Broughton: Lincolnshire, 118

Brychan, 35, 36; Island, 35

Bryn Celli Ddu: Anglesey, 91, 104, 173, 174

Burgh-by-Sands: Cumbria, 24, 27

Burgh-By-Sands: Cumbria, 28, 29, 35, 63, 64, 70, 76, 131, 150, 179, 209

Buxton: Derbyshire, 72, 220

C

Cad Godeu, 38, 180, 211

Caer Bandwy, 148

Caer Beli: Oxfordshire, 73

Caer Caradoc: Wiltshire, 60, 61

Caer Dathal: Gwynedd, 112

Caer Feddwid, 147

Caer Goludd, 148

Caer Ochren, 148

Caer Pedryfan, 147

Caer Rigor, 147

Caer Siddi, 146, 162

Caer Wydr, 147, 162, 209

Caerleon: Gwent, 56

Caernarvon: Gwynedd, 112, 128

Cai, 74, 78, 79, 84

Cailleach, 36, 102

Caintigern, 134, 137, 140

Caledfwlch, 82, 95, 160

Caledonian Wood, 39, 40, 49, 53, 221

Calendar of Oengus, 34

Camboglanna: Cumbria, 27, 28, 94, 221, *See* Castlesteads

Camel: River, 28

Camelot, 56, 57, 77, 98, 221

Camlann: Battle of, 221, 222; Cumbria, 27, 28, 29, 62, 63, 93, 95, 220, *See* Castlesteads

Campus Elleti: Glamorgan, 50, 57

Camulos, 31, 92

Cancer, 221, 222

Canonbie Dick, 45, 46, 48

Capricorn, 74, 221

Caractacus, 61

Carlisle: Cumbria, 45, 76, 93, 94, 97, 109, 130, 142, 172, 222

Carmarthen: Carmarthenshire, 50

Carrowburgh: Northumberland, 109

Carvetii: Tribe, 63, 64, 65, 67, 76

Carwinelow: Cumbria, 40

Cassivellaunus: King, 85

Castlesteads: Cumbria, 27, 63, 220, 221

Cattraeth: Battle of, 115

Catuvellauni: Tribe, 209

Cave of Cruachan: Co.
Roscommon, 31
Celyddon: Battle of, 48, 50, 51, 52,
177, 178, 219, 221
Celyddon Wood, 48, 50, 177, 219
Cenred: King, 90
Ceres, 171
Ceridwen, 80, 102, 113, 152
Cernunnos, 66, 92, 175
Chretien de Troyes, 37, 56, 86
City of the Legion: Battle of, 219,
221
Clackmannan: Clackmannanshire,
100, 101
Clidna, 30, 32
Clydno, 212
Coed Celyddon: Battle, 49
Coligny Calendar, 173, 183, 197,
199
Continuation, 40, 42, 150, 154, 155
Corbridge: Northumberland, 56, 57,
76, 98, 131, 219, 221
Cormorant, 102, 103
Corrievreckan, 35, 36
Cotton Titus A. XIX, 52
Crabapple, 194, 200, 202
Cranes, 107
Creiddylad, 80, 175
Crow, 31, 76, 150
Cuchulainn, 30, 31, 32, 99, 138
Culhwch, 31, 78, 79, 80, 84, 94, 98,
145, 175
Culhwch and Olwen, 31, 78, 79, 84,
94, 98, 112, 145, 149, 175
Cumhail, 31, 92
Cunedda, 69
Cunomaglos, 71, 98
Cunorix, 78, 79
Cynfarch, 27, 88, 109

D

Dalriadan: Tribe, 111, 142
Danby High Moor: Yorkshire, 25

Danu, 81
de Mirabilius Brittanniae, 177
Dechtine, 30, 32, 99
Dee: River, 96
Degasastan: Battle of, 137, 142
Demeter, 171
Diana, 72, 217
Dinas Bran: Denbighshire, 60, 86,
96, 150, 151, 211
Dinas Dinlle: Gwynedd, 45
Dinas Emrys: Gwynedd, 40, 45, 97,
115, 116, 117, 118, 121, 122,
124, 128, 129, 169, 170, 174
Dinas Maelawr: Ceredigion, 54, 56
Diwrnach, 145, 148, 149
Dog, 78, 84, 136
Dolorous Mountain: Mont
Dolorous, 42, 44, 45, 48
Domesday Book, 134
Don, 69, 81
Dore: River, 58
Dragon, 34, 111, 112, 114, 115,
117, 122, 129, 130, 131, 137,
138, 139, 140, 170, 174, 176,
181
Dragon Stone, 138
Drumelzier: Scottish Borders, 39,
40, 46, 48, 52
Dubglas: Battle of, 219, 221
Dumfries: Dumfriesshire, 36, 37,
38, 97, 98, 99, 109, 110
Dumnonii: Tribe, 108
Dunmeller, 39, 53, 54, 56, *See*
Drumelzier
Dylan, 81, 82, 83

E

Eagle, 53, 82, 84, 94, 97, 109, 176,
180
Eamont: Cumbria, 64, 65, 66
Eden: River, 27
Edern, 76
Edinburgh: Lothian, 45, 219

Eigr, 70, 132, 134, 140, 141, 142, 143, 144

Eildon Mid Hill, 42, 43, 44, 45, 48, 50, 52, 57, 221

Eildons: Scottish Borders, 42, 44, 45, 46, 48, 49, 58

Eithne, 45

Elaine, 96

Elder, 191, 192, 195, 202

Elderberry, 190, 195

Eleutherius, 109, 110

Elm, 189, 191, 193, 194, 195, 202

Emain Ablach, 27, 31, 73

Emhain Macha, 27

Eochaid, 111

Epona, 85, 105, 106, 145, 146, 198

Ercing: Herefordshire, 111, 112, 132, 142

Esplumoir, 58, 59

Esus, 53, 106, 107, 175, 208

Etain, 149, 150, 153, 201, 205, 206

Etain Echraide, 149, 180

Ettrick Forest: Selkirkshire, 49

Excalibur, 59

F

Fafnir, 122, 176

False Guinevere, 62

Fergus of Galloway, 40, 41, 42, 44, 48, 57, 109, 110, 142, 143, 160, 161, 166, 167

Fiachna, 134, 135, 136, 137, 139

Findabair, 89, 90, 111, 217

Fionn, 30, 31, 32, 92, 196, 202

Fionn mac Cumhail, 30, 196

Fir, 190, 192

Fisher King, 151, 152, 153, 154, 155

Fortuna, 171

Fountain of Barenton, 58

Frithuwald, 55, 56

Furze, 190, 192

G

Galahad, 96

Galgano Guidotti, 164

Gallizenas, 32, 33

Gangani: Tribe, 68, 69

Gawain, 58, 61, 62, 83

Geiriadur Prifysgol Cymru, 51, 60

Gemini, 221

Genii Loci, 125, 126

Genius, 124, 125, 126, 128, 129, 171

Geoffrey of Monmouth, 28, 30, 32, 38, 39, 49, 50, 52, 56, 58, 60, 61, 62, 70, 73, 86, 87, 88, 89, 93, 95, 96, 108, 109, 110, 111, 112, 113, 114, 117, 131, 132, 139, 162, 164, 165, 170, 172, 178, 222

Geography, 140

Gerald of Wales, 25, 164

Gilfaethwy, 82, 83, 84, 101

Glass Castle, 147

Glast, 30

Glastonbury: Somerset, 25, 26, 28, 30, 147, 150, 162, 163, 164, 165, 209

Glastonbury Tor: Somerset, 71

Gliten, 30

Gliton, 30

Glitonea, 30

Glycon, 171

Goewin, 82, 83, 84, 101, 176

Gofannon, 57, 83, 91

Goibhniu, 57, 83, 153, 211, See Gofannon

Gorlois, 62, 108, 110, 113, 132, 133

Goronwy, 75, 177

Goronwy Pebr, 75

Green Chapel, 58, 61, 62, 147

Guillaume Le Clerc, 40, 44

Guinevere, 62, 89, 91, 95

Guinnion: Battle of, 219, 220, 221

Gundestrup Cauldron, 66

Gwair, 84, 93, 101, 105

Gwalchmai, 83, 84, 96

Gwenddolau, 39, 40, 46, 88, 89,
    215, 216

Gwenddydd, 38, 52, 86, 87, 88, 177

Gwenhwyfar, 89, 90, 91, 111, *See*
    Guinevere

Gwerthmwl, 54, 55, 56

Gwiawn Bach, 102

Gwrwst, 109

Gwyar, 84, 96

Gwyddno Long-shank, 210

Gwydion, 53, 69, 71, 91, 105

Gwyllon, 51, 52, 56

Gwyn, 31, 67, 71, 92, 107, 175

Gwythyr, 80, 89, 90, 106, 107, 175,
    176

H

Hadrian's Wall, 24, 27, 37, 56, 64,
    98, 102, 109, 110, 220

Hafgan, 71, 92, 177

Harleian Genealogies, 91, 92

Hart Fell, 41

Hawthorn, 194, 201

Hazel, 190, 191, 192, 193, 194,
    196, 202

Heather, 191, 195, 202

Heavenfield: Northumberland, 57

Henry II: King, 25

Henwen, 82, 83, 84

Hephaistos, 211

Hera, 128, 141, 143

Hercules, 128, 129, 140, 141, 188,
    208

Herne the Hunter, 92

History of the Britons, 116, 147

History of the Kings of Britain, 28,
    39, 50, 109, 114, 132, 170

History Of The Wars, 50

Holly, 190, 191, 192, 194, 201

Holy Grail, 21, 34, 96, 145, 153,
    156, 184

Hyades, 107

I

Iliad, 77, 117

Imanuentius, 93, 99, 105

Imbolc, 75, 77, 183, 197, 200, 221

Imona, 27, 30, 31, 32, 93, 105, 106,
    152

Inis Cathach, 33, *See* Scattery

Irish Annals, 88

Irthing: River, 27

Isle of Man, 27, 35, 101, 113

Ivy, 190, 191, 192, 194, 195, 202

J

Janus, 144, 199

Jedforest: Scottish Borders, 48

Joseph of Arimathea, 96, 155

Jupiter, 18, 19, 66, 82, 97, 98, 176,
    210

K

King Rhydderch, 40, 41

L

Lady of the Lake, 27, 35, 37, 62,
    87, 96

Lailoken, 39, 52, 53, 54, 56, 62, *See*
    Llallogan

Lance, 154, 155, 156, 157

Lancelot, 45, 58, 91, 94, 95, 96, 217

Lares Familiares, 125, 126

Latis, 27, 35, 37, 62

Lauder Forest: Scottish Borders, 49

Leo, 221

Libra, 221

Life of Merlin, 39, 41, 87

Life of Senan, 34

Life of St. Carannog, 111

Life of St. Collen, 71

Life of St. Gildas, 89

Life of St. Kentigern, 39, 53, 62

Life of St. Padarn, 214
Lightning, 57, 66, 77, 82, 92, 95,
  98, 154, 155, 156, 160, 163, 167,
  194, 201, 204, 205, 210
Lindow Man, 53, 208
Llallogan, 39, 52, 55, 56, 57, 113
Llassar Llaes Gyfnewid, 83, 152,
  153
Llawfrodedd, 212
Lleu, 39, 44, 45, 53, 70, 71, 74, 75,
  82, 83, 87, 91, 93, 95, 97, 101,
  109, 116, 169, 171, 176, 177,
  178, 180, 181, 183, 208, 221, *See*
  Lugh
Lleyn Peninsula: Gwynedd, 68, 69
Lludd, 74, 94, 103, 169, 170, 173,
  See Nudd
Lludd and Lleuelys, 94, 129, 169,
  170, 173, 175
Llyn Cerrig Bach: Anglesey, 82
Llyr, 54, 55, 81, 97, 145, 151
Lochmaben Stane: Dumfriesshire,
  87
Long Meg and Her Daughters, 59,
  88, 109
Longinus, 155, 171
Longtown: Cumbria, 40
Loudoun: East Ayrshire, 45
Lucius Hibernus, 95, 96
Lugh, 32, 39, 44, 45, 52, 53, 56, 57,
  58, 74, 75, 94, 95, 96, 97, 99,
  162, 217
Lughnasadh, 75, 183, 197, 198,
  200, 221
Lugos, 39, 44, 45, 75, 93, 109, 171,
  See Lugh
Lydney Park: Gloucestershire, 78,
  79, 103

M

Mabinogion, 68, 71, 82, 83, 85, 96,
  101, 106, 112, 145, 176

Mabon, 32, 38, 71, 87, 91, 97, 102,
  114
Macha, 27, 30, 31, 32, 36, 49, 70,
  93
Maelor Gawr, 54
Maeswig Gloff, 110
Magister Draconum, 130
Manannan, 27, 99, 100, 101, 106,
  134, 135, 136, 137, 138
Manau Gododdin, 35, 69, 101
Manawydan, 93, 99, 101
Mandubracius, 85, 93, 99, 101, 105,
  145
Maponus, 38, 71, 98, 102, *See*
  Mabon
Mars, 64, 66, 74, 78, 92, 103
Marvels, 132, 142
Math, 82, 83, 92, 97, 101
Math son of Mathonwy, 82, 97, 112,
  176
Matrona, 27, 38, 98, 149
Mayburgh Henge: Cumbria, 65
Mazoe, 30
Medrawd, 91, 93, 95, *See* Modred
Meirchaiun, 109
Merchiawn, 88
Mercury, 80, 92, 171, 175
Merlin, 15, 18, 23, 30, 37, 38, 39,
  40, 41, 42, 44, 46, 48, 49, 50, 52,
  53, 56, 57, 58, 59, 60, 61, 62, 86,
  87, 115, 116, 133, 134, 163, 164,
  178, 221
Metrical Dindshenchas, 35
Midir, 149, 201, 213
Milford Haven: Pembrokeshire, 119
Milky Way, 106, 107, 176
Minerva, 76, 77, 171
Mithras, 171
Modred, 91, 93, 95
Modron, 27, 38, 91, 98, 102, 114,
  149
Moel Benlli: Flintshire, 96
Mogons, 98, 102

Mongan, 134, 135, 136, 137, 138, 139, 140, 181
Mont Dolorous, 42, 44
Morfran, 80, 102
Morgan le Fay, 30, 31, 62, 166
Morgan the Wealthy, 212
Morgen, 30, 31, 62, 166
Moronoe, 30
Morrigan, 30, 31, 36, 50, 62, 70
Morte D'Arthur, 62
Muireann, 30, 31, 32
Muttilow Hill: Cambridgeshire, 118
Myrddin, 15, 23, 38, 39, 46, 48, 50, 51, 52, 54, 56, 58, 62, 63, 86, 88, 113, 116, 132, 177, 178, 181, 188, 200, 202, 209, *See* Merlin

N

Nant Gwrtheyrn: Gwynedd, 59
Nefyn, 38, 59, 68
Nemeton, 19, 23, 66, 72, 73, 79
Nemhain, 36, 38, 62, 68, 87
Nennius, 50, 55, 57, 58, 91, 96, 97, 116, 117, 132, 142, 147, 172, 177, 219, 220
Neptune, 106
Newcastleton: Scottish Borders, 41
Newgrange: County Meath, 32, 99, 104
Nine Queens, 23
Nodens, 74, 78, 79, 103
Noquetran, 41, 42, 44, 48
Notitia Dignitatum, 128
Novantae: Tribe, 36
Nudd, 71, 74, 80, 92, 103, 107, 216, 217
Nyfain, 35, 36, 38

O

Oak, 18, 19, 25, 47, 48, 53, 66, 82, 92, 97, 176, 178, 181, 189, 190,

191, 193, 194, 200, 201, 203, 204, 205
Obsidian, 138, 139
Odgar: King, 145, 148
Odin, 74, 204, 207
Ogma, 188, 207, 208
Olive, 192, 194, 201, 202
Olwen, 98, 103
Orion, 71, 92, 107, 177
Owl, 75

P

Patera, 85, 105, 126, 145, 149, 150, 212
Pennines: Yorkshire, 118
Penshaw Hill: County Durham, 45
Perceval, 42, 59, 60, 61, 86, 96, 148, 151, 156
Perceval Continuation, 42
Peredur, 85, 86, 89, 109, 151, 154
Perilous Forest, 58
Petersfield: Hampshire, 175
Phoebus, 87
Phoenix, 158, 159
Pillar of Eliseg: Denbighshire, 86
Pisces, 221
Pliny, 203, 205
Plover, 69
Pole Star, 114
Pomponius Mela, 32
Porth Cerddin: Dyfed, 145
Poseidon, 106
Procopius, 50
Pryderi, 85, 86, 145
Ptolemy, 140, 143
Pwyll, 85
Pwyll, Prince of Dyfed, 85, 105

Q

Quicken Tree, 190, 191, 194

R

Raven, 75, 76, 150

Ravenna Cosmography, 27, 45

Rawlinson Genealogies, 90

Re Dragon, 131

Red Dragon, 115, 116, 129, 169, 170, 172, 173

Rhagenydd, 211

Rhiannon, 32, 84, 85, 91, 101, 105, 145, 150, 153

Rhun, 177, 216

Rhydderch, 40, 55, 178, 210

Ribble: River, 110

Robert de Boron, 150, 155, 163, 164, 165

Round Table, 23, 64, 65

Rowan, 189, 191, 194, 196, 202

Ruin of Britain, 116

S

Sabazius, 171

Sagittarius, 221

Salisbury: Wiltshire, 19, 39, 60, 61, 87

Salmon, 97, 138, 152, 154, 181, 193, 195, 196, 211

Samhain, 173, 183, 197, 200, 221, 222

Sarapis, 171

Satan, 117

Saturn, 70

Scattery: Island, 33, 34

Scorpio, 92, 177, 221

Seahenge: Norfolk, 18, 19

Segontium. See , See , See , See , See , *See* Caer Dathal

Selgovae: Tribe, 42, 50, 215

Sena: Island, 32, 33

Service Tree, 190, 195, 196

Setantii: Tribe, 210

Shannon: River, 33, 196, 202

Sir Gawain and the Green Knight, 61, 147

Sir Kay, 74

Sloe, 190, 191, 195

Snake, 66, 121, 126, 127, 128, 129, 169, 171, 173, 174, 175, 176

Solway Firth: Cumbria, 27

Song of Amairgen, 180, 181

Sow, 82, 83, 84, 176

Sozomen, 123, 124, 125

Spring Equinox, 107, 183, 197, 221

Spring of Galabes, 58

St. Anne, 72

St. Brendan, 62

St. Brighid, 76

St. Carantoc, 134

St. Dunstan, 26, 164, 165

St. Fintan, 86

St. Galgano, 164, 165

St. Gobban, 152

St. John the Baptist, 155

St. Kentigern, 54, 55

St. Madrun, 98, 149

St. Medan, 149

St. Padarn, 214

St. Senan, 33

St. Tigernach, 148, 149, 213

Stag, 41, 55, 56, 64, 65, 66, 67, 138, 181, 206

Stanwix: Cumbria, 76, 93, 97, 109, 110, 130, 142

Stonehenge: Wiltshire, 19, 39, 60, 73, 74, 87, 97, 116, 117, 170, 172

Sulis, 72

Summer Solstice, 75, 105, 107, 183, 197, 198, 221

T

Tacitus, 91, 203, 205

Tain Bo Cuailnge, 160, 166

Taliesin, 64, 102, 113, 146, 180, 211

Taranis, 18, 53, 98, 113, 208
Tarvotrigaranus, 107
Taurus, 107, 221
Taw: River, 28
Tegau Gold-breast, 217
Test-tree, 190
Teutates, 53, 208
Teviotdale: Scottish Borders, 48
Teyrnon, 85, 91, 106
The Apple Trees, 177
The Death-Song of Uther Ben, 113
*The Dialogue of Myrddin and
    Taliesin*, 51
The Dream of Maxen, 112
The Dream of Rhonabwy, 215
*The Prophecy of Myrddin and
    Gwenddydd, His Sister*, 52
The Spoils of Annwn, 84, 85, 94,
    145, 146, 162, 166
The Voyage of Bran, 137
Thiten, 30
Thomas Malory, 62
Thomas the Rhymer, 45, 47, 48, 49
Thor. *See* Thunor
Thorn, 190
Thunor, 18
Tintagel: Cornwall, 28, 108, 132,
    133, 134, 140, 141, 143
Torridge: River, 28
Tribruit: Battle of, 219, 221
Trinovantes, 145; Tribe, 105, 106
Trioedd Ynys Prydein, 89
Tudwal, 214, 215
Tuireann, 30, 32
Tyr, 74, 78
Tyrnoc the Giant, 213
Tyronoe, 30, 32

U

Uffington White Horse, 73
Urien Rheged, 27, 55, 87
Urn, 117, 118, 119, 120, 121, 122,
    169

Ursa Major, 114
Uther, 60, 62, 70, 88, 108, 109, 110,
    111, 112, 114, 115, 116, 117,
    129, 130, 131, 132, 133, 134,
    137, 142
Uther Pendragon, 99, 102, 108, 115,
    140

V

Valkyries, 76, 78
Venerable Bede, 57
Venus, 80, 87, 88, 217
Vespasian, 60, 61
Vine, 106, 190, 192, 194, 202
Virgo, 220, 221
Vita Sancti Edwardi, 165
Vitiris, 71, 80, 90, 106, 107, 175
Viviane, 35, 38
Volsunga Saga, 122
Vortigern, 18, 49, 57, 59, 86, 96,
    116, 129, 131, 170, 172, 219
Votadini: Tribe, 213
Voyage of Bran, 152, 180
Vulcan, 211

W

Wallop: Hampshire, 40, 59;
    Shropshire, 59
Wayland, 73
Wayland's Smithy, 73
Welsh Annals, 27, 29, 89, 112
White Dragon, 116, 169, 170, 172,
    175
whitethorn. *See* Hawthorn
Whitethorn, 190, 191, 194
Who is the Porter?, 99, 102
Willet: River, 111
William Stukeley, 66
Winter Solstice, 74, 75, 104, 107,
    183, 196, 197, 198, 221
Wllow, 106, 107, 176, 189, 190,
    191, 192, 194, 201, 208

Wolf, 78, 82, 84, 137, 181
Wulfstan of Worcester, 165

Y

Yahweh, 157
Yew, 190, 192, 193, 196, 201, 202, 206

Ygerna, 62, 108, 110, 132, 133, 134, 140
Yggdrasill, 176, 204
Yvain and Perceval, 40

Z

Zeus, 18, 98, 141

LaVergne, TN USA
28 June 2010
187585LV00001B/13/P